On Metaphor

On Metaphor

Edited by Sheldon Sacks

The University of Chicago Press
Chicago and London

The essays in this volume are based on a symposium,"Metaphor: The Conceptual Leap," sponsored by the University of Chicago Extension in February 1978. Most of this volume appeared previously in the Autumn 1978 issue of *Critical Inquiry* (Volume 5, number 1).

The University of Chicago Press, Chicago 60637
The University of Chicago Press, Ltd., London

© 1978, 1979 by The University of Chicago
All rights reserved. Published 1979. Second Impression 1980.
Third Impression 1981.
Printed in the United States of America

Library of Congress Cataloging in Publication Data
Main entry under title:

On metaphor.

"Based on a symposium, 'Metaphor: the conceptual leap,' sponsored by the University of Chicago Extension in February, 1978. Portions of this volume appeared previously in the autumn 1978 issue of Critical inquiry."
    Includes bibliographical references and index.
    1. Metaphor—Addresses, essays, lectures. I. Sacks, Sheldon, 1930–   II. Critical inquiry.
PN228.M405   808   79-5080
ISBN 0-226-73334-3

Contents

Foreword

> But if this is indeed the case—if metaphor, taken in this general
> sense, is not just a certain development of speech, but must be
> regarded as one of its essential conditions—then any effort to un-
> derstand its function leads us back, once more, to the fundamental
> form of verbal *conceiving*.
>
> <div align="right">ERNST CASSIRER, <i>Language and Myth</i></div>

Cassirer's sense that metaphor leads us back "to the fundamental form
of verbal *conceiving*" is reflected in the continuing life of the essays in
this volume, most of which began as lectures or responses to lectures at
the symposium, "Metaphor: The Conceptual Leap," sponsored by the
University of Chicago Extension in February 1978. The second stage in
the life of this symposium was the publication of its proceedings, aug-
mented by several "Afterthoughts on Metaphor" by panelists re-
sponding to the papers, in a special issue of *Critical Inquiry* in the fall of
1978. Now the dialogue has moved to a third stage—the publication of
the present volume—enriched still further by the contributions of two
distinguished philosophers, Nelson Goodman and Max Black, and there
is still no sign that we are nearing the end of the "verbal *conceiving*"
generated by the symposium or its topic.

It is easy enough to notice when a symposium has achieved this kind
of vitality, perhaps a little less easy to explain how it happens. The first
step is, of course, the selection of a topic or problem which has intellectual focus, range, and importance. Metaphor satisfied all these requirements: it is a highly specifiable and definable (although essentially contested and debatable) concept; it permeates the entire range of linguistic
activity and has a rich intellectual history; it has achieved an unprec-
edented importance in modern thought, moving from a place on the
ornamental fringes of discourse to a central position in the understanding of human understanding itself.

The second step in the life of a symposium is the practical matter of
getting the right people to talk to each other under the right conditions.
We solved the problem of "right people" by selecting the participants in
a way that reflects the interdisciplinary nature of the topic in modern
thought, the fact that metaphor has become a central problem not just
for rhetoricians and literary critics but for the most advanced thinkers
in psychology, art history, philosophy, and theology. The problem of
"right conditions" was solved by returning to the authentic, root sense of

the idea of a symposium—that is, "a drinking-party; a convivial meeting for drinking, conversation, and intellectual entertainment" (*OED*). The live-in facilities of the University of Chicago Center for Continuing Education made it possible to create not simply a series of papers by itinerant scholars passing through but a vital intellectual community which engaged in three days of continuous discussions ranging well beyond the scheduled lectures and involving not just the speakers but many of the three hundred participants who attended. It is our hope that the spirit and intellectual fellowship that prevailed in those three days continues to live and grow in this volume, earning it the title of "symposium" in the second sense recorded by the *OED*—"An account of such a meeting or the conversation at it,"—thus making it a catalyst for further discussions and symposia in classrooms and in the intellectual community.

The symposium was held on February 3, 4, and 5, 1978, under the auspices of the University of Chicago Extension, C. Ranlet Lincoln, Dean (who also served as moderator of the symposium). The speakers and panel members were Wayne C. Booth, Ted Cohen, Donald Davidson, Paul de Man, Howard Gardner, Clifford Geertz, Karsten Harries, Bernard Kaplan, W. V. Quine, Paul Ricoeur, Richard Shiff, David Tracy, and Norman Zide. The symposium was conceived and organized by Joan Cowan, Assistant Dean of the Extension, and Joyce Feucht-Haviar. It was funded in part by a grant from the National Endowment for the Humanities. Judging from the reaction of those involved, the symposium was a success, beginning many conversations which continue.

Joan Cowan
Joyce Feucht-Haviar

Metaphor and the Cultivation of Intimacy

Ted Cohen

These are good times for the friends of metaphor. They are *so* salutary that we are in danger of overlooking some very thorny underbrush as we scramble over the high road to figurative glory. Metaphor is a wonderful topic, and its new students are apt to be so enchanted by it that they never learn that the respectable road to its study was blocked until recently. Older students have been quick—perhaps too quick—to suppose that the road has been cleared and that it is the only proper road.

Now that the respectability of metaphor seems to be acknowledged all round, the only serious questions thought open concern how metaphor is to be described: in particular (1) how to understand the relation of "poetic" metaphors to metaphors in ordinary speech and prose (about which Karsten Harries' paper has interesting implications), and (2) how to incorporate an account of metaphor into more general theories of language or meaning (a major ambition of Paul Ricoeur's paper). There are other questions, and to indicate them I will note, very schematically, how we came to these good days.

There has been a very strong line in Western philosophy, especially in that strain running from British empiricism through Vienna positivism, which has denied to metaphors and their study any philosophical seriousness of the first order. Here it is in Hobbes' *Leviathan* (pt. 1, chap. 4):

> The general use of speech, is to transfer our mental discourse into verbal; or the train of our thoughts, into a train of words. . . . Special uses of speech are these; first, to register, what by cogi-

tation, we find to be the cause of any thing, present or past; and what we find things present or past may produce, or effect; which in sum, is acquiring of arts. Secondly, to show to others that knowledge which we have attained, which is, to counsel and teach one another. Thirdly, to make known to others our wills and purposes, that we may have the mutual help of one another. Fourthly, to please and delight ourselves and others, by playing with our words, for pleasure or ornament, innocently.

To these uses, there are also four correspondent abuses. First, when men register their thoughts wrong, by the inconstancy of the signification of their words; by which they register for their conception, that which they never conceived, and so deceive themselves. Secondly, when they used words metaphorically; that is, in other senses than that they are ordained for; and thereby deceive others.

. . . And therefore such [inconstant] names can never be true grounds of any ratiocination. No more can metaphors, and tropes of speech: but these are less dangerous, because they profess their inconstancy; which the other do not.

Far less generous and forgiving is Locke's *Essay* (bk. 3, chap. 10.) (Paul de Man will soon be doing an extraordinary reading of Locke, and perhaps you will hear this passage again. It is, however, a good passage to have more than one look at, and I cannot resist reading it out at a conference where Wayne Booth is present):

34. . . . since wit and fancy find easier entertainment in the world than dry truth and real knowledge, figurative speeches and allusion in language will hardly be admitted as an imperfection or abuse of it. I confess, in discourses where we seek rather pleasure and delight than information and improvement, such ornaments as are borrowed from them can scarce pass for faults. But yet if we would speak of things as they are, we must allow that all the art of rhetoric, besides order and clearness, all the artificial and figurative application of words eloquence hath invented, are for nothing else but to insinuate wrong ideas, move the passions, and thereby mislead the judgment, and so indeed are perfect cheats, and, therefore, however laudable or allowable oratory may render them in harangues and popular addresses, they are certainly, in all discourses that pretend to inform or instruct, wholly to be avoided; and where truth and knowledge are concerned, cannot but be thought a great fault, either of the language or person that makes use of them. What, and how various they are, will be superfluous here to take notice; the books of rhetoric which abound in the

---

Ted Cohen is chairman of the department of philosophy at the University of Chicago. He has written on language, aesthetics, and taste and is currently coediting a collection entitled *Essays in Kant's Aesthetics*.

world will instruct those who want to be informed: only I cannot but observe how little the preservation and improvement of truth and knowledge is the care and concern of mankind; since the arts of fallacy are endowed and preferred. It is evident how much men love to deceive and be deceived, since rhetoric, that powerful instrument of error and deceit, has its established professors, is publicly taught, and has always been had in great reputation: and, I doubt not, but it will be thought great boldness, if not brutality in me, to have said thus much against it. Eloquence, like the fair sex, has too prevailing beauties in it to suffer itself ever to be spoken against. And it is in vain to find fault with those arts of deceiving wherein men find pleasure to be deceived.

Although these remarks of Hobbes and Locke may seem remote, their import has prevailed until quite recently. The works of many twentieth-century positivist philosophers and others either state or imply that metaphors are frivolous and inessential, if not dangerous and logically perverse, by denying to them (1) any capacity to contain or transmit knowledge; (2) any direct connection with facts; or (3) any genuine meaning. In what seems to me a peripheral consequence of the move away from classical positivism, this opinion about metaphor has been abandoned, and it is becoming common—almost customary—to credit metaphors with all three virtues.

This conversion in the estimate of metaphor is very recent. The pivotal text, I think, is Max Black's "Metaphor."[1] It has been an extremely influential and provocative piece and it continues to hold a central position in contemporary discussions. It is also something of a period piece in what its terminology suggests about its presumed readership. Black, refusing to concede that metaphor's only legitimate capacities are emotive, argues for their "cognitive" status. He is thus, up to a point, arguing the case within the categorical constraints imposed by positivist philosophy of language. There is a tacit acceptance of the idea that metaphors are relatively inconsequential unless they are cognitive, that is, unless they meet this canonical test of respectability.

Black's essay became an important stimulus to the theory of metaphor adopted by Nelson Goodman in *Languages of Art*.[2] Goodman very easily credits metaphorical statements with truth values exactly on a par with those possessed by literal statements. Although Goodman does not assign meaning to metaphors,[3] and Black does not explicitly treat them as bearers of truth values, their work, along with that of some others, has created a climate within even the most severely analytical

1. Max Black, "Metaphor," *Proceedings of the Aristotelian Society* 55 (1954–55): 273–94.
2. Nelson Goodman, *Languages of Art* (Indianapolis, Ind., 1968).
3. He is equally reluctant to use any customary conception of meaning in his analyses of literal statements.

circles in which metaphors are treated comfortably as if they were thoroughly "descriptive" (of facts), potential vehicles of knowledge, and possessed a special meaning other than that belonging to their literal readings.

A considerable benefit of this new attitude has been the attraction to the topic of metaphor of a number of talented philosophers and linguists who otherwise might not have been interested. And anyone who, like me, values the topic must be pleased to see it come into its own. Metaphor's elevation in status is precipitate, nonetheless, on two counts. The major straightforward reservation ought to be that it has not yet been argued decisively that metaphors have this logically respectable status. The central, fundamental question concerns meaning. Does a metaphorical statement possess, in addition to its literal meaning (with respect to which the statement will be, typically, absurd or false or pointless), another (metaphorical) meaning wherein resides its capacity to be true as well as to provide the twist of insight we derive from some good metaphors? Or is the magic of metaphors not a matter of the meaning of their words, but a feature of the contexts of their use, of their "pragmatics"? This question cannot be argued completely, or even sensibly for very long, without the background of a general theory of meaning.[4] Both Hobbes and Locke have such theories which dictate their assessments of metaphor. I risk the opinion that only Donald Davidson and Paul Ricoeur, among the speakers at this symposium, possess developed theories of meaning, and their views of the semantics of metaphor are consistent with their general semantic theories. They give opposite answers to the question: Ricoeur invests metaphors with meaning; Davidson denies that they mean anything besides what they mean literally. Each answer has as much to do with a conception of meaning and the theory of meaning as with an attitude toward metaphor.

The other objection to the hasty assimilation of metaphors to the class of semantically normal sentences is oblique and a bit diagnostic. Why quarrel with the negative assessment of the meaning of metaphors? Because it's wrong? That would be a good reason. There has been, however, an equally compelling, implicit reason in the conviction that unless metaphors are full-fledged entities of the preferred sort, there can be nothing in them worth true philosophical investigation. If metaphors are not the sort of thing that bears knowledge, than they could be left to psychologists, anthropologists, and literary critics or theorists but could not support philosophical attention. Locke and others hold a conception of the most, or only, valuable kind of language

---

4. It might seem that the question of whether metaphors have meaning could be settled independently, and then theories of meaning themselves be judged as to whether they give the right answer. I do not see how to do this. What can be done, I think, is to make such a strong case for the indispensability of metaphors that if the best available theory of meaning won't give them any, then it needn't be a defect to be meaning*less*.

and then observe that metaphors do not qualify. The apparently most satisfying response, and what is becoming the dominant one, is to insist upon the qualifications of metaphors; but this is to meet the challenge on its own grounds. The whole progression recalls the Aristotelian response to what is taken to be Plato's denigration of art. If Plato castigates art because it lacks a direct relation to knowledge, then the sharpest possible rebuttal would seem to be one which asserts that art *is* an implement of knowing. But in this response's implication that art is, therefore, worthwhile, there is the further implication that Plato was right about the main point, that knowledge is what matters. Should we accept that point? Should we accept the correlate point about metaphor? Even if we did, and supposed that metaphors could share in the preeminent philosophical prize only if they partook of meaning, truth, and knowledge, it would still be worth knowing whether they serve a lesser good. To learn this we will have to understand better than we do how metaphors are actually created and reacted to, whether or not these are matters of meaning. This is a major concern in the papers of Booth, Harries, de Man, and Ricoeur.

For my part, I will take another look at the half loaf left to metaphor by those who meant to deny it any serious philosophical importance. If metaphors have no "cognitive content" and, therefore, no part in the canonically serious use of language, then of what use are they? Even critics as harsh as Hobbes and Locke cannot think that every metaphor must result from either a lapse in linguistic competence or a perverse wish to mislead or inflame. Then what is the point in making a metaphor? Think of a relatively mundane metaphor. Make it one about which there would be little quarrel: both camps (the detractors and the appreciators) would agree that however things stand with potent, fecund, generative metaphors, this one does nothing spectacular or exotic. It can be paraphrased literally with so little remainder as makes no difference, and those who believe that metaphors say something and have a truth value will concede about this one that the same thing could be said literally.

Then why might you, or anyone, use this metaphor instead of a literal remark? To be eloquent? To decorate? To say something beautiful? Of course these could be your reasons, these "aesthetical impulses," and they are the kind of reasons suggested by those who condemn metaphor outright or consign it to the class of the inconsequential. Because I subscribe to the opinion that metaphors are peculiarly crystallized works of art, I am not surprised by this convergence of arguments about legitimacy. Just as self-appointed followers of Aristotle have swallowed Plato's pill and then found they could treat art with respect only if they could find knowledge in it, so latter-day friends of metaphor have thought that only if metaphors have all the semantic possibilities of literal language—and more—could metaphors be intellectually respectable. Otherwise they could be nothing more than small-scale art. But why? Is knowledge the only, or even the most important, concern? Is its formal semantics all that matters in the use of language, or the only correct and proper subject? Is a joke less important than a theorem even if it's a good joke and a trivial theorem?

I want to suggest a point in metaphor which is independent of the question of its cognitivity and which has nothing to do with its aesthetical character. I think of this point as the achievement of intimacy. There is a unique way in which the maker and the appreciator of a metaphor are drawn closer to one another. Three aspects are involved: (1) the speaker issues a kind of concealed invitation; (2) the hearer expends a special effort to accept the invitation; and (3) this transaction constitutes the acknowledgment of a community. All three are involved in any communication, but in ordinary literal discourse their involvement is so pervasive and routine that they go unremarked. The use of metaphor throws them into relief, and there is a point in that.

An appreciator of a metaphor must do two things: he must realize that the expression is a metaphor, and he must figure out the point of the expression. His former accomplishment induces him to undertake the latter. Realizing the metaphorical character of an expression is often easy enough; it requires only the assumption that the speaker is not simply speaking absurdly or uttering a patent falsehood. But it can be a more formidable task: not every figurative expression which can survive a literal reading is a mere play on words. (You will not find more artful changes rung on this theme than those in the first sentence of Joyce's "The Dead": "Lily, the caretaker's daughter, was literally run off her feet.")

In both tasks—realizing that the expression is intended metaphorically, and seeing what to make of it—the hearer typically employs a number of assumptions about the speaker: what the speaker believes, what the speaker believes about what the hearer believes (which includes beliefs about what the speaker thinks the hearer can be expected to believe about the speaker).

During a departmental meeting you call your chairman a bolshevik. How does he take that? He does not think you are simply describing his formal political persuasion. Why not? Because he knows that you know he isn't a bolshevik.[5] So you aren't transmitting a fact because there is no fact, and everyone knows that and knows that everyone else knows that. Thus the chairman knows that you were not bent on reporting or recording a fact: you were speaking figuratively.

This sounds very complex, and of course nothing like the time and difficult effort suggested are actually undergone by the chairman just to

5. It would be different if he were a ninety-year-old immigrant, formerly Lenin's auxiliary (as some chairmen may be), but even then you would likely be up to something besides recording that long- and well-known fact.

realize that your expression is a metaphor; but, thought of as a reconstruction, this, or something like it, must underlie the chairman's realization that he has been offered a metaphor.

Once the chairman knows that you speak figuratively, he has then to unpack the figure to understand why you call him a bolshevik. In doing this he again moves through a network of assumptions, hypotheses, and inferences, *at the core of which is the literal sense of the expression* and some part of which overlaps the complex gone through earlier in achieving his realization that the utterance was a metaphor. I have toyed with the idea that there is an inverse correlation here, that the complexity of the reasoning which leads to "*p* is a metaphor" is inversely related to the complexity of unpacking *p* once it's seen to require unpacking—the idea being that the more unearthed in order to detect a metaphor, the less has to be added to decipher it. This is not the place to explore this idea; nor will I say anything about what must be called into play by the hearer when he works out the metaphor—what is meant by "bolshevik," what the speaker knows the hearer believes about bolsheviks, and the rest—for you can set that out as well as I.

The question is, Why do you put the chairman to all that trouble? Why does the chairman allow it and expend the effort? What is gained? One answer is that a transaction is precipitated in which you and the chairman actively engage one another in coping with a piece of language. He must penetrate your remark, so to speak, in order to explore you yourself, in order to grasp the import, for that import is not exactly *in* the remark itself. Furthermore, you know that he is doing this; you have invited him to do it; you have, in fact, required him to do it. He accepts the requirement, and you two become an intimate pair.

There is certainly intimacy in the literal use of language. Not even the most routine literal exchanges are passive—on either side. And the idea that language, used only literally, keeps us from really reaching one another's minds—because language is conventional and static, predetermining what can be said regardless of what we may want to say—is typically not only a sophomoric idea, but a deeply confused and mistaken one. And yet sometimes there is this wish to say something special, not to arouse, insinuate, or mislead, and not to convey an exotic meaning, but to initiate explicitly the cooperative act of comprehension which is, in any view, something more than a routine act of understanding.

The sense of close community results not only from the shared awareness that a special invitation has been given and accepted, but also from the awareness that not everyone could make that offer or take it up. In general, and with some obvious qualifications, it must be true that all literal use of language is accessible to all whose language it is. But a figurative use can be inaccessible to all but those who share information about one another's knowledge, beliefs, intentions, and attitudes. I think the community can be as small as you like, even a solitary pair: perhaps only the chairman knows enough of what you think and feel (along with knowing that you know that he knows this) to take the point of your remark. And the group might be even smaller: surely the self-dialogue of the soul is often figurative.

In these respects metaphors are surprisingly like jokes. With a joke, too, there is first the realization that it *is* a joke and then the understanding—what's called getting the joke. I have refrained from supplying examples of metaphor, but I won't resist the chance to recite some jokes (for illustration only). I give three, in an effort to associate myself with Kant.

1. In the Soviet Union it is time for the national elections. Finding their voting machines in much the same condition as their combines at the time of the Russian wheat harvest, the Soviet election officials are unable to proceed. But then, availing themselves of detente, they appeal to the United States' Department of State. The State Department discovers some unused voting machines in Chicago and lends them to the Soviets. The election is held on schedule, and Mayor Daley becomes a member of the Praesidium.

Understanding this joke requires little more than a very general background. It is not even necessary to know who Mayor Daley was, although knowing that will add something, as will knowing that he is no longer alive. Metaphors are often like this. It requires little beyond the most elementary linguistic competence to detect and comprehend the metaphor in "Juliet is the sun," but the more you know about the sun, the more you will make of the metaphor.

2. What is Sacramento?
It is the stuffing in a Catholic olive.[6]

This will be understood by considerably fewer people than grasp the first joke. Children, for instance, are unlikely to get it, even children who know of the Sacrament, for "pimento" is one of those words children seldom can recall. It is like the first joke in requiring two relatively discrete apprehensions: first, understanding that it is a joke and what the joke is, and then, second, finding it funny (if one does). This separation is even sharper in the second example, for there it is easier to imagine someone understanding perfectly well how the wordplay goes and yet finding nothing funny because the thrust seems anti-Catholic, or otherwise offensive. A metaphor is like this when, although it is clear enough what connections are intended and how they are supposed to be made, there is still no magic click, no real point in forcing those connections.

6. Thanks to Richard Bernstein for at least half this joke, and a good bit more.

3. What is a goy?
   An answer recently current at M.I.T. is that a goy is a girl if examined at or before time *t,* and a boy if examined after *t.*[7]

This joke is radically esoteric. It is, accordingly, understood by a very few people. A more interesting consequence of its hermetic character is that grasping it seems to be an all-or-nothing matter. There is not a sharp difference between understanding what the joke is and finding it funny. The recognition that it is a joke and the comprehension of just what the joke is are very nearly all there is to a complete response. Jokes of this kind are the ones most clearly undermined by any need for instruction in the background material. Some jokes can survive a preface of the form "First you will need to know that . . . ," but example three is of a kind that can't. I suspect that metaphors are like this when they must, to be effective, deliver their twist compactly and all at once, without exegesis.

The property in common with metaphors that all three jokes are meant to illustrate is the capacity to form or acknowledge a (progressively more select) community and thereby to establish an intimacy between the teller and the hearer. There may be more features in common. In particular, I am tempted to infer that there can be no effective procedures for dealing with metaphors. This means that there can be no routine method for (1) detecting metaphors when they appear, just as there are no foolproof rules for determining when someone is joking, or (2) unpacking the metaphor once it is known to be one, just as there is no standard method for explaining a joke.[8] This must be related to the fact that often a paraphrase fails to do the job of its metaphor in much the same way that an explanation fails to replace a joke.

Before leaving off and commending to you this topic of linguistic intimation,[9] I would like to warn against a possible misstep. Intimacy sounds like a good thing, and I have been urging attention to the use of metaphor in its cultivation. It is not, however, an invariably friendly thing, nor is it intended to be. Sometimes one draws near another in

7. This joke was purveyed and, I think, created by George Boolos, who is free to decline both credits. Guides to its hermeneutics may be found in Nelson Goodman's *Fact, Fiction, & Forecast* (Cambridge, Mass., 1955), pp. 74–75, and Leo Rosten's *Joys of Yiddish* (New York, 1968), p. 141.

8. In earlier papers, while claiming that there is no determinate routine for constructing the meaning or point of a metaphor, I suggested that there is a general scheme for identifying metaphors. I no longer think that must be so.

9. Professor Marrie Bergmann, a member of the conference, referred me to Martin Joos' *The Five Clocks* (Indiana University Research Center in Anthropology, Folklore, and Linguistics, publication no. 22 [Bloomington, Ind., 1962]); it is a remarkably interesting study which discusses ways in which intimacy is achieved by means of linguistic style. Joos is not concerned with figurative uses, but with the use of "incorrect" language—jargon, for instance; but the similarities are worth pursuing.

order to deal a penetrating thrust. When the device is a hostile metaphor or a cruel joke requiring much background and effort to understand, it is all the more painful because the victim has been made a complicitor in his own demise. Do not, therefore, suppose that jokes are always for shared amusement, or metaphors always for communal insight. Some of the most instructive examples will be ones in which intimacy is sought as a means to a lethal and one-sided effect. I leave the construction of examples to you.

I have just begun to open this topic for myself and hope to participate in elaborating two of its themes. As precisely and delicately as we can describe it, what is the character of this linguistic intimacy, and how, in general and in detail, is it attained? And then what good is it—what is it for? Perhaps you will find these questions useful when mulling over the rich variety of example metaphors used in the papers to come.

The Epistemology of Metaphor

Paul de Man

Metaphors, tropes, and figural language in general have been a perennial problem and, at times, a recognized source of embarrassment for philosophical discourse and, by extension, for all discursive uses of language including historiography and literary analysis. It appears that philosophy either has to give up its own constitutive claim to rigor in order to come to terms with the figurality of its language or that it has to free itself from figuration altogether. And if the latter is considered impossible, philosophy could at least learn to control figuration by keeping it, so to speak, in its place, by delimiting the boundaries of its influence and thus restricting the epistemological damage that it may cause. This attempt stands behind recurrent efforts to map out the distinctions between philosophical, scientific, theological, and poetic discourse and informs such institutional questions as the departmental structure of schools and universities. It also pertains to the received ideas about differences between various schools of philosophical thought, about philosophical periods and traditions, as well as about the possibility of writing a history of philosophy or of literature. Thus, it is customary to assume that the common sense of empirical British philosophy owes much of its superiority over certain continental metaphysical excesses to its ability to circumscribe, as its own style and decorum demonstrate, the potentially disruptive power of rhetoric. "The Skywriters," says a contemporary literary critic (with tongue in cheek) in a recent polemical article, "march under the banner of Hegel and Continental Philosophy, while the Common Sense school [of literary criticism] is content with no philosophy, unless it be that of Locke and a homespun organicism."[1]

The mention of Locke in this context certainly does not come unexpected since Locke's attitude toward language, and especially toward the rhetorical dimensions of language, can be considered as exemplary or, at any rate, typical of an enlightened rhetorical self-discipline. At times it seems as if Locke would have liked nothing better than to be allowed to forget about language altogether, difficult as this may be in an essay having to do with understanding. Why would one have to concern oneself with language since the priority of experience over language is so obvious? "I must confess then," writes Locke in the *Essay Concerning Human Understanding*, "that, when I first began this discourse of the understanding, and a good while after, I had not the least thought that any consideration of words was at all necessary to it."[2] But, scrupulous and superb writer that he is, by the time he reaches book 3 of his treatise, he can no longer ignore the question:

> But when, having passed over the original and composition of our *ideas*, I began to examine the extent and certainty of our knowledge, I found it had so near a connexion with words that, unless their force and manner of signification were first well observed, there could be very little said clearly and pertinently concerning knowledge, which, being conversant about truth, had constantly to do with propositions. And though it terminated in things, yet it was, for the most part, so much by the intervention of words that they seemed scarce separable from our general knowledge. At least they interpose themselves so much between our understandings and the truth which it would contemplate and apprehend that, like the *medium* through which visible objects pass, their obscurity and disorder does not seldom cast a mist before our eyes and impose upon our understandings. [Bk. 3, chap. 9, pp. 87–88]

1. Geoffrey Hartman, "The Recognition Scene of Criticism," *Critical Inquiry* 4 (Winter 1977): 409.
2. Locke, *An Essay Concerning Human Understanding*, ed. John W. Yolton, 2 vols. (London and New York, 1961), 2:bk. 2, chap. 9, p. 87. All further references will appear in the text.

Paul de Man, Tripp Professor in the humanities and chairman of the comparative literature department of Yale University, is the author of *Blindness and Insight: Essays in the Rhetoric of Contemporary Criticism* and *Allegories of Reading*.

Neither is there any question about what it is in language that thus renders it nebulous and obfuscating: it is, in a very general sense, the figurative power of language. This power includes the possibility of using language seductively and misleadingly in discourses of persuasion as well as in such intertextual tropes as allusion, in which a complex play of substitutions and repetitions takes place between texts. The following passage is famous but always deserves extensive quotation:

> Since wit and fancy finds easier entertainment in the world than dry truth and real knowledge, *figurative speeches* and allusions in language will hardly be admitted as *an* imperfection or *abuse* of it. I confess, in discourses where we seek rather pleasure and delight than information and improvement, such ornaments as are borrowed from them can scarce pass for faults. But yet, if we would speak of things as they are, we must allow that all the art of rhetoric, besides order and clearness, all the artificial and figurative application of words eloquence hath invented, are for nothing else but to insinuate wrong *ideas,* move the passions, and thereby mislead the judgment, and so indeed are perfect cheat; and therefore however laudable or allowable oratory may render them in harangues and popular addresses, they are certainly, in all discourses that pretend to inform or instruct, wholly to be avoided and, where truth and knowledge are concerned, cannot but be thought a great fault either of the language or person that makes use of them. What and how various they are will be superfluous here to take notice, the books of rhetoric which abound in the world will instruct those who want to be informed; only I cannot but observe how little the preservation and improvement of truth and knowledge is the care and concern of mankind, since the arts of fallacy are endowed and preferred. It is evident how much men love to deceive and be deceived, since rhetoric, that powerful instrument of error and deceit, has its established professors, is publicly taught, and has always been had in great reputation; and I doubt not but it will be thought great boldness, if not brutality, in me to have said thus much against it. *Eloquence,* like the fair sex, has too prevailing beauties in it to suffer itself ever to be spoken against. And it is in vain to find fault with those arts of deceiving wherein men find pleasure to be deceived. [Bk. 3, chap. 10, pp. 105–6]

Nothing could be more eloquent than this denunication of eloquence. It is clear that rhetoric is something one can decorously indulge in as long as one knows where it belongs. Like a woman, which it resembles ("like the fair sex"), it is a fine thing as long as it is kept in its proper place. Out of place, among the serious affairs of men ("if we would speak of things as they are"), it is a disruptive scandal—like the appearance of a real woman in a gentlemen's club where it would only be

tolerated as a picture, preferably naked (like the image of Truth), framed
and hung on the wall. There is little epistemological risk in a flowery,
witty passage about wit like this one, except perhaps that it may be taken
too seriously by dull-witted subsequent readers. But when, on the next
page, Locke speaks of language as a "conduit" that may "corrupt the
fountains of knowledge which are in things themselves" and, even worse,
"break or stop the pipes whereby it is distributed to public use," then this
language, not of poetic "pipes and timbrels" but of a plumber's handy-
man, raises, by its all too graphic concreteness, questions of propriety.
Such far-reaching assumptions are then made about the structure of the
mind that one may wonder whether the metaphors illustrate a cognition
or if the cognition is not perhaps shaped by the metaphors. And indeed,
when Locke then develops his own theory of words and language, what
he constructs turns out to be in fact a theory of tropes. Of course, he
would be the last man in the world to realize and to acknowledge this.
One has to read him, to some extent, against or regardless of his own
explicit statements; one especially has to disregard the commonplaces
about his philosophy that circulate as reliable currency in the intellectual
histories of the Enlightenment. One has to pretend to read him ahistori-
cally, the first and necessary condition if there is to be any expectation of
ever arriving at a somewhat reliable history. That is to say, he has to be
read not in terms of explicit statements (especially explicit statements
about statements) but in terms of the rhetorical motions of his own text,
which cannot be simply reduced to intentions or to identifiable facts.

Unlike such later instances as Warburton, Vico, or, of course, Her-
der, Locke's theory of language is remarkably free of what is now referred to as "cratylic" delusions. The arbitrariness of the sign as signifier
is clearly established by him, and his notion of language is frankly
semantic rather than semiotic, a theory of signification as a substitution
of words for "ideas" (in a specific and pragmatic sense of the term) and
not of the linguistic sign as an autonomous structure. "Sounds have no
natural connexion with our *ideas,* but have all their signification from
the arbitrary imposition of men. . . ." Consequently, Locke's reflection
on the use and abuse of words will not start from the words themselves,
be it as material or as grammatical entities, but from their meaning. His
taxonomy of words will therefore not occur, for example, in terms of
parts of speech but will espouse his own previously formulated theory of
ideas as subdivided in simple ideas, substances, and mixed modes,[3] best
paraphrased in this order since the first two, unlike the third, pertain to
entities that exist in nature.

On the level of simple ideas, there seem to be no semantic or

3. An apparent exception to this principle would be bk. 3, chap. 7, where Locke
pleads for the necessity of studying particles of speech as well as nouns. But the assimilation of particles to "some action or insinuation of the mind" of which they are "tracks"
reintegrates them at once into the theory of ideas (p. 73).

epistemological problems since the nominal and the real essence of the species designated by the word coincide; since the idea is simple and undivided, there can in principle be no room for play or ambivalence between the word and the entity, or between property and essence. Yet this lack of differential play immediately leads to a far-reaching consequence: "The *names of simple* ideas *are not capable of any definitions* . . ." (bk. 3, chap. 4, p. 26). Indeed not, since definition involves distinction and is therefore no longer simple. Simple ideas are, therefore, in Locke's system, simpleminded; they are not the objects of understanding. The implication is clear but comes as something of a shock, for what would be more important to understand than single ideas, the cornerstones of our experience?

In fact, we discourse a great deal about simple ideas. Locke's first example is the term "motion," and he is well aware of the extent to which metaphysical speculation, in the scholastic as well as in the more strictly Cartesian tradition, centers on the problem of the definition of motion. But nothing in this abundant literature could be elevated to the level of a definition that would answer the question: What is motion? "Nor have the modern philosophers, who have endeavored to throw off the *jargon* of the Schools and speak intelligibly, much better succeeded in defining simple *ideas,* whether by explaining their causes or any otherwise. The *atomists,* who define motion to be a *passage from one place to another,* what do they more than put one synonymous word for another? For what is *passage* other than *motion*? And if they were asked what passage was, how would they better define it than by *motion*? For is it not at least as proper and significant to say *passage is a motion from one place to another* as to say *motion is a passage,* etc. This is to translate and not to define . . ." (bk. 3, chap. 4, p. 28). Locke's own "passage" is bound to continue this perpetual motion that never moves beyond tautology: motion is a passage and passage is a translation; translation, once again, means motion, piles motion upon motion. It is no mere play of words that "translate" is translated in German as "*übersetzen*" which itself translates the Greek "*meta phorein*" or metaphor. Metaphor gives itself the totality which it then claims to define, but it is in fact the tautology of its own position. The discourse of simple ideas is figural discourse or translation and, as such, creates the fallacious illusion of definition.

Locke's second example of a word for a simple idea is "light." He takes pains to explain that the word "light" does not refer to the perception of light and that to understand the causal process by which light is produced and perceived is not at all the same as to understand light. In fact, to understand light is to be able to make this very distinction between the actual cause and the idea (or experience) of a perception, between aperception and perception. When we can do this, says Locke, then the *idea* is that which is *properly* light, and we come as close as we can come to the proper meaning of "light." To understand light as idea is to understand light properly. But the word "idea" (*eide*), of course, itself means light, and to say that to understand light is to perceive the idea of light is to say that understanding is to see the light of light and is therefore itself light. The sentence: to understand the idea of light would then have to be translated as to light the light of light (*das Licht des Lichtes lichten*), and if this begins to sound like Heidegger's translations from the Pre-Socratics, it is by chance. Etymons have a tendency to turn into the repetitive stutter of tautology. Just as the word "passage" translates but fails to define motion, "idea" translates but does not define light and, what is worse, "understand" translates but does not define understanding. The first idea, the simple idea, is that of light in motion or figure, but the figure is not a *simple* idea but a delusion of light, of understanding, or of definition. This complication of the simple will run through the entire argument which is itself the motion of this complication (of motion).

   Things indeed get more complex as one moves from simple ideas to substances. They can be considered in two perspectives: either as a collection of properties or as an essence which supports these properties as their ground. The example for the first model of a substance is "gold," not unrelated, in some of its properties, to the solar light in motion. The structure of substances considered as a collection of properties upsets the convergence of nominal and real essences that made the utterer of simple ideas into something of a stuttering idiot but, at least from an epistemological point of view, a happy one. For one thing, properties are not just the idea of motion, they actually move and travel. One will find gold in the most unexpected places, for instance in the tail of peacock. "I think all agree to make [gold] stand for a body of a certain yellow shining colour; which being the *idea* to which children have annexed that name, the shining yellow part of a peacock's tail is properly to them gold" (bk. 3, chap. 9, p. 85). The closer the description comes to that of metaphor, the more dependent Locke becomes on the use of the word "properly." Like the blind man who cannot understand the idea of light, the child who cannot tell the figural from the proper keeps recurring throughout eighteenth-century epistemology as barely disguised figures of our universal predicament. For not only are tropes, as their name implies, always on the move—more like quicksilver than like flowers or butterflies which one can at least hope to pin down and insert in a neat taxonomy—but they can disappear altogether, or at least appear to disappear. Gold not only has a color and a texture, but it is also soluble. "For by what right is it that fusibility comes to be a part of the essence signified by the word *gold,* and solubility but a property of it? . . . That which I mean is this: that these being all but properties, depending on its real constitution, and nothing but powers either active or passive in reference to other bodies, no one has authority to determine the signification of the word *gold* (as referred to such a body existing in nature)

. . ." (bk. 3, chap. 9, pp. 85–86). Properties, it seems, do not properly totalize, or, rather, they totalize in a haphazard and unreliable way. It is indeed not a question of ontology, of things as they are, but of authority, of things as they are decreed to be. And this authority cannot be vested in any authoritative body, for the free usage of ordinary language is carried, like the child, by wild figuration which will make a mockery of the most authoritarian academy. We have no way of defining, of policing, the boundaries that separate the name of one entity from the name of another; tropes are not just travellers, they tend to be smugglers and probably smugglers of stolen goods at that. What makes matters even worse is that there is no way of finding out whether they do so with criminal intent or not.

Perhaps the difficulty stems from a misconceived notion of the paradigm "substance." Instead of being considered as a collection, as a summation of properties, the accent should perhaps fall on the link that binds the properties together. Substances can be considered as the support, the ground of the properties (*hypokeimenon*). Here Locke's example will be "man"; the question to be accounted for then becomes: What essence is the proper of man? The question in fact amounts to whether the proper, which is a linguistic notion, and the essence, which exists independently of linguistic mediation, can coincide. As the creature endowed with conceptual language, "man" is indeed the entity, the place where this convergence is said to take place. The epistemological stakes are therefore higher in the case of the example "man" than in the case of "gold." But so are the difficulties, for, in answer to the question "What essence is the proper of man," the tradition confronts us with two perhaps incompatible answers. Man can be defined in terms of his outward appearance (as in Plato: *animal implume bipes latis unguibus*) but also in terms of his inner soul or being. "For though the sound *man*, in its own nature, be as apt to signify a complex *idea* made up of animality and rationality, united in the same subject, as to signify any other combination: yet, used as a mark to stand for a sort of creatures we count of our own kind, perhaps the outward shape is as necessary to be taken into our complex *idea*, signified by the word *man*, as any other we find in it . . . for it is the shape, as the leading quality, that seems more to determine that species than a faculty of reasoning, which appears not at first and in some never" (bk. 3, chap. 11, p. 115). The problem is that of a necessary link between the two elements in a binary polarity, between "inside" and "outside," that is to say, by all accounts, that of metaphor as the figure of complementarity and correspondence. One now sees that this figure is not only ornamental and aesthetic but powerfully coercive since it generates, for example, the ethical pressure of such questions as "to kill or not to kill." "And if this be not allowed to be so," says Locke, "I do not know how they can be excused from murder who kill monstrous births (as we call them) because of an un-

ordinary shape, without knowing whether they have a rational soul
or no, which can be no more discerned in a well-formed than ill-shaped
infant as soon as born" (bk. 3, chap. 11, p. 115). The passage is, of course,
primarily a mock argument, a hyperbolical example to unsettle the un-
questioned assumption of definitional thought. Yet it has its own logic
which will have to run its course. For how could anyone "allow" something
to be if it is not necessarily the case that it is? For it is not necessarily the
case that the inner and the outer man are the same man, that is to say,
are "man" at all. The predicament (to kill or not to kill the monstrous
birth) appears here in the guise of a purely logical argument. But not
much further along in the *Essay,* what is "only" an argument in book 3
becomes an ethically charged issue in book 4, chapter 4, which is entitled
"Of the Reality of Knowledge."[4] The problem there under discussion
is what to do with the "changeling"; the simpleminded child so called
because it would be natural for anyone to assume that this child has been
substituted by mistake for his real offspring. The substitutive text of
tropes now has extended to reality.

> The well-shaped *changeling* is a man, has a rational soul, though it
> appear not: this is past doubt, say you. Make the ears a little longer
> and more pointed, and the nose a little flatter than ordinary, and
> then you begin to boggle; make the face yet narrower, flatter, and
> longer, and then you are at a stand; add still more and more of the
> likeness of a brute to it, and let the head be perfectly that of some
> other animal, then presently it is a *monster,* and it is demonstration
> with you that it hath no rational soul and must be destroyed. Where
> now (I ask) shall be the just measure, which the utmost bounds of
> that shape that carries with it a rational soul? For since there have
> been human *foetuses* produced, half-beast and half-man, and others
> three parts one and one part the other, and so it is possible they
> may be in all the variety of approaches to the one or the other
> shape and may have several degrees of mixture of the likeness of a
> man or a brute, I would gladly know what are those precise linea-
> ments which, according to this hypothesis, are or are not capable of
> a rational soul to be joined to them. What sort of outside is the
> certain sign that there is or is not such an inhabitant within? [Bk. 4,
> chap. 4, p. 175]

If we then are invited by Locke, in conclusion, to "quit the common
notion of species and essences," this would reduce us to the mindless
stammer of simple ideas and make us into a philosophical "changeling,"
with the unpleasant consequences that have just been conjectured. As we

4. Examples used in logical arguments have a distressing way of lingering on with a
life of their own. I suppose no reader of J. L. Austin's paper, "On Excuses," has ever been
quite able to forget the "case" of the inmate in an insane asylum parboiled to death by a careless guard.

move from the mere contiguity between words and things in the case of simple ideas to the metaphorical correspondence of properties and essences in substances, the ethical tension has considerably increased.

Only this tension could account for the curious choice of examples selected by Locke when he moves on to the uses and possible abuses of language in mixed modes. His main examples are manslaughter, incest, parricide, and adultery—when any nonreferential entity such as mermaid or unicorn would have done just as well.[5] The full list of examples—"motion," "light," "gold," "man," "manslaughter," "parricide," "adultery," "incest"—sounds more like a Greek tragedy than the enlightened moderation one tends to associate with the author of *On Government.* Once the reflection on the figurality of language is started, there is no telling where it may lead. Yet there is no way *not* to raise the question if there is to be any understanding. The use and the abuse of language cannot be separated from each other.

"Abuse" of language is, of course, itself the name of a trope: catachresis. This is indeed how Locke describes mixed modes. They are capable of inventing the most fantastic entities by dint of the positional power inherent in language. They can dismember the texture of reality and reassemble it in the most capricious of ways, pairing man with woman or human being with beast in the most unnatural shapes. Something monstrous lurks in the most innocent of catachreses: when one speaks of the legs of the table or the face of the mountain, catachresis is already turning into prosopopeia, and one begins to perceive a world of potential ghosts and monsters. By elaborating his theory of language as a motion from simple ideas to mixed modes, Locke has deployed the entire fan-shape or (to remain within light imagery) the entire spectrum or rainbow of tropological totalization, the anamorphosis of tropes which has to run its full course whenever one engages, however reluctantly or tentatively, the question of language as figure. In Locke, it began in the arbitrary, metonymic contiguity of word-sounds to their meanings, in which the word is a mere token in the service of the natural entity, and it concludes with the catachresis of mixed modes in which the word can be said to produce of and by itself the entity it signifies and that has no equivalence in nature. Locke condemns catachresis severely: "he that hath *ideas* of substances disagreeing with the real existence of things, so far wants the materials of true knowledge in his understanding, and hath instead thereof *chimeras.* . . . He that thinks the name *centaur* stands for some real being, imposes on himself and mistakes words for things" (bk. 3, chap. 10, p. 104). But the condemnation, by Locke's own argu-

5. In the general treatment of mixed modes, Locke lists "adultery" and "incest" (p. 34). In the subsequent discussion of the abuses of language, he returns to the problem of mixed modes and gives as examples manslaughter, murder, and parricide, as well as the legal term often associated with manslaughter, "chance medley." Mermaids and unicorns are mentioned in another context in bk. 3, chap. 3, p. 25.

ment, now takes all language for its target, for at no point in the course of the demonstration can the empirical entity be sheltered from tropological defiguration. The ensuing situation is intolerable and makes the soothing conclusion of book 3, entitled "Of the Remedies of the Foregoing Imperfections and Abuses [of Language]," into one of the least convincing sections of the *Essay*. One turns to the tradition engendered by Locke's work in the hope of finding some assistance out of the predicament.

* * *

Condillac's *Essai sur l'origine des connaissances humaines* constantly advertises, perhaps even exaggerates, its dependence on Locke's *Essay*. It contains at least two sections that explicitly deal with the question of language; in fact, its systematic commitment to a theory of mind that is in fact a theory of the sign makes it difficult to isolate any part of the treatise that is not modeled on a linguistic structure. Two sections, however, openly and explicitly deal with language: the chapter on the origins of language, "Du langage et de la méthode," which makes up the second part of the *Essai,* and another section, "Des abstractions" (pt. 1, section 5). From Rousseau to Michel Foucault, the former section (which elaborates the notion of *"langage d'action"*) has received much attention. But the chapter on abstract terms also deals with language in a more inclusive way than its title would seem to indicate. It can be shown, though this is not my present purpose, that the subsequent chapters on *"langage d'action"* are a special case of the more inclusive model and history set up in this section. Read in conjunction with Locke's "On Words," it allows for a wider perspective on the tropological structure of discourse.

At first sight, the brief chapter seems to deal with only one rather specialized use of language, that of conceptual abstractions. But "abstractions" are defined from the start in a way that considerably expands the semantic field covered by the term. They come into being, says Condillac, "by ceasing to think [*en cessant de penser*] of the properties by which things are distinguished in order to think only of those in which they agree [or correspond: the French word is '*conviennent*'] with each other."[6] The structure of the process is once more precisely that of metaphor in its classical definition. Some hundred and thirty years later, Nietzsche will make the very same argument to show that a word such as "leaf" (*Blatt*) is formed by "making what is different equal [*Gleichsetzen des Nichtgleichen*]" and by "arbitrarily dropping individual differences

---

6. Condillac, *Essai sur l'origine des connaissances humaines* (1746), ed. Charles Porset (Paris, 1973), bk. 1, sec. 2, p. 194. All further references will be from bk. 1, chap. 5 and will appear in the text; here and elsewhere, my translation.

[beliebiges Fallenlassen der individuellen Verschiedenheiten]."[7] And a few years
after Condillac, Rousseau will make the same argument in his analysis of
denomination in the second *Discourse*.[8] It is entirely legitimate to conclude that when Condillac uses the term "abstraction," it can be "translated" as metaphor or, if one agrees with the point that was made with
reference to Locke about the self-totalizing transformation of all tropes,
as trope. As soon as one is willing to be made aware of their epistemological implications, concepts are tropes and tropes concepts.

Condillac spells out these implications in what reads like the plot of a
somewhat odd story. He implicitly acknowledges the generalized meaning of the term "abstraction" by insisting that no discourse would be
conceivable that does not make use of abstractions: "[abstractions] are
certainly absolutely necessary *[elles sont sans doute absolument nécessaires]*"
(sec. 2, p. 174). On the other hand, he cautions at once against the threat
their seductive power constitutes for rational discourse: just as certainly
as they are indispensable, they are necessarily defective or even
corruptive—"however corruptive *[vicieux]* this contradiction may be, it is
nevertheless necessary" (sec. 6, p. 176). Worse still, abstractions are capable of infinite proliferation. They are like weeds, or like a cancer; once
you have begun using a single one, they will crop up everywhere. They
are said to be "marvelously fecund" (sec. 7, p. 177), but there is something of Rappaccini's garden about them, something sinister about those
vigorous plants that no gardener can do without nor keep in check. Even
after their ambivalent nature has been analyzed on an advanced level of
critical understanding, there is very little hope they can be mastered: "I
don't know if, after all that I have said, it will at last be possible to forego
all these 'realized' abstractions: many reasons make me fear the opposite
is true" (sec. 12, p. 179).[9] The story is like the plot of a Gothic novel in
which someone compulsively manufactures a monster on which he then
becomes totally dependent and does not have the power to kill.
Condillac (who after all went down in the anecdotal history of philosophy as the inventor of a mechanical statue able to smell roses) bears a
close resemblance to Ann Radcliffe or Mary Shelley.

From the recognition of language as trope, one is led to the telling
of a tale, to the narrative sequence I have just described. The temporal
deployment of an initial complication, of a structural knot, indicates the
close, though not necessarily complementary, relationship between trope

7. Nietzsche, *Über Wahrheit und Lüge im aussermoralischen Sinn*, ed. Karl Schlecta, 3 vols.
(München, 1969), 3:313.
8. Rousseau, *Deuxième Discours (Sur l'origine et les fondements de l'inégalité)*, in *Oeuvres
complètes*, ed. Jean Starobinski, 5 vols. (Paris, 1964), 3:148.
9. The French word *"réaliser"* is used in a precise technical sense. The abstractions are
mistaken for "real" objects in the same way Locke speaks of the danger of mistaking words
for things. The reason for this error becomes clear later in the text.

and narrative, between knot and plot. If the referent of a narrative is indeed the tropological structure of its discourse, then the narrative will be the attempt to account for this fact. This is what happens in the most difficult, but also the most rewarding, section of Condillac's text.

Paragraph 6 starts out with a description of first or simple ideas in a manner reminiscent of Locke; the main stress is on *ideas* rather than on *first*, for Condillac stresses the conceptual aspect of all ideas, regardless of order. He contrasts a reality, which is presumably that of things in themselves, with what he calls, somewhat tautologically, "a true reality [*une vraie réalité*]." This true reality is not located in things but in the subject, which is also the mind as *our* mind (*notre esprit*). It is the result of an operation the mind performs upon entities, an aperception ("*apercevoir en nous*") and not a perception. The language which describes this operation in Condillac's text is consistently, and more so than in Locke's, a language of mastery of the subject over entities: things become "truly real" only by being appropriated and seized upon with all the etymological strength implied in *Begriff*, the German word for concept. To understand is to seize (*begreifen*) and not to let go of what one has thus taken hold of. Condillac says that impressions will be considered by the mind only if they are "locked up [*renfermées*]" in it. And as one moves from the personal subject "*nous*" to the grammatical subject of all the sentences ("*notre esprit*"), it becomes clear that this action of the mind is also the action of the subject.

Why does the subject have to behave in such a potentially violent and authoritarian way? The answer is clear: this is the only way in which it can constitute its own existence, its own ground. Entities, in themselves, are neither distinct nor defined; no one could say where one entity ends and where another begins. They are mere flux, "modifications." By considering itself as the place where this flux occurs, the mind stabilizes itself as the ground of the flux, the *lieu de passage* through which all reality has to pass: ". . . these 'modifications' change and follow each other incessantly in [our mind's] being, which then appears to itself as a ground [*un certain fond*] that remains forever the same" (sec. 6, p. 176). The terminology is a mixture of Locke and Descartes (or Malebranche). The subject seen as a compulsive stabilization that cannot be separated from an unsettling action upon reality performed by this very subject is a version of a Cartesian *cogito*—except that the function performed in Descartes' second and third "Meditation" by hyperbolic doubt becomes here, in the tradition of Locke, a function of empirical perception. Hyperbolic doubt, a mental act in Descartes, now extends to the entire field of empirical experience.

The self-constitutive act of the subject has, in Condillac (as in Descartes), a much more openly reflexive status than in Locke. The verb most frequently associated with the subject "mind" is "to reflect [*réfléchir*]": "since our mind is too limited to *reflect* . . ."; "the mind cannot *reflect* on nothing. . . ." To reflect is an analytical act that distinguishes differences and articulates reality; these articulations are called abstractions, and they would have to include any conceivable act of denomination or predication. This is also the point at which an act of ontological legerdemain enters the system: the subject (or mind) depends on something which is not itself, here called "modifications" ("certain sensations of light, color, etc., or certain operations of the soul . . ."), in order to be at all, but these modifications are themselves as devoid of being as the mind—cut off from its differentiating action, they are nothing. As the other of the mind, they are devoid of being, but by recognizing them as similar to itself in this negative attribute, the mind sees them, as in a specular reflection, as being both itself and not itself at the same time. The mind "is" to the extent that it "is like" its other in its inability to be. The attribute of being is dependent on the assertion of a similarity which is illusory, since it operates at a stage that precedes the constitution of entities. "How will these experiences, taken abstractly, or separately, from the entity [the mind] to which they belong and to which they correspond only to the extent that they are locked up in it, how will these experiences become the object of the mind? Because the mind persists in considering them as if they were entities in themselves. . . . The mind contradicts itself. On the one hand, it considers these experiences without any relation to its own being, and then they are nothing at all; on the other hand, because nothingness cannot be comprehended, it considers them as if they were something, and persists in giving them the same reality with which it at first perceived them, although this reality can no longer correspond to them." Being and identity are the result of a resemblance which is not in things but posited by an act of the mind which, as such, can only be verbal. And since to be verbal, in this context, means to allow substitutions based on illusory resemblances (the determining illusion being that of a shared negativity) then mind, or subject, is the central metaphor, the metaphor of metaphors. The power of the tropes, which Locke sensed in a diffuse way, is here condensed in the key metaphor of the subject as mind. What was a general and implicit theory of tropes in Locke becomes in Condillac a more specific theory of metaphor. Locke's third personal narrative about things in the world becomes here the autobiographical discourse of the subject. Different as the two narratives may be, they are still the allegory of the same tropological aporia. It now also becomes more directly threatening since we, as subjects, are explicitly inscribed within the narrative. One feels more than ever compelled to turn elsewhere for assistance and, staying in the same philosophical tradition, Kant would seem to be the obvious place.

* * *

Kant rarely discusses the question of tropes and rhetoric directly but comes closest in a passage from the *Critique of Judgment* that deals with the distinction between schemata and symbolic language. He starts out from the term "hypotyposis" which, used, as he does, in a very inclusive way, designates what, after Peirce, one might call the iconic element in a representation. Hypotyposis makes present to the senses something which is not within their reach, not just because it does not happen to be there but because it consists, in whole or in part, of elements too abstract for sensory representation. The figure most closely akin to hypotyposis is that of prosopopeia; in its most restricted sense, prosopopeia makes accessible to the senses, in this case the ear, a voice which is out of earshot because it is no longer alive. In its most inclusive and also its etymological sense, it designates the very process of figuration as giving face to what is devoid of it.

In section 59 of the *Critique of Judgment* ("Of the Beautiful as a Symbol of Public Morality"), Kant is primarily concerned with the distinction between schematic and symbolic hypotyposes. He begins by objecting to the improper use of the term "symbolic" for what we still call today *symbolic* logic. Mathematical symbols used in algorithms are in fact semiotic indices. They should not be called symbols because "they contain nothing that belongs to the representation [*Anschauung*] of the object." There is no relationship whatever between their iconic properties and those of the object, if it has any. Things are different in the case of a genuine hypotyposis. A relationship exists but it can differ in kind. In the case of schemata, which are objects of the mind (*Verstand*), the corresponding aperception is a priori, as would be the case, presumably, for a triangle or any other geometrical shape. In the case of symbols, which are objects of reason (*Vernunft*) comparable to Condillac's abstractions, no sensory representation would be appropriate (*"angemessen,"* i.e., sharing a common ratio), but such a similarity is "understood" to exist by analogy (*"unterlegt,"* which could be translated by saying that an "underlying" similarity is created between the symbol and the thing symbolized). Kant then illustrates at some length the distinction between an actual and an analogical resemblance. In an analogy, the sensory properties of the *analogon* are not the same as those of the original, but they function according to a similar formal principle. For example, an enlightened state will be symbolized by an organic body in which part and whole relate in a free and harmonious way, whereas a tyranny will be properly symbolized by a machine such as a treadmill. Everyone understands that the state *is* not a body or a machine but that it functions like one, and that this function is conveyed more economically by the symbol than by lengthy abstract explanations. We seem at last to have come closer to controlling the tropes. This has become possible because there seem to be, for Kant, tropes that are epistemologically reliable. The denominative noun "triangle," in geometry, is a trope, a hypotyposis which allows for the representation of an abstraction by a substitutive figure, yet the representation is fully rational and *"angemessen."* By showing that one can move from the symbolic order, which is indeed imprecise and therefore exists in the restrictive mode of the *only* (the word *"blosz"* recurs four times in the passage), to the rational precision of the schemata, while remaining within the general tropological field defined by the hypotyposis, the epistemological threat that disturbed Locke and Condillac seems to have been laid to rest. The solution is dependent, however, on a decisive either/or distinction between symbolic and schematic language. Representation is either schematic or symbolic (*"entweder Schemata oder Symbole"*), and the critical mind can decisively distinguish between both.

At this point in the argument, Kant interrupts his exposition for a digression on the all-too-often-overlooked prevalence of figures in philosophical discourse, an important question which "would deserve a more exhaustive examination." But this is not the time nor place for such an examination—which he, in fact, never undertook in a systematic way. The terminology of philosophers is full of metaphors. Kant cites several examples, all of them having to do with grounding and standing: "ground [*Grund*]," "to depend [*abhängen*]," "to follow from [*fliessen*]" and, with a reference to Locke, "substance." All these hypotyposes are symbolic and not schematic, which means that they are not reliable from an epistemological point of view. They are "a mere translation [*Übertragung*] from a reflexion upon a represented object into an entirely different concept, to which *perhaps* no representation could ever correspond [*dem* vielleicht *nie eine Anschauung direkt korrespondieren kann*]" (emphasis mine). The appearance of the word "perhaps" in this sentence, even though it sounds like a casual side remark, is most surprising. It has been the point of the entire argument that we know for certain whether a representation directly corresponds to a given concept or not. But the "perhaps" raises the question of how such a decision can be made, whether it is in the nature of things or whether it is merely assumed (*unterlegt*). Is the distinction between schemata and symbol itself a priori or is it merely "understood" in the hope of having it perform the definitional work that cannot be performed directly? From the moment this decision can be said, even in passing, to be "perhaps" possible, the theory of a schematic hypotyposis loses much of its power of conviction. Things happen, in the text, as if Kant had not at first been aware of the metaphorical status of his own term *"unterlegen"* when he used it in support of a crucial distinction between two modes of support. The considerations about the possible danger of uncontrolled metaphors, focused on the cognate figures of support, ground, and so forth, reawaken the hidden uncertainty about the rigor of a distinction that does not hold if the language in which it is stated reintroduces the elements of indetermination it sets out to eliminate. For it is not obvious that the iconic representation that can be used to illustrate a rational concept is indeed a figure. In the second *Discourse,* Rousseau confronts a similar question[10] but concludes that the particular representation that any general concept necessarily engenders is a psychological epiphenomenon related to memory and to the imagination and not a conceptual trope that belongs to the realm of language and knowledge. What Kant calls a schematic hypotyposis would then not be a cognition at all but a mere mnemotechnic device, the equivalent of the mathematical sign in the area of the psychology of perception rather than of language. In that case, the sentence which emphasizes that the decision as to whether a representation can be adequate to its object is of the order of the "perhaps," is more rigorous than the either/or distinction, despite or rather because of its vagueness. If the distinction between a priori and symbolic judgments can only be stated by means of metaphors that are themselves symbolic, then Locke's and Condillac's difficulties have not been overcome. Not only our knowledge of God, to which the passage under examination returns at the end, but the knowledge of knowledge is then bound to remain symbolic. He who takes it for schematic and gives it the attributes of predictability and transcendental authority that pertain to the objective reality of entities unmediated by language is guilty of reification (the opposite figure of prosopopeia); and he who thinks that the symbolic can be considered a stable property of language, that language, in other words, is purely symbolic and nothing else, is guilty of aestheticism—"whereby nothing is seen as it is, not in practice either."

In all three instances, we started out from a relatively self-assured attempt to control tropes by merely acknowledging their existence and circumscribing their impact. Locke thought that all we needed to banish rhetoric from the councils of the philosophers was an ethical determination of high seriousness coupled with an alert eye for interlopers. Condillac limits the discussion to the sphere of abstractions, a part of language that appeals neither to poets nor to empirical philosophers; he seems to claim that all will be well if we abstain from taking these cumbersome terms for realities. Kant seems to think that the entire question lacks urgency and that tidy critical housekeeping can rehabilitate rhetoric and make it epistemologically respectable. But, in each case, it turns out to be impossible to maintain a clear line of distinction between rhetoric, abstraction, symbol, and all other forms of language. In each case, the resulting undecidability is due to the asymmetry of the binary model that opposes the figural to the proper meaning of the figure. The ensuing anxiety surfaces obliquely in the case of Locke and Condillac; it would take a much longer demonstration to indicate that Kant's critical philosophy is disturbed by similar hesitations, but the somewhat surpris-

10. Rousseau, p. 150.

ing theological allusion at the end of our passage may be a symptom. The manifest effacement of such anxiety-traces in the texts is much less important, however, than the contradictory structures of the texts themselves, as it is brought out by a reading willing to take their own rhetoric into consideration.

* * *

As Kant just taught us, when things run the risk of becoming too difficult, it is better to postpone the far-reaching consequences of an observation for a later occasion. My main point stresses the futility of trying to repress the rhetorical structure of texts in the name of uncritically preconceived text models such as transcendental teleologies or, at the other end of the spectrum, mere codes. The existence of literary codes is not in question, only their claim to represent a general and exhaustive textual model. Literary codes are subcodes of a system, rhetoric, that is not itself a code. For rhetoric cannot be isolated from its epistemological function however negative this function may be. It is absurd to ask whether a code is true or false but impossible to bracket this question when tropes are involved—and this always seems to be the case. Whenever the question is repressed, tropological patterns reenter the system in the guise of such formal categories as polarity, recurrence, normative economy, or in such grammatical tropes as negation and interrogation. They are always again totalizing systems that try to ignore the disfiguring power of figuration. It does not take a good semiotician long to discover that he is in fact a rhetorician in disguise.

The implications of these parallel arguments for literary history and for literary aesthetics are equally controversial. An historian caught in received models of periodization may find it absurd to read texts that belong to the Enlightenment as if one were reading Nietzsche's *Über Wahrheit und Lüge im aussermoralischen Sinn* or Jacques Derrida's *La Mythologie blanche*. But if we assume, just for the sake of argument, that these same historians would concede that Locke, Condillac, and Kant can be read as we have here read them, then they would have to conclude that our own literary modernity has reestablished contact with a "true" Enlightenment that remained hidden from us by a nineteenth-century Romantic and realist epistemology that asserted a reliable rhetoric of the subject or of representation. A continuous line could then be said to extend from Locke to Rousseau to Kant and to Nietzsche, a line from which Fichte and Hegel, among others, would very definitely be excluded. But are we so certain that we know how to read Fichte and Hegel in the properly rhetorical manner? Since we assume that it is possible to coordinate Locke and Nietzsche by claiming that their similarly ambivalent attitudes toward rhetoric have been systematically overlooked, there is no reason to assume a priori that a similar argument could not be made with regard to Fichte or Hegel. It would have to be a very different argument, of course, especially in the case of Hegel, but it is not inconceivable that it can be made. And if one accepts, again merely for the sake of argument, that syntagmatic narratives are part of the same system as paradigmatic tropes (though not necessarily complementary), then the possibility arises that temporal articulations, such as narratives or histories, are a correlative of rhetoric and not the reverse. One would then have to conceive of a rhetoric of history prior to attempting a history of rhetoric or of literature or of literary criticism. Rhetoric, however, is not in itself an historical but an epistemological discipline. This may well account for the fact that patterns of historical periodization are at the same time so productive as heuristic devices yet so demonstratively aberrant. They are one way of access, among others, to the tropological structure of literary texts and, as such, they necessarily undermine their own authority.

Finally, our argument suggests that the relationship and the distinction between literature and philosophy cannot be made in terms of a distinction between aesthetic and epistemological categories. All philosophy is condemned, to the extent that it is dependent upon figuration, to be literary and, as the depository of this very problem, all literature is to some extent philosophical. The apparent symmetry of these statements is not as reassuring as it sounds since what seems to bring literature and philosophy together is, as in Condillac's argument about mind and object, a shared lack of identity or specificity.

Contrary to common belief, literature is not the place where the unstable epistemology of metaphor is suspended by aesthetic pleasure, although this attempt is a constitutive moment of its system. It is rather the place where the possible convergence of rigor and pleasure is shown to be a delusion. The consequences of this lead to the difficult question whether the entire semantic, semiological, and performative field of language can be said to be covered by tropological models, a question which can only be raised after the proliferating and disruptive power of figural language has been fully recognized.

What Metaphors Mean

Donald Davidson

Metaphor is the dreamwork of language and, like all dreamwork, its interpretation reflects as much on the interpreter as on the originator. The interpretation of dreams requires collaboration between a dreamer and a waker, even if they be the same person; and the act of interpretation is itself a work of the imagination. So too understanding a metaphor is as much a creative endeavor as making a metaphor, and as little guided by rules.

These remarks do not, except in matters of degree, distinguish metaphor from more routine linguistic transactions: all communication by speech assumes the interplay of inventive construction and inventive construal. What metaphor adds to the ordinary is an achievement that uses no semantic resources beyond the resources on which the ordinary depends. There are no instructions for devising metaphors; there is no manual for determining what a metaphor "means" or "says"; there is no test for metaphor that does not call for taste.[1] A metaphor implies a kind and degree of artistic success; there are no unsuccessful metaphors, just as there are no unfunny jokes. There are tasteless metaphors, but these are turns that nevertheless have brought something off, even if it were not worth bringing off or could have been brought off better.

This paper is concerned with what metaphors mean, and its thesis is

---

1. I think Max Black is wrong when he says, "The rules of our language determine that some expressions must count as metaphors." He allows, however, that what a metaphor "means" depends on much more: the speaker's intention, tone of voice, verbal setting, etc. "Metaphor," in his *Models and Metaphors* (Ithaca, N.Y., 1962), p. 29.

29

that metaphors mean what the words, in their most literal interpretation, mean, and nothing more. Since this thesis flies in the face of contemporary views with which I am familiar, much of what I have to say is critical. But I think the picture of metaphor that emerges when error and confusion are cleared away makes metaphor a more, not a less, interesting phenomenon.

The central mistake against which I shall be inveighing is the idea that a metaphor has, in addition to its literal sense or meaning, another sense or meaning. This idea is common to many who have written about metaphor: it is found in the works of literary critics like Richards, Empson, and Winters; philosophers from Aristotle to Max Black; psychologists from Freud and earlier to Skinner and later; and linguists from Plato to Uriel Weinreich and George Lakoff. The idea takes many forms, from the relatively simple in Aristotle to the relatively complex in Black. The idea appears in writings which maintain that a literal paraphrase of a metaphor can be produced, but it is also shared by those who hold that typically no literal paraphrase can be found. Some stress the special insight metaphor can inspire and make much of the fact that ordinary language, in its usual functioning, yields no such insight. Yet this view too sees metaphor as a form of communication alongside ordinary communication; it conveys truths or falsehoods about the world much as plainer language does, though the message may be considered more exotic, profound, or cunningly garbed.

The concept of metaphor as primarily a vehicle for conveying ideas, even if unusual ones, seems to me as wrong as the parent idea that a metaphor has a special meaning. I agree with the view that metaphors cannot be paraphrased, but I think this is not because metaphors say something too novel for literal expression but because there is nothing there to paraphrase. Paraphrase, whether possible or not, is appropriate to what is *said:* we try, in paraphrase, to say it another way. But if I am right, a metaphor doesn't say anything beyond its literal meaning (nor does its maker say anything, in using the metaphor, beyond the literal). This is not, of course, to deny that a metaphor has a point, nor that that point can be brought out by using further words.

In the past those who have denied that metaphor has a cognitive content in addition to the literal have often been out to show that metaphor is confusing, merely emotive, unsuited to serious, scientific, or

Donald Davidson is University Professor of philosophy at the University of Chicago. He is the author of many important essays, including "Actions, Reasons and Causes," "Causal Relations," and "Truth and Meaning," coauthor of *Decision-Making: An Experimental Approach,* and coeditor of *Words and Objections, Semantics of Natural Language,* and *The Logic of Grammar.*

philosophic discourse. My views should not be associated with this tradition. Metaphor is a legitimate device not only in literature but in science, philosophy, and the law; it is effective in praise and abuse, prayer and promotion, description and prescription. For the most part I don't disagree with Max Black, Paul Henle, Nelson Goodman, Monroe Beardsley, and the rest in their accounts of what metaphor accomplishes, except that I think it accomplishes more and that what is additional is different in kind.

My disagreement is with the explanation of how metaphor works its wonders. To anticipate: I depend on the distinction between what words mean and what they are used to do. I think metaphor belongs exclusively to the domain of use. It is something brought off by the imaginative employment of words and sentences and depends entirely on the ordinary meanings of those words and hence on the ordinary meanings of the sentences they comprise.

It is no help in explaining how words work in metaphor to posit metaphorical or figurative meanings, or special kinds of poetic or metaphorical truth. These ideas don't explain metaphor, metaphor explains them. Once we understand a metaphor we can call what we grasp the "metaphorical truth" and (up to a point) say what the "metaphorical meaning" is. But simply to lodge this meaning in the metaphor is like explaining why a pill puts you to sleep by saying it has a dormative power. Literal meaning and literal truth conditions can be assigned to words and sentences apart from particular contexts of use. This is why adverting to them has genuine explanatory power.

I shall try to establish my negative views about what metaphors mean and introduce my limited positive claims by examining some false theories of the nature of metaphor.

A metaphor makes us attend to some likeness, often a novel or surprising likeness, between two or more things. This trite and true observation leads, or seems to lead, to a conclusion concerning the meaning of metaphors. Consider ordinary likeness or similarity: two roses are similar because they share the property of being a rose; two infants are similar by virtue of their infanthood. Or, more simply, roses are similar because each is a rose, infants, because each is an infant.

Suppose someone says "Tolstoy was once an infant." How is the infant Tolstoy like other infants? The answer comes pat: by virtue of exhibiting the property of infanthood, that is, leaving out some of the wind, by virtue of being an infant. If we tire of the phrase "by virtue of," we can, it seems, be plainer still by saying the infant Tolstoy shares with other infants the fact that the predicate "is an infant" applies to him; given the word "infant," we have no trouble saying exactly how the infant Tolstoy resembles other infants. We could do it without the word "infant"; all we need is other words that mean the same. The end result is the same. Ordinary similarity depends on groupings established by the ordinary meanings of words. Such similarity is natural and un-surprising to the extent that familiar ways of grouping objects are tied to usual meanings of usual words.

A famous critic said that Tolstoy was "a great moralizing infant." The Tolstoy referred to here is obviously not the infant Tolstoy but Tolstoy the adult writer; this is metaphor. Now in what sense is Tolstoy the writer similar to an infant? What we are to do, perhaps, is think of the class of objects which includes all ordinary infants and, in addition, the adult Tolstoy and then ask ourselves what special, surprising prop-erty the members of this class have in common. The appealing thought is that given patience we could come as close as need be to specifying the appropriate property. In any case, we could do the job perfectly if we found words that meant exactly what the metaphorical "infant" means. The important point, from my perspective, is not whether we can find the perfect other words but the assumption that there is something to be attempted, a metaphorical meaning to be matched. So far I have been doing no more than crudely sketching how the concept of meaning may have crept into the analysis of metaphor, and the answer I have suggested is that since what we think of as garden variety similarity goes with what we think of as garden variety meanings, it is natural to posit unusual or metaphorical meanings to help explain the similarities metaphor promotes.

The idea, then, is that in metaphor certain words take on new, or what are often called "extended," meanings. When we read, for exam-ple, that "the Spirit of God moved upon the face of the waters," we are to regard the word "face" as having an extended meaning (I disregard further metaphor in the passage). The extension applies, as it happens, to what philosophers call the extension of the word, that is, the class of entities to which it refers. Here the word "face" applies to ordinary faces, and to waters in addition.

This account cannot, at any rate, be complete, for if in these con-texts the words "face" and "infant" apply correctly to waters and to the adult Tolstoy, then waters really do have faces and Tolstoy literally was an infant, and all sense of metaphor evaporates. If we are to think of words in metaphors as directly going about their business of applying to what they properly do apply to, there is no difference between metaphor and the introduction of a new term into our vocabulary: to make a metaphor is to murder it.

What has been left out is any appeal to the original meaning of the word. Whether or not metaphor depends on new or extended meanings, it certainly depends in some way on the original meanings; an adequate account of metaphor must allow that the primary or original meanings of words remain active in their metaphorical setting.

Perhaps, then, we can explain metaphor as a kind of ambiguity: in the context of a metaphor, certain words have either a new or an original meaning, and the force of the metaphor depends on our uncertainty as we waver between the two meanings. Thus when Melville writes that "Christ was a chronometer," the effect of metaphor is produced by our taking "chronometer" first in its ordinary sense and then in some extraordinary or metaphorical sense.

It is hard to see how this theory can be correct. For the ambiguity in the word, if there is any, is due to the fact that in ordinary contexts it means one thing and in the metaphorical context it means something else; but in the metaphorical context we do not necessarily hesitate over its meaning. When we do hesitate, it is usually to decide which of a number of metaphorical interpretations we shall accept; we are seldom in doubt that what we have is a metaphor. At any rate, the effectiveness of the metaphor easily outlasts the end of uncertainty over the interpretation of the metaphorical passage. Metaphor cannot, therefore, owe its effect to ambiguity of this sort.[2]

Another brand of ambiguity may appear to offer a better suggestion. Sometimes a word will, in a single context, bear two meanings where we are meant to remember and to use both. Or, if we think of wordhood as implying sameness of meaning, then we may describe the situation as one in which what appears as a single word is in fact two. When Shakespeare's Cressida is welcomed bawdily into the Grecian camp, Nestor says, "Our general doth salute you with a kiss." Here we are to take "general" two ways: once as applying to Agamemnon, who is the general; and once, since she is kissing everyone, as applying to no one in particular, but everyone in general. We really have a conjunction of two sentences: our general, Agamemnon, salutes you with a kiss; and everyone in general is saluting you with a kiss.

This is a legitimate device, a pun, but it is not the same device as metaphor. For in metaphor there is no essential need of reiteration; whatever meanings we assign the words, they keep through every correct reading of the passage.

A plausible modification of the last suggestion would be to consider the key word (or words) in a metaphor as having two different kinds of meaning at once, a literal and a figurative meaning. Imagine the literal meaning as latent, something that we are aware of, that can work on us without working in the context, while the figurative meaning carries the direct load. And finally, there must be a rule which connects the two

2. Nelson Goodman says metaphor and ambiguity differ chiefly "in that the several uses of a merely ambiguous term are coeval and independent" while in metaphor "a term with an extension established by habit is applied elsewhere under the influence of that habit"; he suggests that as our sense of the history of the "two uses" in metaphor fades, the metaphorical word becomes merely ambiguous *(Languages of Art* [Indianapolis, Ind., 1968], p. 71). In fact in many cases of ambiguity, one use springs from the other (as Goodman says) and so cannot be coeval. But the basic error, which Goodman shares with others, is the idea that two "uses" are involved in metaphor in anything like the way they are in ambiguity.

meanings, for otherwise the explanation lapses into a form of the ambiguity theory. The rule, at least for many typical cases of metaphor, says that in its metaphorical role the word applies to everything that it applies to in its literal role, and then some.[3]

This theory may seem complex, but it is strikingly similar to what Frege proposed to account for the behavior of referring terms in modal sentences and sentences about propositional attitudes like belief and desire. According to Frege, each referring term has two (or more) meanings, one which fixes its reference in ordinary contexts and another which fixes its reference in the special contexts created by modal operators or psychological verbs. The rule connecting the two meanings may be put like this: the meaning of the word in the special contexts makes the reference in those contexts to be identical with the meaning in ordinary contexts.

Here is the whole picture, putting Frege together with a Fregean view of metaphor: we are to think of a word as having, in addition to its mundane field of application or reference, two special or supermundane fields of application, one for metaphor and the other for modal contexts and the like. In both cases the original meaning remains to do its work by virtue of a rule which relates the various meanings.

Having stressed the possible analogy between metaphorical meaning and the Fregean meanings for oblique contexts, I turn to an imposing difficulty in maintaining the analogy. You are entertaining a visitor from Saturn by trying to teach him how to use the word "floor." You go through the familiar dodges, leading him from floor to floor, pointing and stamping and repeating the word. You prompt him to make experiments, tapping objects tentatively with his tentacle while rewarding his right and wrong tries. You want him to come out knowing not only that these particular objects or surfaces are floors but also how to tell a floor when one is in sight or touch. The skit you are putting on doesn't *tell* him what he needs to know, but with luck it helps him to learn it.

Should we call this process learning something about the world or learning something about language? An odd question, since what is learned is that a bit of language refers to a bit of the world. Still, it is easy to distinguish between the business of learning the meaning of a word and using the word once the meaning is learned. Comparing these two activities, it is natural to say that the first concerns learning something about language, while the second is typically learning something about the world. If your Saturnian has learned how to use the word "floor," you may try telling him something new, that *here* is a floor. If he has mastered the word trick, you have told him something about the world.

Your friend from Saturn now transports you through space to his

---

3. The theory described is essentially that of Paul Henle, "Metaphor," in *Language, Thought, and Culture,* ed. Henle (Ann Arbor, Mich., 1958).

home sphere, and looking back remotely at earth you say to him, nodding at the earth, "floor." Perhaps he will think this is still part of the lesson and assume that the word "floor" applies properly to the earth, at least as seen from Saturn. But what if you thought he already knew the meaning of "floor," and you were remembering how Dante, from a similar place in the heavens, saw the inhabited earth as "the small round floor that makes us passionate"? Your purpose was metaphor, not drill in the use of language. What difference would it make to your friend which way he took it? With the theory of metaphor under consideration, very little difference, for according to that theory a word has a new meaning in a metaphorical context; the occasion of the metaphor would, therefore, be the occasion for learning the new meaning. We should agree that in some ways it makes relatively little difference whether, in a given context, we think a word is being used metaphorically or in a previously unknown, but literal way. Empson, in *Some Versions of Pastoral,* quotes these lines from Donne: "As our blood labours to beget / Spirits, as like souls as it can, . . . / So must pure lover's soules descend. . . ." The modern reader is almost certain, Empson points out, to take the word "spirits" in this passage metaphorically, as applying only by extension to something spiritual. But for Donne there was no metaphor. He writes in his *Sermons,* "The spirits . . . are the thin and active part of the blood, and are a kind of middle nature, between soul and body." Learning this does not matter much; Empson is right when he says, "It is curious how the change in the word [that is, in what we think it means] leaves the poetry unaffected."[4]

The change may be, in some cases at least, hard to appreciate, but unless there is a change, most of what is thought to be interesting about metaphor is lost. I have been making the point by contrasting learning a new use for an old word with using a word already understood; in one case, I said, our attention is directed to language, in the other, to what language is about. Metaphor, I suggested, belongs in the second category. This can also be seen by considering dead metaphors. Once upon a time, I suppose, rivers and bottles did not, as they do now, literally have mouths. Thinking of present usage, it doesn't matter whether we take the word "mouth" to be ambiguous because it applies to entrances to rivers and openings of bottles as well as to animal apertures, or we think there is a single wide field of application that embraces both. What does matter is that when "mouth" applied only metaphorically to bottles, the application made the hearer *notice* a likeness between animal and bottle openings. (Consider Homer's reference to wounds as mouths.) Once one has the present use of the word, with literal application to bottles, there is nothing left to notice. There is no similarity to seek because it consists simply in being referred to by the same word.

4. William Empson, *Some Versions of Pastoral* (London, 1935), p. 133.

Novelty is not the issue. In its context a word once taken for a metaphor remains a metaphor on the hundredth hearing, while a word may easily be appreciated in a new literal role on a first encounter. What we call the element of novelty or surprise in a metaphor is a built-in aesthetic feature we can experience again and again, like the surprise in Haydn's Symphony no. 94, or a familiar deceptive cadence.

If metaphor involved a second meaning, as ambiguity does, we might expect to be able to specify the special meaning of a word in a metaphorical setting by waiting until the metaphor dies. The figurative meaning of the living metaphor should be immortalized in the literal meaning of the dead. But although some philosophers have suggested this idea, it seems plainly wrong. "He was burned up" is genuinely am-biguous (since it may be true in one sense and false in another), but although the slangish idiom is no doubt the corpse of a metaphor, "He was burned up" now suggests no more than that he was very angry. When the metaphor was active, we would have pictured fire in the eyes or smoke coming out of the ears.

We can learn much about what metaphors mean by comparing them with similes, for a simile tells us, in part, what a metaphor merely nudges us into noting. Suppose Goneril had said, thinking of Lear, "Old fools are like babes again"; then she would have used the words to assert a similarity between old fools and babes. What she did say, of course, was "Old fools are babes again," thus using the words to intimate what the simile declared. Thinking along these lines may inspire another theory of the figurative or special meaning of metaphors: the figurative mean-ing of a metaphor is the literal meaning of the corresponding simile. Thus "Christ was a chronometer" in its figurative sense is synonymous with "Christ was like a chronometer," and the metaphorical meaning once locked up in "He was burned up" is released in "He was like some-one who was burned up" (or perhaps "He was like burned up").

There is, to be sure, the difficulty of identifying the simile that corresponds to a given metaphor. Virginia Woolf said that a highbrow is "a man or woman of thoroughbred intelligence who rides his mind at a gallop across country in pursuit of an idea." What simile corresponds? Something like this, perhaps: "A highbrow is a man or woman whose intelligence is like a thoroughbred horse and who persists in thinking about an idea like a rider galloping across country in pursuit of . . . well, something."

The view that the special meaning of a metaphor is identical with the literal meaning of a corresponding simile (however "corresponding" is spelled out) should not be confused with the common theory that a metaphor is an elliptical simile.[5] This theory makes no distinction in

5. J. Middleton Murray says a metaphor is a "compressed simile," *Countries of the Mind*, 2d ser. (Oxford, 1931), p. 3. Max Black attributes a similar view to Alexander Bain, *English Composition and Rhetoric*, enl. ed. (London, 1887).

meaning between a metaphor and some related simile and does not provide any ground for speaking of figurative, metaphorical, or special meanings. It is a theory that wins hands down so far as simplicity is concerned, but it also seems too simple to work. For if we make the literal meaning of the metaphor to be the literal meaning of a matching simile, we deny access to what we originally took to be the literal meaning of the metaphor, and we agreed almost from the start that *this* meaning was essential to the working of the metaphor, whatever else might have to be brought in in the way of a nonliteral meaning.

Both the elliptical simile theory of metaphor and its more sophisticated variant, which equates the figurative meaning of the metaphor with the literal meaning of a simile, share a fatal defect. They make the hidden meaning of the metaphor all too obvious and accessible. In each case the hidden meaning is to be found simply by looking to the literal meaning of what is usually a painfully trivial simile. This is like that— Tolstoy like an infant, the earth like a floor. It is trivial because everything is like everything, and in endless ways. Metaphors are often very difficult to interpret and, so it is said, impossible to paraphrase. But with this theory, interpretation and paraphrase typically are ready to the hand of the most callow.

These simile theories have been found acceptable, I think, only because they have been confused with a quite different theory. Consider this remark by Max Black:

> When Schopenhauer called a geometrical proof a mousetrap, he was, according to such a view, *saying* (though not explicitly): "A geometrical proof is *like* a mousetrap, since both offer a delusive reward, entice their victims by degrees, lead to disagreeable surprise, etc." This is a view of metaphor as a condensed or elliptical *simile*.[6]

Here I discern two confusions. First, if metaphors are elliptical similes, they say *explicitly* what similes say, for ellipsis is a form of abbreviation, not of paraphrase or indirection. But, and this is the more important matter, Black's statement of what the metaphor says goes far beyond anything given by the corresponding simile. The simile simply says a geometrical proof is like a mousetrap. It no more *tells* us what similarities we are to notice than the metaphor does. Black mentions three similarities, and of course we could go on adding to the list forever. But is this list, when revised and supplemented in the right way, supposed to give the *literal* meaning of the simile? Surely not, since the simile declared no more than the similarity. If the list is supposed to provide the figurative meaning of the simile, then we learn nothing about metaphor

6. Black, p. 35.

from the comparison with simile—only that both have the same figurative meaning. Nelson Goodman does indeed claim that "the difference between simile and metaphor is negligible," and he continues, "Whether the locution be 'is like' or 'is,' the figure *likens* picture to person by picking out a certain common feature. . . ."[7] Goodman is considering the difference between saying a picture is sad and saying it is like a sad person. It is clearly true that both sayings liken picture to person, but it seems to me a mistake to claim that either way of talking "picks out" a common feature. The simile says there is a likeness and leaves it to us to pick out some common feature or features; the metaphor does not explicitly assert a likeness, but if we accept it as a metaphor, we are again led to seek common features (not necessarily the same features the associated simile suggests; but that is another matter).

Just because a simile wears a declaration of similitude on its sleeve, it is, I think, far less plausible than in the case of metaphor to maintain that there is a hidden second meaning. In the case of simile, we note what it literally says, that two things resemble one another; we then regard the objects and consider what similarity would, in the context, be to the point. Having decided, we might then say the author of the simile intended us—that is, meant us—to notice that similarity. But having appreciated the difference between what the words meant and what the author accomplished by using those words, we should feel little temptation to explain what has happened by endowing the words themselves with a second, or figurative, meaning. The point of the concept of linguistic meaning is to explain what can be done with words. But the supposed figurative meaning of a simile explains nothing; it is not a feature of the word that the word has prior to and independent of the context of use, and it rests upon no linguistic customs except those that govern ordinary meaning.

What words do do with their literal meaning in simile must be possible for them to do in metaphor. A metaphor directs attention to the same sorts of similarity, if not the same similarities, as the corresponding simile. But then the unexpected or subtle parallels and analogies it is the business of metaphor to promote need not depend, for their promotion, on more than the literal meanings of words.

Metaphor and simile are merely two among endless devices that serve to alert us to aspects of the world by inviting us to make comparisons. I quote a few stanzas of T. S. Eliot's "The Hippopotamus":

> The broad-backed hippopotamus
> Rests on his belly in the mud;
> Although he seems so firm to us
> He is merely flesh and blood.

7. Goodman, pp. 77–78.

Flesh and blood is weak and frail,
Susceptible to nervous shock;
While the True Church can never fail
For it is based upon a rock.

The hippo's feeble steps may err
In compassing material ends,
While the True Church need never stir
To gather in its dividends.

The 'potamus can never reach
The mango on the mango-tree;
But fruits of pomegranate and peach
Refresh the Church from over sea.

Here we are neither told that the Church resembles a hippopotamus (as in simile) nor bullied into making this comparison (as in metaphor), but there can be no doubt the words are being used to direct our attention to similarities between the two. Nor should there be much inclination, in this case, to posit figurative meanings, for in what words or sentences would we lodge them? The hippopotamus really does rest on his belly in the mud; the True Church, the poem says literally, never can fail. The poem does, of course, intimate much that goes beyond the literal meanings of the words. But intimation is not meaning. *too simple*

The argument so far has led to the conclusion that as much of metaphor as can be explained in terms of meaning may, and indeed must, be explained by appeal to the literal meanings of words. A consequence is that the sentences in which metaphors occur are true or false in a normal, literal way, for if the words in them don't have special meanings, sentences don't have special truth. This is not to deny that there is such a thing as metaphorical truth, only to deny it of sentences. Metaphor does lead us to notice what might not otherwise be noticed, and there is no reason, I suppose, not to say these visions, thoughts, and feelings inspired by the metaphor, are true or false.

If a sentence used metaphorically is true or false in the ordinary sense, then it is clear that it is usually false. The most obvious semantic difference between simile and metaphor is that all similes are true and most metaphors are false. The earth is like a floor, the Assyrian did come down like a wolf on the fold, because everything is like everything. But turn these sentences into metaphors, and you turn them false; the earth is like a floor, but it is not a floor; Tolstoy, grown up, was like an infant, but he wasn't one. We use a simile ordinarily only when we know the corresponding metaphor to be false. We say Mr. S. is like a pig because we know he isn't one. If we had used a metaphor and said he was a pig, this would not be because we changed our mind about the facts but because we chose to get the idea across a different way.

What matters is not actual falsehood but that the sentence be taken to be false. Notice what happens when a sentence we use as a metaphor, believing it false, comes to be thought true because of a change in what is believed about the world. When it was reported that Hemingway's plane had been sighted, wrecked, in Africa, the New York *Mirror* ran a headline saying, "Hemingway Lost in Africa," the word "lost" being used to suggest he was dead. When it turned out he was alive, the *Mirror* left the headline to be taken literally. Or consider this case: a woman sees herself in a beautiful dress and says, "What a dream of a dress!"—and then wakes up. The point of the metaphor is that the dress is like a dress one would dream of and therefore isn't a dream-dress. Henle provides a good example from *Anthony and Cleopatra* (2. 2):

> The barge she sat in, like a burnish'd throne
> Burn'd on the water

Here simile and metaphor interact strangely, but the metaphor would vanish if a literal conflagration were imagined. In much the same way the usual effect of a simile can be sabotaged by taking the comparison too earnestly. Woody Allen writes, "The trial, which took place over the following weeks, was like a circus, although there was some difficulty getting the elephants into the courtroom."[8]

Generally it is only when a sentence is taken to be false that we accept it as a metaphor and start to hunt out the hidden implication. It is probably for this reason that most metaphorical sentences are *patently* false, just as all similes are trivially true. Absurdity or contradiction in a metaphorical sentence guarantees we won't believe it and invites us, under proper circumstances, to take the sentence metaphorically.

Patent falsity is the usual case with metaphor, but on occasion patent truth will do as well. "Business is business" is too obvious in its literal meaning to be taken as having been uttered to convey information, so we look for another use; Ted Cohen reminds us, in the same connection, that no man is an island.[9] The point is the same. The ordinary meaning in the context of use is odd enough to prompt us to disregard the question of literal truth.

Now let me raise a somewhat Platonic issue by comparing the making of a metaphor with telling a lie. The comparison is apt because lying, like making a metaphor, concerns not the meaning of words but their use. It is sometimes said that telling a lie entails saying what is false; but this is wrong. Telling a lie requires not that what you say be false but that

8. Woody Allen, *New Yorker*, 21 November 1977, p. 59.
9. Ted Cohen, "Figurative Speech and Figurative Acts," *Journal of Philosophy* 72 (1975): 671. Since the negation of a metaphor seems always to be a potential metaphor, there may be as many platitudes among the potential metaphors as there are absurds among the actuals.

you think it false. Since we usually believe true sentences and disbelieve false, most lies are falsehoods; but in any particular case this is an accident. The parallel between making a metaphor and telling a lie is emphasized by the fact that the same sentence can be used, with meaning unchanged, for either purpose. So a woman who believed in witches but did not think her neighbor a witch might say, "She's a witch," meaning it metaphorically; the same woman, still believing the same of witches and her neighbor but intending to deceive, might use the same words to very different effect. Since sentence and meaning are the same in both cases, it is sometimes hard to prove which intention lay behind the saying of it; thus a man who says "Lattimore's a Communist" and means to lie can always try to beg off by pleading a metaphor.

What makes the difference between a lie and a metaphor is not a difference in the words used or what they mean (in any strict sense of meaning) but in how the words are used. Using a sentence to tell a lie and using it to make a metaphor are, of course, totally different uses, so different that they do not interfere with one another, as say, acting and lying do. In lying, one must make an assertion so as to represent oneself as believing what one does not; in acting, assertion is excluded. Metaphor is careless to the difference. It can be an insult, and so be an assertion, to say to a man "You are a pig." But no metaphor was involved when (let us suppose) Odysseus addressed the same words to his companions in Circe's palace; a story, to be sure, and so no assertion—but the word, for once, was used literally of men.

No theory of metaphorical meaning or metaphorical truth can help explain how metaphor works. Metaphor runs on the same familiar linguistic tracks that the plainest sentences do; this we saw from considering simile. What distinguishes metaphor is not meaning but use—in this it is like assertion, hinting, lying, promising, or criticizing. And the special use to which we put language in metaphor is not—cannot be—to "say something" special, no matter how indirectly. For a metaphor *says* only what shows on its face—usually a patent falsehood or an absurd truth. And this plain truth or falsehood needs no paraphrase—it is given in the literal meaning of the words.

What are we to make, then, of the endless energy that has been, and is being, spent on methods and devices for drawing out the content of a metaphor? The psychologists Robert Verbrugge and Nancy McCarrell tell us that:

> Many metaphors draw attention to common systems of relationships or common transformations, in which the identity of the participants is secondary. For example, consider the sentences: *A car is like an animal, Tree trunks are straws for thirsty leaves and branches.* The first sentence directs attention to systems of relationships among energy consumption, respiration, self-induced

motion, sensory systems, and, possibly, a homunculus. In the second sentence, the resemblance is a more constrained type of transformation: suction of fluid through a vertically oriented cylindrical space from a source of fluid to a destination.[10]

Verbrugge and McCarrell don't believe there is any sharp line between the literal and metaphorical uses of words; they think many words have a "fuzzy" meaning that gets fixed, if fixed at all, by a context. But surely this fuzziness, however it is illustrated and explained, cannot erase the line between what a sentence literally means (given its context) and what it "draws our attention to" (given its literal meaning as fixed by the context). The passage I have quoted is not employing such a distinction: what it says the sample sentences direct our attention to are facts expressed by paraphrases of the sentences. Verbrugge and McCarrell simply want to insist that a correct paraphrase may emphasize "systems of relationships" rather than resemblances between objects.

According to Black's interaction theory, a metaphor makes us apply a "system of commonplaces" associated with the metaphorical word to the subject of the metaphor: in "Man is a wolf" we apply commonplace attributes (stereotypes) of the wolf to man. The metaphor, Black says, thus "selects, emphasizes, suppresses, and organizes features of the principal subject by implying statements about it that normally apply to the subsidiary subject."[11] If paraphrase fails, according to Black, it is not because the metaphor does not have a special cognitive content, but because the paraphrase "will not have the same power to inform and enlighten as the original. . . . One of the points I most wish to stress is that the loss in such cases is a loss in cognitive content; the relevant weakness of the literal paraphrase is not that it may be tiresomely prolix or boringly explicit; it fails to be a translation because it fails to give the insight that the metaphor did."[12]

How can this be right? If a metaphor has a special cognitive content, why should it be so difficult or impossible to set it out? If, as Owen Barfield claims, a metaphor "says one thing and means another," why should it be that when we try to get explicit about what it means, the effect is so much weaker—"put it that way," Barfield says, "and nearly all the tarning, and with it half the poetry, is lost."[13] Why does Black think a literal paraphrase "inevitably says too much—and with the wrong emphasis"? Why inevitably? Can't we, if we are clever enough, come as close as we please?

10. Robert R. Verbrugge and Nancy S. McCarrell, "Metaphoric Comprehension: Studies in Reminding and Resembling," *Cognitive Psychology* 9 (1977): 499.

11. Black, pp. 44–45.

12. Ibid., p. 46.

13. Owen Barfield, "Poetic Diction and Legal Fiction," in *The Importance of Language*, ed. Max Black (Englewood Cliffs, N.J., 1962), p. 55.

For that matter, how is it that a simile gets along without a special intermediate meaning? In general, critics do not suggest that a simile says one thing and means another—they do not suppose it *means* anything but what lies on the surface of the words. It may make us think deep thoughts, just as a metaphor does; how come, then, no one appeals to the "special cognitive content" of the simile? And remember Eliot's hippopotamus; there there was neither simile nor metaphor, but what seemed to get done was just like what gets done by similes and metaphors. Does anyone suggest that the *words* in Eliot's poem have special meanings?

Finally, if words in metaphor bear a coded meaning, how can this meaning differ from the meaning those same words bear in the case where the metaphor *dies*—that is, when it comes to be part of the language? Why doesn't "He was burned up" as now used and meant mean *exactly* what the fresh metaphor once meant? Yet all that the dead metaphor means is that he was very angry—a notion not very difficult to make explicit.

There is, then, a tension in the usual view of metaphor. For on the one hand, the usual view wants to hold that a metaphor does something no plain prose can possibly do and, on the other hand, it wants to explain what a metaphor does by appealing to a cognitive content—just the sort of thing plain prose is designed to express. As long as we are in this frame of mind, we must harbor the suspicion that it *can* be done, at least up to a point.

There is a simple way out of the impasse. We must give up the idea that a metaphor carries a message, that it has a content or meaning (except, of course, its literal meaning). The various theories we have been considering mistake their goal. Where they think they provide a method for deciphering an encoded content, they actually tell us (or try to tell us) something about the *effects* metaphors have on us. The common error is to fasten on the contents of the thoughts a metaphor provokes and to read these contents into the metaphor itself. No doubt metaphors often make us notice aspects of things we did not notice before; no doubt they bring surprising analogies and similarities to our attention; they do provide a kind of lens or lattice, as Black says, through which we view the relevant phenomena. The issue does not lie here but in the question of how the metaphor is related to what it makes us see.

It may be remarked with justice that the claim that a metaphor provokes or invites a certain view of its subject rather than saying it straight out is a commonplace; so it is. Thus Aristotle says metaphor leads to a "perception of resemblances." Black, following Richards, says a metaphor "evokes" a certain response: "a suitable hearer will be led by a metaphor to construct a . . . system."[14] This view is neatly summed up by

14. Black, p. 41.

what Heracleitus said of the Delphic oracle: "It does not say and it does not hide, it intimates."[15]

I have no quarrel with these descriptions of the effects of metaphor, only with the associated views as to *how* metaphor is supposed to produce them. What I deny is that metaphor does its work by having a special meaning, a specific cognitive content. I do not think, as Richards does, that metaphor produces its result by having a meaning which results from the interaction of two ideas; it is wrong, in my view, to say, with Owen Barfield, that a metaphor "says one thing and means another"; or with Black that a metaphor asserts or implies certain complex things by dint of a special meaning and *thus* accomplishes its job of yielding an "insight." A metaphor does its work through other intermediaries—to suppose it can be effective only by conveying a coded message is like thinking a joke or a dream makes some statement which a clever interpreter can restate in plain prose. Joke or dream or metaphor can, like a picture or a bump on the head, make us appreciate some fact—but not by standing for, or expressing, the fact.

If this is right, what we attempt in "paraphrasing" a metaphor cannot be to give its meaning, for that lies on the surface; rather we attempt to evoke what the metaphor brings to our attention. I can imagine someone granting this and shrugging it off as no more than an insistence on restraint in using the word "meaning." This would be wrong. The central error about metaphor is most easily attacked when it takes the form of a theory of metaphorical meaning, but behind that theory, and statable independently, is the thesis that associated with a metaphor is a cognitive content that its author wishes to convey and that the interpreter must grasp if he is to get the message. This theory is false, whether or not we call the purported cognitive content a meaning.

It should make us suspect the theory that it is so hard to decide, even in the case of the simplest metaphors, exactly what the content is supposed to be. The reason it is often so hard to decide is, I think, that we imagine there is a content to be captured when all the while we are in fact focusing on what the metaphor makes us notice. If what the metaphor makes us notice were finite in scope and propositional in nature, this would not in itself make trouble; we would simply project the content the metaphor brought to mind onto the metaphor. But in fact there is no limit to what a metaphor calls to our attention, and much of what we are caused to notice is not propositional in character. When we try to say what a metaphor "means," we soon realize there is no end to what we want to mention.[16] If someone draws his finger along a coastline on a

15. I use Hannah Arendt's attractive translation of "σημαίνει"; it clearly should not be rendered as "mean" in this context.

16. Stanley Cavell mentions the fact that most attempts at paraphrase end with "and so on" and refers to Empson's remark that metaphors are "pregnant" (*Must We Mean What We Say?* [New York, 1969], p. 79). But Cavell doesn't explain the endlessness of paraphrase

map, or mentions the beauty and deftness of a line in a Picasso etching, how many things are drawn to your attention? You might list a great many, but you could not finish since the idea of finishing would have no clear application. How many facts or propositions are conveyed by a photograph? None, an infinity, or one great unstatable fact? Bad question. A picture is not worth a thousand words, or any other number. Words are the wrong currency to exchange for a picture.

It's not only that we can't provide an exhaustive catalogue of what has been attended to when we are led to see something in a new light; the difficulty is more fundamental. What we notice or see is not, in general, propositional in character. Of course it *may* be, and when it is, it usually may be stated in fairly plain words. But if I show you Wittgenstein's duck-rabbit, and I say, "It's a duck," then with luck you see it as a duck; if I say, "It's a rabbit," you see it as a rabbit. But no proposition expresses what I have led you to see. Perhaps you have come to realize that the drawing can be seen as a duck or as a rabbit. But one could come to know this without ever seeing the drawing as a duck or as a rabbit. Seeing as is not seeing that. Metaphor makes us see one thing as another by making some literal statement that inspires or prompts the insight. Since in most cases what the metaphor prompts or inspires is not entirely, or even at all, recognition of some truth or fact, the attempt to give literal expression to the content of the metaphor is simply misguided.

The theorist who tries to explain a metaphor by appealing to a hidden message, like the critic who attempts to state the message, is then fundamentally confused. No such explanation or statement can be forthcoming because no such message exists.

Not, of course, that interpretation and elucidation of a metaphor are not in order. Many of us need help if we are to see what the author of a metaphor wanted us to see and what a more sensitive or educated reader grasps. The legitimate function of so-called paraphrase is to make the lazy or ignorant reader have a vision like that of the skilled critic. The critic is, so to speak, in benign competition with the metaphor maker. The critic tries to make his own art easier or more transparent in some respects than the original, but at the same time he tries to reproduce in others some of the effects the original had on him. In doing this the critic also, and perhaps by the best method at his command, calls attention to the beauty or aptness, the hidden power, of the metaphor itself.

---

as I do, as can be learned from the fact that he thinks it distinguishes metaphor from some ("but perhaps not all") literal discourse. I hold that the endless character of what we call the paraphrase of a metaphor springs from the fact that it attempts to spell out what the metaphor makes us notice, and to this there is no clear end. I would say the same for any use of language.

Metaphor as Rhetoric:
The Problem of Evaluation

Wayne C. Booth

1

There were no conferences on metaphor, ever, in any culture, until our own century was already middle-aged. As late as 1927, John Middleton Murry, complaining about the superficiality of most discussions of metaphor, could say, "There are not many of them."[1] If we take what he said at face value, what we are doing in this symposium appears as part of an intellectual movement that is—to use the word that Thucydides uses to set things up for his history—one of the "greatest" in the history of thought. Explicit discussions of something called metaphor have multiplied astronomically in the past fifty years. This increase is not simply parallel to the vast general increase in scholarly and critical writing. Shakespeareans have multiplied too, as have scholars of Homer, of Dickens, and of Charles the Second. But students of metaphor have positively pullulated. The bibliographies show more titles for 1977, for example, than for—well, the truth is that I refuse to do the counting to make this point, but I'll wager a good deal that the year 1977 produced more titles than the entire history of thought before 1940. We shall soon no doubt have more metaphoricians than metaphysicians—or should that be metamorticians, the embalmers of dead metaphor? I have in fact extrapolated with my pocket calculator to the year 2039; at that point there will be more students of metaphor than people.

1. John Middleton Murry, "Metaphor," in *John Clare and Other Studies* (1927; London and New York, 1950), pp. 85–97; reprinted in Warren Shibles' *Essays on Metaphor* (Whitewater, Wis., 1972), p. 27.

But of course we can never take such explosions at face value. We must discount this one in at least two ways. First, there have been many more discussions of what people from the Greek philosophers on *called* metaphor than any bibliography could show. Almost all such discussions before this century were either short sections in treatises on rhetoric or style or incidental complaints and warnings by philosophers seeking an unequivocal language. For almost everyone, metaphor was one kind of figurative device among many, not the generic term for all similitudes. The total number of discussions must be almost as great as the total number of treatises on the resources available to the rhetorician or poet. And that would make a fair number of "titles."

On the other hand, if we take metaphor to be what people *now call* metaphor, we must discount even more. Along with the immense increase in bibliography about something previously *called* metaphor has gone an immense explosion of meanings for the word. If I listed what was said about metaphor before Murry's statement, defining it as "whatever people *now* mean by the word," I would in fact be forced to list pages from every philosopher, grammarian, rhetorician, and logician from the Pre-Socratics on.

Even when we do all the discounting possible, however, the fact remains that all of us here are part of a very curious, perhaps finally inexplicable, intellectual movement. No matter how we define it, metaphor seems to be taking over not only the world of humanists but the world of the social and natural sciences as well.[2]

Perhaps this broadening of meanings and explosion of interest are all to the good. If we love metaphor, we surely should not complain when we find thousands of students taking it seriously. But there is a problem for students of any subject when the word for that subject expands to cover everything. And that is precisely what has happened to this word. Metaphor has by now been defined in so many ways that there is no human expression, whether in language or any other medium, that would not be metaphoric in *someone's* definition. This could mean that the word has become useless and that we should all take up some other line of inquiry. Surely when a word can mean everything it risks meaning nothing. But the interesting thing is that in spite of differences in the scope of our definitions, we all meet everyday certain statements that everyone recognizes as metaphor and calls by that name. We seem to

2. For evidence, see the table of contents of *Essays on Metaphor* or leaf through Shibles' immense compendium *Metaphor: An Annotated Bibliography and History* (Whitewater, Wis., 1971).

Wayne C. Booth's most recent book is *Critical Understanding: The Powers and Limits of Pluralism.*

have a kind of common-sense agreement about a fairly narrow definition, one that survives even while our theory expands the original concept beyond recognition.

In a seminar that I cannot claim to be running—rather, it runs me—the students and I have so far not found any one definition of metaphor that we all could possibly agree on. But we have found innumerable instances of what all of us happily call metaphors regardless of our definitions. In Paul Ricoeur's metaphoric definition, they are "full-fledged": "Man is a wolf to man"; "Chicago is a dungheap"; "You're the cream in my coffee." We have also found many that are metaphors only in definitions that are not universally accepted: "I'll defend that position"; "God is love." And of course there are many that look metaphoric but that could in some contexts be quite literal: "Mary is an elephant"; "Jeffrey is a rat"; "Something's rotten in the state of Denmark." If I said, "We have here three different breeds of cat," everyone would agree that I had attempted a metaphor. But we would begin to dispute if I asked for a clear vote about whether this sentence I am now delivering contains no metaphors. Some of us would note that "delivering" and "contains" and "clear" still have some metaphoric sense whether I intended it or not. Others would want to add further words, like "sentence" itself or "metaphor," that I did not intend metaphorically.

Classical rhetoricians—if by an odd chance we had any among us—would say that the sentence contains *no* metaphors; dead ones are not just dead, they are no longer metaphors. Metaphor for them is generally not contrasted with literal speech but with normal or ordinary or usual, *un*twisted, speech. Since the words "delivery" and "contain" have become one usual way of saying what I wanted to say, they are not dead metaphors but nonmetaphors. At the other extreme, some would claim that all my terms were metaphors, and they would seek, though not always find, philological evidence to prove that they were originally "motivated." Or they might, like Paul de Man, seek to show the inescapable metaphorical quality of all human discourse. We might even find among us someone who would want to argue for the once popular theological view that not only is all language metaphorical but that the whole of our life is but a metaphor—what used to be called an analogy—for God's truth.

2

Suppose we confine our attention for a while to examples that we would all call metaphors and ask the question that would have occurred first to Demetrius, say, or Quintilian: Which are the good ones?

Most writers on metaphor imply that they know how to answer that question; some actually give their criteria. But why is it that so few give any real help to the writer or reader of metaphor? Where would you send me now for assistance in determining which metaphors should be celebrated and which should be hanged from the neck until dead? Donald Davidson might say that to ask the question is to pursue a wild goose or will-o'-the-wisp. There are no unsuccessful metaphors, he says, only tasteless ones. If he wishes, we can change the question to Where do I go for help in improving my taste?

Let's choose an easy metaphor for a close look. A lawyer friend of mine was hired to defend a large Southern utility against a suit by a small one, and he thought at first that he was doing fine. All of the law seemed to be on his side, and he felt that he had presented his case well. Then the lawyer for the small utility said, speaking to the jury, almost as if incidentally to his legal case, "So now we see what it is. They got us where they want us. They holding us up with one hand, their good sharp fishin' knife in the other, and they sayin', 'you jes set still, little catfish, we're *jes* going to *gut* ya.'" At that moment, my friend reports, he knew he had lost the case. "I was in the hands of a genius of metaphor."

It is not too difficult to figure out ways of talking about why this metaphor is a good one. Our sense of its mastery is indeed quick and intuitive, but it is useful to slow down a bit and see if we can discover the grounds of our assurance.

In the first place, we have isolated a particular kind of metaphor from all the other things called metaphor. We are thus forced to put aside a variety of definitions that we may for other occasions want to use. For the purpose of explaining the power of "catfish," we get no help from classing it (1) with all symbolic expressions that claim similarity or likeness, or, narrowing down a bit, with (2) all nonliteral language, whether intended to be recognized as "figured" or "troped" or "twisted" or not, or, still narrowing, with (3) all symbolic inventions, whether in language or other media, that *are* intended to be taken nonliterally. Our catfish does belong, of course, in all these increasingly smaller classes, but the classes are still so large that they cannot, in themselves, lead us toward discriminations of quality among their members. Even the notion of human intention, added in the third class, does not help us much, until we take the obvious next step and ask *what* intention, thus importing the rhetorical notion of *purpose* into the philosophical problem of intentions. If the lawyer's purpose was to tell the truth in a new and interesting way, then we might discover the metaphor's work by inquiring into its truth, and we might try to decide whether his metaphor said anything more than "They're trying to cheat us." Or if his purpose was to be accurate and clear, we might, as many modern guides to writing tell us to do, find fault with his mixed metaphors, pointing out that catfish don't set, or even sit. But his purpose is obviously to forge a weapon in order to win, and that weapon is thus in a class of metaphors that classical rhetorical treatises took as a large part of their province.

Suppose that instead of attempting a formal definition of the class we simply list the marks of this beast, so that we can then judge its "points," in the hope that the same procedure may enable us to mark off other kinds that will yield different criteria. Whether or not we finally decide that the various species of what we call metaphor belong to a single genus or simply bear family resemblances to each other will not matter much for our various special inquiries into quality, though it will of course continue to matter to us in our philosophical endeavors. (Since most of the papers at the symposium seem to assume that metaphor is, finally, a single determinate concept, I suppose I should, without providing argument, declare myself on that issue. I am pretty sure that the many things we call metaphor are not mutually compatible under a single determinate definition; at most they bear family resemblances to some other members of the family, and some of them are in fact essentially different from some others. One obvious clash, for example, is that between any "weapon metaphor" chosen to produce the greatest possible shock, with heightened contempt for the victim, and any "sublime metaphor" embodied in a culture [not chosen by a particular author] and expressing the greatest possible spiritual heightening: for example, all myths and rituals. We may all want to legislate against certain uses of the word in order to distinguish what true metaphor is. But in fact people will go on calling these disparate things metaphor, and we should not use the word without acknowledging its inescapable indeterminacy.)

Here, then, are some marks of the catfish metaphor:

1. It is a part of an intended communication, not primarily a piece of self-expression or an attempt at formal beauty.
2. What is being communicated is context-dependent: the full meaning of the metaphor cannot be determined without reference to the rhetorical situation. *That* it is a metaphor everyone will see without a context. *What* it says or does depends on a rhetorical situation.
3. That context reveals to everyone a clear persuasive purpose: to win.
4. That *purpose* can be paraphrased regardless of what theorists say about whether the *metaphor* can be. There are many different synonymous ways of describing the lawyer's intent to win his case.
5. The metaphor is itself also *largely* paraphrasable, but the contrast is not necessarily with some literal meaning but rather with some less striking or more everyday way of putting the point. Other metaphors might be invented, more or less effective for the same purpose.
6. What is being compared are two things, not just two words: in this

case they are two *situations* which could be unpacked as an elaborate analogy: large utility is to fisherman as small utility is to catfish; knife is to catfish's vital center as large utilities' measures are to small utility's vital center; and so on.

7. Unlike the metaphors Paul Ricoeur prefers to talk about, this one is stable, in the sense that once the jury has recognized the comparison, no further act of interpretation is required, no further underminings of normal readings invited. Though analysis will reveal immense complexity in the rhetorical moment, the invitation to reconstruct one comparison out of another comparison is sharply limited by implicit standards of relevance. Hundreds of associations with fish, knives, fishermen, gutting, and utilities are simply and flatly declared irrelevant. To pursue them would be a mistaken extension of the metaphorical process.

8. It is thus local or finite: there is no direct invitation to speculate about meanings, profound or otherwise, about metaphor, about life, about the universe, not even about capitalist exploitation. Our attention is held to the battle of utilities. The metaphor adds no new truth, not in any obvious way. (This does not mean that a probing thinker cannot see how the metaphor is "really" related to larger matters, just as he can render the metaphor's stability unstable without half trying.)

9. Yet implicit in all this is a mark that this kind of metaphor shares with all other deliberate rhetorical deviations: more is communicated than the words literally say. What the more is cannot be easily described. Aristotle and others called it energy, which does put us in the right direction. Whether the metaphor communicates more than the nonmetaphor is not mainly a question of cognitive content or meaning, though we might still want to debate about that. What is unquestionable is that when weapon metaphors succeed, more passes from speaker to hearer than would have passed otherwise. I shall want to return in a few moments to look at what that more might be, but for now it is enough to repeat what Ted Cohen has said: part of what is communicated does not depend on the metaphor succeeding in the sense of winning or even in the sense of being thought good. The speaker has performed a task by yoking what the hearer had not yoked before, and the hearer simply cannot resist joining him; they thus perform an identical dance step, and the metaphor accomplishes at least part of its work even if the hearer then draws back and says, "I shouldn't have allowed that!"

10. Finally, we find a mark that clearly distinguishes this figure from what I have elsewhere called stable irony. It is true that the act of reconstruction begins, as it does with irony, in a recognition that literal, discrete, or "ordinary" meanings alone will not make sense of the passage—a new relation must be actively sought. But after the

auditor has reconstructed such acceptable meanings, they are not, with this kind of metaphor, separated from the *stated* meanings and then in some sense repudiated, as they must be in receiving irony. Having moved from the gutting of catfish to the gutting of small utilities, the mind is not then asked to rule out what it first saw, a wrong reading. The original meaning, what might be called the uninterpreted picture, remains as part of the final picture in a way that is not true of stable ironies. The big utility is forever a knife-wielding threat.

These seem the marks that are essential in the sense that whenever I find them applicable I will be able to derive criteria for success with weapon metaphors: an unusual or surprising comparison of two things, part of a communication in a context that reveals a predetermined purpose that can be paraphrased, intended to be recognized and reconstructed with stable, local meanings that can thus be evaluated as contributing to that purpose.

It is curious that the difference between metaphor and simile, essential in the study of some kinds of metaphor, seems here to become extremely unimportant. It is perhaps true that adding a "like" or "as" to the catfish picture will weaken it somewhat. But this addition does not change the nature of the picture, and one is not surprised to find that classical theorists, unlike many modern philosophers with different purposes in view, have seen the choice between simile and metaphor as minor, as depending simply on whether the speaker profits from seeming more or less daring.[3]

3

Once we have a metaphoric species clearly in mind—and I remind you that I have begun with one of the simplest kinds—we can easily discover criteria for effectiveness. In fact, we can easily invent other metaphors designed for the same purpose and then judge their relative quality. Suppose the lawyer had said, "And so the big utilities are proceeding to disembowel the company I represent, right before our eyes." Or: "The big utilities just expect us to stand looking on helplessly while they sap our vital forces." Or, finally, to make one that is a closer rival: "They got us where they want us. They holding us up with one hand, their good sharp fishin' knife in the other, and they sayin', 'you jes' hang quiet, little bass, we're *jes'* going to *gut* ya.'"

Where can I go for help in choosing between "bass" and "catfish"?

3. See, e.g., Demetrius, *On Style:* "When the metaphor seems daring, let it for greater security be converted into a simile . . . [By adding 'like'] we obtain a simile and a less risky expression."

Philosophical discussions seldom deal with any metaphor more complex than "Man is a wolf," "My sweetheart is my Schopenhauer," and "Smith is a pig" and they almost never give me a rhetorical context that would determine my standards of success. Even when such discussions deal with complexities and offer evaluations, they seem to reduce all criteria to two, truth and coherence, sometimes adding novelty, or a novel truth that reveals new incoherence. And I find the same poverty, somewhat surprisingly, when I turn to authors who explicitly promise to be helpful about such matters. All modern guides to writing have a word to say about metaphor, or at most two: "cliché" and "mixed." That is to say, most modern writing guides that fall into the hands of the young have only two standards to be applied to my examples: novelty and coherence. (Note that they tend to drop the philosopher's concern for truth.) New metaphors are good, the newer the better; old ones are clichés, if they are not so old that they are actually dead, in which case they don't matter unless we happen to remember the etymology. At this point the second criterion comes in: metaphors should be coherent, that is, metaphors should not be mixed.

Well, I have made my bass metaphor more coherent, with "hang quiet" instead of "set still." Have I improved it? And as for novelty, surely it is just as novel to talk of gutting a bass in that situation as gutting a catfish. It is not even clear to me that it matters, for those on the jury, whether they have all heard that comparison before: so much depends on *other* qualities.

One of the subtlest of modern guides, Fowler, adds two criteria. He is against "overdone" metaphors no matter how coherent and he quotes Samuel Richardson's long passage with disapproval: "Tost to and fro by the high winds of passionate control, I behold the desired port, the single state, into which I would fain steer. . . . " And on for eight lines of sailing. Second, he is against "spoilt metaphors," by which he means that our metaphors should be accurate: "Yet Jaurès was the Samson who upheld the pillars of the Bloc"—Samson, you may or may not remember, did not exactly *uphold* pillars.

It would take the rest of this paper to describe the criteria that leap to mind to be added to or subtracted from these, now that we know what we are looking for. But they need not leap to mind unaided. The classical rhetoricians are a rich source of suggestions about such matters, and it is a pity that because rhetoric has so often been degraded into mere lists of devices we have let ourselves lose what it could teach. Here is a short list that one could dig out of almost any rhetoric text from Aristotle to Whately.

1. Good metaphors of this kind are *active,* lending the energy of animated things to whatever is less energetic or more abstract. As Demetrius says, they introduce "inanimate things in a state of activity as

though they were animate." "Catfish" and "bass" both win easily here over my other versions.

2. Good weapon metaphors are *concise.* All the rhetoricians had a strong sense of what Herbert Spencer later described, at length, as a law of stylistic economy: the more you can convey in a given number of words, the better. Indeed, that is one reason for using metaphor rather than ordinary language: it says more with less. If I try to unpack "catfish" I find that a full paragraph or two will be required to describe what it manages to convey. "Bass" is as economical, but my "disembowel" version is less economical (though shorter) because it says so much less. Even it is better, however, than simply saying, "They're trying to destroy us."

3. Good metaphors are *appropriate,* in their grandeur or triviality, to the task in hand. If the point is to heighten sublimity, then trivial metaphors must be avoided. But if diminishment is desired, vice versa. Now in our example what is needed is a heightening of power- ful, hypocritical destructiveness on the one hand, and of helpless in- nocence on the other. On the face of it neither a catfish nor a bass is an *especially* good metaphor for innocence. But both are innocent enough, and catfish is a bit better than bass for squirming helpless- ness, since it is not a game fish but an easily caught harmless scavenger.[4]

4. It is not enough that the metaphor be appropriate to the task, and thus to other elements in the text. It must be properly *accommodated to the audience,* in this case a Southern jury. It is not hard to think of hearers for whom some other innocent victim would be preferable, and there might even be some juries for whom the very vulgarity that makes "catfish" so powerful should be diminished.

5. Finally such a metaphor should build a proper *ethos* for the speaker, building or sustaining his character as someone to be trusted. Here we approach something difficult to talk about indeed. But once we think about it we realize that every speaker who uses any figure with the intent that it be recognized *as* a figure, instead of using it as an art that disguises art, calls attention to himself in ways that the user of "ordinary, usual," untwisted language does not. Every speaker, of course, makes a character, an *ethos* for himself, whether he is using figurative language or not. He may even choose to build a character like the Jonathan Swift Samuel Johnson described—the sort of "rogue" who "never hazards a metaphor." But this kind of metaphor, like all kinds that invite recognition, builds a character in a further sense: the *ethos* of what we call a "real character," in this case a colorful jester who identifies, in a kind of humorous helplessness, with the little fellow. He makes us almost forget that the little fellow is actually

4. I am indebted to an anonymous voice from the audience for these data about catfish.

a utility, something that cannot suffer, and that the lawyer is paid to invent metaphors like this.

4

This by no means exhausts the criteria we could discover and apply to weapon metaphors. I think that with a year or two of thought one might work out those criteria, and it would be worth doing in a world that for want of rhetorical attention writes and speaks mainly blobs of verbal spaghetti. But it is time to turn to even more complicated matters. I want first to suggest larger and more important relations between metaphor and character than were implied in my final mark of weapon metaphors, larger in fact than even the classical rhetoricians seem to have recognized.

I invite you a second time to ask where, in all that you have read about metaphor, you would go for assistance in deciding not whether any part of the following is good or bad as craft but whether the whole passage is an admirable conclusion to a book. The one-page chapter, "The Metaphor Delivered," concludes a book about the protest march on Washington during the Vietnam War.

> Whole crisis of Christianity in America that the military heroes were on one side, and the unnamed saints on the other! Let the bugle blow. The death of America rides in on the smog. America— the land where a new kind of man was born from the idea that God was present in every man not only as compassion but as power, and so the country belonged to the people; for the will of the people—if the locks of their life could be given the art to turn—was then the will of God. Great and dangerous idea! If the locks did not turn, then the will of the people was the will of the Devil. Who by now could know where was what? Liars controlled the locks.
>
> Brood on that country who expresses our will. She is America, once a beauty of magnificence unparalleled, now a beauty with a leprous skin. She is heavy with child—no one knows if legitimate—and languishes in a dungeon whose walls are never seen. Now the first contractions of her fearsome labor begin—it will go on: no doctor exists to tell the hour. It is only known that false labor is not likely on her now, no, she will probably give birth, and to what?—the most fearsome totalitarianism the world has ever known? or can she, poor giant, tormented lovely girl, deliver a babe of a new world brave and tender, artful and wild? Rush to the locks. God writhes in his bonds. Rush to the locks. Deliver us from our curse. For we must end on the road to that mystery where courage, death, and the dream of love give promise of sleep.[5]

5. Norman Mailer, *The Armies of the Night* (New York, 1968), p. 288.

Now it may at first appear that Norman Mailer's passage uses several metaphors of the catfish kind: weapons designed to win adherents and destroy enemies. "Let the bugle blow." "Bugle" is to "U.S. Army troops" as "my plea" to "the army of saints." "Vietnam protesters" are to "saints" as "military heroes" to—well, we must be careful, because it is not clear that Mailer means "heroes" to be turned into "devils." Can we say that America, the "beauty with the leprous skin" is to "unpredictable future" as "pregnant woman languishing in prison" is to "unpredictable, perhaps illegitimate babe"? Already things are getting too complicated for literal analysis. And suddenly the leprous woman becomes a lovely giant, who, though lacking a doctor, is sure to deliver either a fearsome totalitarianism or a "babe of a new world brave and tender, artful and wild," a babe that may or may not be identified with the God who is writhing in his bonds—no doubt suffering in the smog on which the death of America rides. The last sentence alone defies close analysis, because if it is true that we must end on the road where there is promise of sleep, it is not at all clear why we should rush to what locks, or who is to deliver us from our curse.

(I cannot know, of course, how readers will respond to this passage out of context. But it may be useful to underline its intensities by reporting on a contrast between my expectations in reading this paper to the original audience and the actual response. I had written for delivery, immediately following my attempt at a neutral reading, the following:

> I cannot know, of course, how you feel about the passage by now. But I should be much surprised if most of you do not think it a terrible piece of metaphoric jumbling. . . . I shall not try to reverse your judgment completely, but I do want to think a bit about the grounds for that judgment.

My actual surprise was of a different kind. The audience began laughing much too early and too hard for my own comfort. At "tormented lovely girl" I interrupted the reading with a plea for a fair hearing: "You're spoiling the pleasure for those who like the passage." But the laughter continued to mount. When I said, at the end, "I tried very hard to read that neutrally, so that I would not give an opinion about it in advance, and I was surprised by the laughter," the comment itself produced *more* laughter. Finally, in something of a flurry, I asked: "Was there anyone who *resented* the laughter?" The question was first met with silence.

"Not a single person in this room thinks that the passage is a good way to end a book?"

At that point a voice said "Yes," and I said, "At last! Who is it? Ah, Mr. Strier [my colleague, Richard Strier]. Well, we'll hear from you later."

In the discussion after the talk, Strier said that "if Booth had wanted to, he could have made this audience laugh at *any* author. His reading was *not* neutral. He did not let us know that the author was Mailer, and the passage was thus wrenched out of its context, taken out of its historical moment and put into a new context, where attention was focused on deliberately scrambled metaphor as a thing in itself."

I welcomed the rather warm discussion that followed, and I accept Strier's point—it is in fact one of my theses about metaphor that it cannot be judged without reference to a context. The interchange is worth reporting here, however, primarily because it illustrated the high emotional involvement we display in our judgments of metaphor. Having laughed in contempt at the passage, many in the audience reported themselves extremely uncomfortable. When they learned that the author was Mailer and that I thought the passage really quite skillful ["much better than I could have managed if I had attempted a book like that"], they were left confused, their emotional investment without a clear object.

In any case, even if we finally decide that Mailer's attempt is not as successful as he would have hoped, the reason can surely not be that Mailer has mixed his metaphors as aggressively as Shakespeare often did. It would not be hard to find passages in many great authors which, as Strier said, would make an audience laugh if read out of context.)

In judging a passage of this intricate kind, then, we must think hard about what the kind really is, and about how contexts work. Almost all of the marks that we found in "catfish" have here been changed. It is true that we still have metaphors that are clearly intended and that seem to serve *some* rhetorical purpose. But everything else is different. I won't bore you this time by running through all of the marks, but we must note that whatever was covert about "catfish" is not only overt here but positively brandished, as a stage magician would brandish his saw before hacking his assistant to pieces. Trumpets blaring, Mailer openly promises his metaphor and proclaims its "delivery" with a blaring pun on the woman's delivery.

Note secondly that the metaphors are so grotesquely scrambled that one cannot believe the scrambling accidental. Our schoolteacherly norms are deliberately violated, and we cannot easily tell whether, or at what point, the naughty boy is writing with his pen in his cheek. As it were.

Such metaphor, we should not forget as we analyze, has proved itself to have great power in our time. *Armies of the Night* received mostly rave reviews, and you may remember that the world on the whole palpitated to what was said—quite inaccurately—to be Mailer's invention of a new literary genre: the novel as history, history as a novel. Richard Gilman, reviewing for *The New Republic* wrote, "All the rough force of his imagination, his brilliant gifts of observation, his ravishing if often cal-culating honesty, his daring and his *chutzpah* are able to flourish on the steady ground of a newly coherent subject . . . history and personality confront each other with a new sense of liberation."

The key word here is personality. Such metaphoric muddlings, "rough," "brilliant," "ravishing," "calculating," "honest," "daring," are designed to flaunt personality—that is, a special *ethos.* The "character of the speaker" is flaunted to a degree that prevents our determining whether the passage is designed to win members to the antiwar camp or to construct another of Mailer's "advertisements" for himself. We have no way of knowing how many converts to the cause Mailer's book made, but we have plenty of evidence that it was immensely successful in selling Mailer.

I can remember trying to convince a student when the book first came out that it was cheaply self-serving, though it was for me on the "right side." I got nowhere, of course, because to her my judgment against Mailer's art meant that I was not really committed to opposing the war. Another graduate student confessed last week that when he first read the book years ago he found the experience overwhelmingly mov-ing and that when he rereads this page now he feels embarrassed about his earlier gullibility.

What kind of creature is it that can shift like that under our gaze? And how could we ever arrive at defensible judgments of its quality, not simply expressions of our prejudice?

One possible answer to the first question is that Mailer has turned the *ethos,* which in "catfish" was a means to practical ends, into an end in itself. You will note that if we accepted that answer we would have transported the passage out of the domains of rhetoric into the clear pure air of poetry—at least we would have done so according to one traditional way of distinguishing the two. Obviously the means-end dis-tinction doesn't help us very much; if it is true that Mailer is making and advertising a self in such passages, he would surely have a right to insist that such a project is an essential part of his effort to attack the warlords.

To complicate things further, it is clear that Mailer is attempting, however desperately, to remake the *ethos* of America; though his metaphors call attention to him when we look at them critically, they are explicitly addressed to the reader's view of America's rebirth. Read un-critically, as my graduate student originally read them, the metaphors did their work, and their work was an inextricable mixture of argument about the war, portraiture of Mailer, and promise-threat about a glorious-gruesome future society.

Such metaphors are far more obviously constitutive of characters and societies than are the catfish kind. It is true that even the simplest weapon metaphor of the catfish kind will reveal to the perceptive critic the constitution of characters, both of the speaker and of the victim. But metaphors of Mailer's kind do not simply allow the critic to think of such matters; they require every reader to do so.

I needn't tell you that Mailer was not the first rhetor to attempt such immense metaphoric identifications of a constituted self and a constituted cause. Every great political speech or pamphlet reveals similar grand fusions. Toward the end of Edmund Burke's *Reflections on the Revolution in France,* for example, he attempts a metaphoric heightening appropriate to his antirevolutionary cause:

> Our people will find employment enough for a truly patriotic, free, and independent spirit, in guarding what they possess [the British Constitution], from violation. I would not exclude alteration neither; but even when I changed, it should be to preserve. I should be led to my remedy by a great grievance. In what I did, I should follow the example of our ancestors. I would make the reparation as nearly as possible in the style of the building. A politic caution, a guarded circumspection, a moral rather than a complexional timidity were among the ruling principles of our forefathers in their most decided conduct. Not being illuminated with the light of which gentlemen of France tell us they have got so abundant a share, they acted under a strong impression of the ignorance and fallibility of mankind. He that had made them thus fallible, rewarded them for having in their conduct attended to their nature. Let us imitate their caution, if we wish to deserve their fortune, or to retain their bequests. Let us add, if we please, but let us preserve what they have left; and, standing on the firm ground of the British constitution, let us be satisfied to admire rather than attempt to follow in their desperate flights the aëronauts of France.
>
> I have told you [the ostensible French correspondent receiving Burke's "reflections"] candidly my sentiments. I think they are not likely to alter yours. I do not know that they ought. You are young; you cannot guide, but must follow the fortune of your country. But hereafter they may be of some use to you, in some future form which your commonwealth may take. In the present it can hardly remain; but before its final settlement it may be obliged to pass, as one of our poets says, "through great varieties of untried being," and in all its transmigrations to be purified by fire and blood.
>
> I have little to recommend my opinions, but long observation and much impartiality. They come from one who has been no tool of power, no flatterer of greatness; and who in his last acts does not wish to belie the tenor of his life. They come from one, almost the whole of whose public exertion has been a struggle for the liberty of others; from one in whose breast no anger durable or vehement has ever been kindled, but by what he considered as tyranny; and who snatches from his share in the endeavors which are used by good men to discredit opulent oppression, the hours he has employed on your affairs; and who in so doing persuades himself he

has not departed from his usual office: they come from one who desires honours, distinctions, and emoluments, but little; and who expects them not at all; who has no contempt for fame, and no fear of obloquy; who shuns contention, though he will hazard an opinion: from one who wishes to preserve consistency; but who would preserve consistency by varying his means to secure the unity of his end; and, when the equipoise of the vessel in which he sails, may be endangered by overloading it upon one side, is desirous of carrying the small weight of his reasons to that which may preserve its equipoise.

Despite the obvious differences, the similarities are close enough to justify comparison. Burke's metaphors are also mixed, though less wildly than Mailer's: remodelled buildings, lights, bequests, firm ground, desperate flights, fire and blood, steady tenors, kindled fires, overloaded vessels. The tone of self-advertisement as a passionately concerned, distressed citizen is thus similar, though Burke calls attention to himself much more explicitly. And, like Mailer, Burke implies that the fate of the whole nation depends on embracing a *national* character that will match the *personal ethos* of the speaker.

If we feel a difference in quality between them, we cannot, then, explain it with general rules of metaphoric practice. We cannot even employ that old and useful criterion, decorum: though Mailer's style might be considered indecorous according to general standards, it is entirely appropriate to its context. There is nothing out of keeping, either with the book that has preceded the passage or with the situation as Mailer has portrayed it: any reader who has followed Mailer this far will be offended if the speaker does *not* come close to losing control; only shouting, perhaps even shrieking, can do justice to the total vision he has tried to portray.

With a phrase like "total vision" I betray the immensity of the tasks concealed behind the search for a way to appraise metaphors. The metaphors we care for most are always embedded in metaphoric structures that finally both depend on and constitute selves and societies; any critic who presumes to say that Burke's concluding passage is superior to Mailer's, not just as a matter of "personal preference" but for reasons testable in public discourse, must claim to practice a criticism adequate to differences of quality among selves and societies.

What might such a criticism of metaphorical worlds conceivably be? Most obviously it will not be peculiar to what we ordinarily call metaphor. It is likely, on the face of it, to make use of every art we have for criticizing cultures and it is certain to reveal that special kind of reflexivity that all cultural criticism reveals: the quality of the culture that produces the criticism. But if this is so, the dual criticism of metaphor that we seek—of the self-created characters and of the cultures made by metaphorists—will itself be a mode of preserving and improving our culture. I seem to be moving toward an immense thesis: the quality of any culture will in part be measured both by the quality of the metaphors it induces or allows and the quality of the judges of metaphor that it educates and rewards.[6] Such a thesis obviously suggests several lifetimes of inquiry, but since I seem to be stuck with it, let me now suggest, without attempting demonstration, some of the consequences we face if we take it seriously.

Whatever you may think about the implausibility of the quest for a reasoned discourse about metaphoric selves and cultures, it should be obvious from the word "quest" that I am shifting consciously to a radically different kind of inquiry. Studies of metaphor can themselves be thought about under at least four basic metaphors. We can wield a scalpel to analyze the nature of the beast regardless of whether it lives or dies. (If that seems too hostile a way of putting it, find your own metaphoric tool for what one does when specific metaphors are isolated from daily life and literary culture and probed for what or how they mean.) Moving to a slightly "warmer" classroom, study of metaphor can be the solving of a puzzle, taking literally Aristotle's statement that metaphors are like enigmas or riddles. Study of this kind will differ greatly, of course, depending on whether the puzzle solver expects what he finds to fit what he knew when he began or hopes for something new. If the former, he is like an explorer or anthropologist or missionary who has his conclusions fixed in advance and merely seeks new data to support predetermined causes; if the latter, he is more like a third kind of student, an explorer hoping to find a better way to live, or an anthropologist who, like Lévi-Strauss in *Tristes tropiques,* hopes that somehow his quest will allow him to return a wiser if not a better man.

In spite of an obvious hierarchy among these three, I see no reason to assume any of them to be illegitimate. But the study of metaphor is for me better described by a fourth kind of metaphor: a quest for ways to improve my culture and myself; that is, a search for a cure. And I am acutely aware that this might suggest Mailer's own way of employing metaphor. It is thus not hard to think of metaphoric ridicule for what I am suggesting: you are, I can hear a mocking voice say, turning the library into a spiritual culture emporium; or, you want to be both athletic coach and referee of the game. You will turn the critic and scholar into hollow prophetic voices rivaling the already too plentiful prophets on our scene. Let the bugle blow! God writhes in his bonds! Rush to the locks!

Let us take the point as a warning, but then remind ourselves that we are, if I am right, forced into something like this kind of talk if we

6. Ted Cohen has shown me an emphatic restatement by E. L. Doctorow of this claim that metaphorists are the unacknowledged legislators of the world: "And I am led to an even more pugnacious view—that the development of civilizations is essentially a progression of metaphors." "False Documents," *American Review* 26 (1977): 231–32.

respond to metaphor seriously. Mailer's extravagant style has forced us to bring into the open a mark of all figurative language. It is fairly easy to ignore this mark when dealing with metaphors out of context. But nobody can read Mailer's two paragraphs without discovering that regardless of whatever subject is ostensibly being aggrandized or diminished they call Norman Mailer on stage and demand of us that we deal with him personally, as we say, deal with him as a larger figure than he would have seemed had he followed any "normal" stylistic path. And we cannot claim to deal with him if we avoid judging his actual "size." We may detest or love or fear or emulate the giant figure that emerges; we may indeed conclude that his effort to appear large has in fact turned him into a ridiculous dwarf or imp. But we cannot ignore his character, not only his character as a writer who aspires to special effects but his *ethos* as a human being who writes. Once we have as much attention called to the writer as these metaphors demand of us, we cannot stop our inferences about the person who has been responsible for all this. He will either bond us to him or alienate us, the very intimacy of the bonding increasing our distress. And immense consequences for our psyches, and hence for our culture, will result from our choice of direction.

In short, the question is not *whether* we will judge the character of metaphorists and the societies that produce and sustain them. We all are forced to do that all the time, as the responses to Mailer illustrate. To *understand* a metaphor is by its very nature to *decide* whether to join the metaphorist or reject him, and that is simultaneously to decide either to be shaped in the shape his metaphor requires or to resist. The only question is thus whether to attempt reasoned critical discourse about such judgments.

Modern Western society is the only one in the history of mankind in which many thinkers, perhaps a majority, have assumed that criticism of character, and of cultures as they feed or destroy characters, is inherently nonrational. We are the first to have proclaimed that since we cannot use Locke's recommended scientific language for judgments of Mailer's or Burke's *ethos*, we can do no more than express our feelings and preferences about it. I have not, of course, proved here that we have been wrong in that assumption. But suppose we assume, as many inquirers have recently claimed, that we have been.[7] *If* we have been wrong, *if* rational criticism of values is possible, however difficult, then we have an immense obligation to build and improve our repertory of

7. I have argued this point, partly by presenting many "witnesses," in *Modern Dogma and the Rhetoric of Assent* (Notre Dame, Ind. and Chicago, 1974), esp. the appendix "Two-Score and More of Witnesses against the Fact-Value Split." Witnesses have multiplied since 1974. See, e.g., Alan Donagan's *The Theory of Morality* (Chicago, 1977). I think it is fair to say that most professional philosophers in 1978, in contrast with the world of, say, 1958, would claim that to repudiate ethical argument as necessarily irrational is to contradict reason.

standards and of our ways of talking about standards. In this perspective, criticism of metaphoric worlds, or visions, becomes one clear and important—perhaps the clearest and most important—instance of a general human project of improving life by criticizing it. And it is a project that will necessarily entail the use of metaphor; literal propositions will not be adequate to convey many of the judgments that our criticism must attempt. I can now only hint at what such a claim for a metaphorical criticism of metaphor might mean.

5

What I am calling for is not as radically new as it may sound to ears that are still tuned to positivist frequencies. A very large part of what we value as our cultural monuments can be thought of as metaphoric criticism of metaphor and the characters who make them. The point is perhaps most easily made about the major philosophies. Stephen Pepper has argued, in *World Hypotheses,*[8] that the great philosophies all depend on one of four "root metaphors," formism, mechanism, organicism, and contextualism, and they are great precisely because they have so far survived the criticism of rival metaphors. Each view of the totality of things claims supremacy, but none has been able to annihilate the others. They all thus survive as still plausible, pending further criticism through further philosophical inquiry. In this view, even the great would-be literalists like Hobbes and Locke are finally metaphorists—simply committed to another kind of metaphor, one that to them seems literal. Without grossly oversimplifying we could say that the whole work of each philosopher amounts to an elaborate critique of the inadequacy of all other philosophers' metaphors. What is more, the very existence of a tradition of a small group of great philosophies is a sign that hundreds of lesser metaphors for the life of mankind have been tested in the great philosophical—that is, critical—wars and found wanting.

In fact we find in every major philosophy not just this implicit critique of all rival metaphors but quite explicit consideration of the validity of particular metaphors. When Thrasymachus, for example, tries to take over the inquiry in *The Republic* by offering as a metaphor for justice the relation of shepherd and sheep, Socrates (and Plato) are much too wise to dismiss him, as many moderns might do, by claiming that metaphors prove nothing. Instead, the dialogue painstakingly explores what such a picture means, gradually substitutes rival metaphors, and argues for their superiority. If we think of justice, for example, as like the relation of pilot to ship and passengers, we can suggest thereby that the pilot has

---

8. *World Hypotheses: A Study in Evidence* (Berkeley, 1942). In *Concept and Quality: A World Hypothesis* (Lasalle, Ill., 1966), Pepper suggests that "the purposive act" is a fifth root metaphor.

a personal stake binding him to the welfare of the passengers: if the ship goes down, he goes with it, and serious consequences for the course of the inquiry follow. That metaphor in turn can be criticized by inventing others, until, by the end of *The Republic,* the parts of the soul, the parts of the state, and the organization of the universe itself have been richly analogized and illuminated. No one who has ever seriously pursued justice with Socrates through *The Republic* could ever again defend Thrasymachus' position, at least not in the simple form that has been permanently unmasked by Plato's critique of metaphor.

One can conceive then, of a philosophical critique of Mailer's entire metaphoric effort, one that would place his implied embattled "self" onstage shouting his view of justice and injustice in the world and subject that self to steady questioning in the light of alternative metaphors. Such a critique would, no doubt, convince only those with a taste for philosophical argument; the Mailers of the world might ignore it. But surely all of us here would be receptive to it.

Perhaps more pertinent to the audience that was originally swayed by Mailer's pregnant giant and all that preceded her in the book would be a second kind of critique, the kind practiced by all good historians when they attempt to tell rival stories. I have several times implied that the effectiveness of Mailer's final page cannot really be determined aside from the whole of the work that leads to it. Another way of saying the same thing is to say that the adequacy of Mailer's metaphors is in part tested by their capacity to serve as a conclusion to an account of *these* events treated in *this* way. The fact that an intelligent and gifted author could face these events and build a relatively coherent and persuasive work about them, a work that moves with *some* success toward this deliberate jumble of metaphors at the end, is in itself evidence for some pertinence in the view that emerges. Many a metaphoric view of the Vietnam crisis could not survive the "proving" applied by this interesting (and exasperating) mind: "The national conflict about Vietnam is a tempest in a teapot"; "American intervention in Vietnam has been a Sunday school picnic"; "The marchers on Washington were a pack of self-serving, mercenary lackeys." Anyone who tries to write so much as three pages about that march, leading to any one of these three metaphors as climax, will see that Mailer's effort has, by its very existence, already earned the right to a serious critique. Thus any historical critique that is to offer a genuine challenge must be equally serious in attempting adequacy to the magnitude of the events.

It is entirely beyond my competence to suggest what such a rival history would contain, let alone to invent a final metaphoric page to surpass Mailer's; the difficulties in such a task are precisely the mark of why accomplishing it, or failing to, would constitute a valid kind of criticism of Mailer's own achievement.

For most of us a more plausible direction would be a third kind of critique, a literary history that would tell the story not of the protest march itself but of this kind of literary work, describing it in careful detail and placing it with its siblings in the history of apocalyptic protest. My reference to Burke's final pages is only a hint toward what such a history would look for: the range of devices and effects achieved by similar rhetors attempting to produce a similar sense of crisis. As Samuel Johnson insisted, all criticism of human achievements must at some point be comparative: What have other authors been able to accomplish with similar tasks? What have been the advantages and disadvantages of jumbling metaphors at the moment of greatest passion? What are the uses of explicit avowals of one's own character, as in Burke's climax and in so many pages of Mailer's? Which specific metaphors for a nation in agony have shown the greatest power to survive the criticism provided by other metaphors? M. H. Abrams' great literary history *Natural Super-naturalism* might be a kind of model for anyone seeking to place Mailer's vision in the history of apocalyptic and revolutionary metaphor.[9]

It should be clear from these three examples that almost every discipline can provide some of the criticism of metaphor that we are calling for. Every theology entails a metaphor for man's relation to God, and the great theologies are those that have survived after generations of criticism. Every anthropology entails metaphors for man's relation to man and to nature and culture, and a great deal of anthropological writing is devoted to criticizing bad metaphors. Marshall Sahlins' recent *Culture and Practical Reason,* for example, can be viewed as an extended critique of functional metaphors for how we invent our cultures.[10]

Similarly, most important literary critics have a good deal to say about how to distinguish the pusillanimous from the magnanimous, the metaphors that diminish us from those that enlarge us. And the major psychologists all develop ways of criticizing each other's metaphors for the soul. (Why have Freud's metaphors for the soul's working parts proved so much more appealing to the modern world than, say, a psy-

---

9. See my "M. H. Abrams: Historian as Critic, Critic as Pluralist," *Critical Inquiry* 2 (Spring 1976): 411–45. In Abrams' other great work of "metaphoric criticism," *The Mirror and the Lamp: Romantic Theory and the Critical Tradition* (New York, 1953), he engages in very little explicit judging of metaphors as he marshals diverse historical descriptions of poets as mirrors, fountains, instruments, makers of objects, teachers, lamps, and what not. He lets history do the judging for him as the useful, enduring metaphors are brought forth in quotation from those whose lives were energized by thinking through or with them. Another excellent example of criticism disguised as history is Arthur Lovejoy's *The Great Chain of Being* (Cambridge, Mass., 1933). The power of a metaphor like the "great chain" to survive Lovejoy's sustained historical scrutiny does not, in our usual way of thinking, say anything about its truth. But once we begin to take seriously the task of criticizing metaphor, we must re-open the question of whether the metaphors that have recently replaced God's plenum—mechanistic evolution, for example—have not sacrificed a good deal of general truth for what they have gained in local validity.

10. Marshall Sahlins, *Culture and Practical Reason* (Chicago, 1976).

chology of the four humours? And why, at the other extreme, has the metaphor of the conditioned response, or operant conditioning, appealed to thousands of inquirers as the only truly literal way of talking about human behavior? It is interesting that those who advocate the simplest metaphors for man's soul are likely to prove most simplistic when they turn to criticism of souls and societies. B. F. Skinner, for example, lays about him freely with charges against our society's way of making its citizens; though he doesn't use the word "soul," which for him would be a metaphoric disguise for "behavior," his program, as announced most popularly in *Beyond Freedom and Dignity,* could be described as an aggressive critique both of freedom and autonomy metaphors for individual people and of the social measures that such metaphors lead us to practice.)

6

The study of metaphor would, as I have said, be only one part of any revived practice of the two ethical criticisms: of characters and of societies that make characters. But there is one important fact about our society that makes metaphor an even more important part of such criticism for us than for any previous culture. For the first time in history, a society finds itself offering immense rewards to a vast number of hired metaphorists, hired to make metaphors that will accomplish a predetermined end regardless of what they say about our character or do to it. Advertisers are hired to make some possession stand for happiness or well-being. I am of course not neutral on the question of whether we are on the whole harmed by their ministrations. There is an essentially corrupting, diminishing process in inducing desire for a predetermined happiness, a happiness that depends on possessing something. But one needn't accept my particular judgment, which would take some tall arguing to prove, to see that we have a totally new cultural situation that invites an army of critics to study and judge its effects.

All metaphorists in all cultures have hoped to be rewarded for their successes. Patronage and sometimes immense wealth have been freely given to those who could invent metaphoric visions of human life and happiness in that life. But those metaphorists were not paid to keep their visions small and precisely centered on possession. What they invented to *stand for* human happiness could best be described as having a kind of reflexive quality. All of the great poets seem to be saying something like this: my vision of what *stands for* human happiness is itself the activity of sharing pictures of what human life is or can be. Metaphor in this view is not a means to other ends but one of the main ends of life; sharing metaphors becomes one of the experiences we live for.

From this point of view, the great plays and narratives, like the great lyric poems, are themselves metaphors for what life is or can be; and they are thus a further great resource of criticism of what life is and of what other poets' metaphors say it is. We need not have explicit statements that "life is" this or that.

> Our birth is but a sleep and a forgetting:
> The Soul that rises with us, our Life's Star,
> Hath had elsewhere its setting,
> And cometh from afar: . . .

Taken as a literal statement about preexistence, such comments are too easily rejected with counterstatements: no, our birth is much more (or less) than a sleep and a forgetting; the soul did *not* have elsewhere its setting; and so on. To argue with Wordsworth in that way would be like attempting to say to Mailer, "No, America is not much like a pregnant giant lost in the smog." Rather than such direct debate about propositions, good literature, whether or not it presents either literal or allegorical *statements* about life, provides an *experience* that takes place literally and yet somehow stands for or represents what life might be or ought to be.

I don't pretend to know what Aristotle really had in mind when he called poetry more philosophical than history because it is more "universal." But there is a sense in which every poem, whether overtly didactic or not, presents a claim to universal truth by implying a prologue for itself: "If you ask what life *is*, the best answer I can give at the moment is this representative slice of what it feels like—not a slice of life itself, as in the old formula, but a slice of representation, a metonymic bit:

> What shall I do with this absurdity—
> Oh heart, O troubled heart—this caricature,
> Decrepit age that has been tied to me
> As to a dog's tail?"

The truth in Yeats' metaphoric vision of old age is, to be sure, of a kind that cannot be placed into direct contradiction with Wordsworth's radically different vision of childhood and youth. But that does not mean that the two visions claim no truth value. The metaphors criticize each other, in a sense contradict each other, but without the effort at mutual annihilation that logical contradictions imply.

It is no doubt this inherent aspiration of all literature to metaphoric truth that accounts for our tendency in modern times, as the old religious metaphors have weakened their hold on us, to turn literature to overt religious uses. When critics like Matthew Arnold found themselves treating poetry as the religion of the future, they were in fact simply expressing a kind of rivalry that was implicit in all secular metaphoric enterprises from the beginning: my story, though it may present no visible Gods and no expressions of piety, inevitably rivals yours that begins, "In the beginning was the Word." Our stories criticize each other as expressions of how life is.

The enduring religions have survived, one could argue, because the narrated myths that represent them have proved invulnerable to the criticism offered by rival myths. And the literary works that become classics are precisely those that have survived the unrelenting criticism presented by the literature of each new generation. Viewed in this perspective, even the most secular literary work is engaged in the religious exchange. The most innocent nonsense poem or nonreferential aleatoric verbal game says to us, "Life as it is, or as it ought to be, is best known as you experience me. I stand for bigger things." And every such work is in turn criticized by every other work. Bellow's *Herzog* says to Robbe-Grillet's *Project for a Revolution in New York,* "Your absurdist view is absurd and immoral, negatively sentimental." *Project* replies, "Your affirmation is a sentimental lie."

In calling for a criticism that would take such matters seriously I am, of course, violating the aesthetic presuppositions of many modern literary critics. I am saying that there can be no "innocent" art, no art that can be considered free of ethical responsibility. Since every work of art will, to the degree that it succeeds, change the character of individuals and thus of cultures, and since culture will, to the degree that it is viable, determine the production of this or that kind of art, critics cannot honestly dodge the task of attempting to judge, dangerous and difficult as that task will always be. And the judgment will always entail criticism of metaphor.

The great critics have all accepted this responsibility, in one form or another. The great artists have all known it. And from the beginning they have often, though not always, dramatized within their works their awareness of how their art presented a metaphoric vision of life and thus a critique of life without art and of other artists' visions.

There is a fine moment illustrating this kind of reflexivity quite early in *The Odyssey.* Odysseus has landed, after many troubles, on the island ruled by Alkinoos. He is wined and dined, and then he listens to a blind minstrel, a "man of song / whom the Muse cherished; by her gift he knew / the Good of life, and evil— / for she who lent him sweetness made him blind." The minstrel sings an account of Odysseus and Achilles, and of Ares' dalliance with Aphrodite, and "Odysseus, / listening, found sweet pleasure in the tale." Finally, after further dancing and singing of tales, Odysseus approaches the moment when he must tell his *own* story:

> . . . how beautiful this is, to hear a minstrel
> gifted as yours: a god he might be, singing!
> There is no boon in life more sweet, I say,
> than when a summer joy holds all the realm,
> and banqueters sit listening to a harper

in a great hall, by rows of tables heaped . . .
Here is the flower of life, it seems to me!

Homer is of course describing what he himself is doing, and we can be sure that he expects to be paid for it in one way or another. But he is not, like too many of our bards, describing a vision of human happiness that is in ineradicable conflict with what he is being paid to induce in others: the flower of life is for him the creating of pictures of the flower of life (I am told that the word "flower" in Fitzgerald's translation is not found in the Greek, but my point is not affected by the fact).

Metaphors as courtroom weapons; metaphors as advertisements for myself; metaphors as sales pitches, or as potential firebombs capable of destroying entire cultures overnight in primetime; metaphors as love letters to readers; metaphors as visions of how making metaphor itself redeems our lives. . . . Any criticism that attempts to discriminate among the problems and possibilities in such an assemblage will not be easy and it will not be precise. It will be neither univocal in its methods nor certain in its conclusions. It will itself be a part of the process it studies.

All serious study of anything is, no doubt, life-justifying. But there might be a special flowering about a criticism that pursued the two kinds of ethical criticism I have adumbrated: discriminating among the characters and cultures that metaphors build, in the belief that the quality of any culture is in large part the quality of the metaphorists that it creates and sustains.

Metaphor and Transcendence

Karsten Harries

Challenging Aristotle's claim that "a good metaphor implies an intuitive perception of the similarity in dissimilars," recent discussions have often insisted that, in poetry at least, metaphor joins dissimilars not so much to let us perceive in them some previously hidden similarity but to create something altogether new. As C. Day Lewis claims, "we find poetic truth struck out by the collision rather than the collusion of images."[1] Despite the obvious difficulties we have in drawing a sharp distinction between collision and collusion, despite the play that always joins the two, I would grant the usefulness of this and similar distinctions, grant also that Lewis' assertion is easily supported: today critics and poets alike do tend to emphasize collision rather than collusion. Such emphasis has not always characterized poetry and criticism. The preference for tension, for metaphors of opposition and collision, is, if not exclusively, a modern phenomenon which rests on a particular approach to poetry.[2] In this paper I want to sketch and then question that approach and some of its presuppositions.

1

It is a commonplace to say that a poem should be a complete whole. "Unity," we read in the *Princeton Encyclopedia of Poetry and Poetics,* "is the

1. C. Day Lewis, *The Poetic Image* (London, 1947), p. 72.
2. Metaphysical poetry, with its farfetched metaphors, comes most readily to mind. But despite an undeniable similarity, which lets Gustav René Hocke claim that we are

most fundamental and comprehensive aesthetic criterion, upon which all others depend."[3] Almost equally common is the claim that metaphor is "the life-principle of poetry, the poet's chief test and glory."[4] Yet generally accepted as these two claims may be, it is nevertheless difficult to reconcile the insistence on metaphor with the demand for unity. To be sure, discussions of metaphor have rightly stressed its power to connect, associate, and gather together; metaphor would thus seem to be a force tending towards unity, an agent, perhaps even the chief agent, of the kind of unity demanded of the poem. But the demand that the poem be a self-sufficient whole leaves little room for what I will call the ontological function of metaphor.[5]

Ever since Aristotle, metaphor has been placed in the context of a mimetic theory of language and of art. Metaphors are in some sense about reality. The poet uses metaphor to help reveal what is. He, too, serves the truth, even if his service is essentially lacking in that "Metaphor consists in giving the thing a name that belongs to something else."[6] Thus it is an improper naming. This impropriety invites a movement of interpretation that can come to rest only when metaphorical has been replaced with a more proper speech. This is not to say, however, that such replacement is possible nor that interpretation can ever come to rest. What metaphor names may transcend human understanding so that our language cannot capture it. In that case, proper speech would be denied to man. But regardless of whether we seek proper speech with man, for example, with the philosopher, or locate it beyond man with God, or think it only an idea that cannot find adequate realization, as long as we understand metaphor as an improper naming, we place its telos beyond poetry.

In such a view metaphor has to open the work of art to a dimension that transcends it; thus, it destroys our experience of the work of art as a

---

dealing with a perennial mannerism, an "anticlassical and antinaturalistic constant of European intellectual history" (*Manierismus in der Literatur* [Hamburg, 1959], p. 301), the phenomena seem to me different and to rest on different presuppositions.

3. Richard Harter Fogle, "Unity," *Princeton Encyclopedia of Poetry and Poetics,* ed. Alex Preminger (Princeton, N.J., 1974), p. 880.

4. Lewis, *The Poetic Image,* p. 17.

5. For a fuller discussion of the distinction between "ontological" and "aesthetic" approaches to art, see my "Hegel on the Future of Art," *Review of Metaphysics* 27 (June 1974): 680–84.

6. Aristotle *Poetics* 21. 1457b. 6–7.

Karsten Harries, chairman of the department of philosophy at Yale University, is the author of several works on aesthetics, including *The Meaning of Modern Art: A Philosophical Interpretation.*

self-sufficient whole. Given such considerations we may well want to agree with Jonathan Culler when he denies that the power of literature lies in metaphor and claims that, on the contrary, "it is precisely literature's resistance to metaphor, resistance to replacement operations, which is the source of this power."[7] Resistance here cannot mean immunity. Poetic language is metaphorical. And yet, the demand that the poem be a self-sufficient whole, that poetry be autotelic, implies the demand that it struggle against metaphor. It is this struggle, made unavoidable by the acceptance of unity as "the most fundamental and comprehensive aesthetic criterion," that helps to account for the preference for metaphors of collision. To show this, however, requires first a more thorough examination of the implications of the acceptance of unity as an aesthetic criterion.

2

A particularly suggestive discussion of unity is found in Alexander Gottlieb Baumgarten's *Reflections on Poetry* (1735), a work that not only helped to inaugurate a characteristically modern approach to poetry, and indeed to all art, but also gave us the term "aesthetics" to characterize that approach. In the course of that discussion Baumgarten offers the reader a simile: a poem is said to be like a world, more precisely, like the world as described by rationalist philosophers, by Leibniz, for example, who understood the cosmos as a perfectly ordered whole having its sufficient reason in God.[8] In it nothing is superfluous nor is anything missing. The same, according to Baumgarten, ought to be true of the poem. Given the infant state of the science of aesthetics, the simile promised rapid progress. One only had to appropriate the insights of the metaphysicians. Thus, Baumgarten claims, just as the world has its sufficient reason in God, the poem has its sufficient reason in the theme.

Baumgarten's simile, quite traditional in its suggestion that the poet is a second God, seems innocent enough: after all, a work of art is supposed to have unity. To be sure, this is not to deny complexity, tension, and incongruity, but order should triumph so that what may at first appear to be discordant elements are in the end recognized to have been absolutely necessary. In a successful work of art nothing is superfluous, while it is impossible to add anything without weakening or destroying the aesthetic whole. The task of the observer or the reader is only to open himself to the artist's creation. Emphasis on the unity of the aesthetic object thus implies aesthetic distance, that separation of art from life on which Kant was to insist in the *Critique of Judgment*.

7. Jonathan Culler, "Commentary," *New Literary History* 6 (Autumn 1974): 229.
8. Alexander Gottlieb Baumgarten, *Reflections on Poetry*, trans. Karl Aschenbrenner and William B. Holther (Berkeley and Los Angeles, 1954), p. 63.

The self-sufficiency of the aesthetic experience corresponds to the unity of the work of art. Aristotle had already suggested that we do not need art to survive. But while art cannot be considered useful in any obvious sense, it is precisely this uselessness that gives it a special appeal. Just because the aesthetic experience justifies itself, because it does not have an instrumental function and is not a means to some end, it can give us a sense of being at one with ourselves that we are denied as long as anticipation binds us to an uncertain future. Emphasis on the completeness of the aesthetic object thus leads to the interpretation of the aesthetic realm as an autonomous sphere, removed from morality, religion, or the state, removed even from reality. Only as long as the work of art is governed by the demands of its own aesthetic perfection does it remain pure. This aesthetic approach to art demands resistance to all mimetic accounts of its essence.

In Baumgarten's view the work of the poet resembles that of the metaphysician in that both imitate the world. Both capture something of the perfection of God's creation. But there is a decisive difference: the metaphysician's descriptions are essentially inadequate in that he has to content himself with abstract ideas, with a mirror that cannot capture the richness of God's creation. For the sake of clarity and distinctness he surrenders the concrete and sensuous. The poet does not make that sacrifice. His work is not a pale representation of the world but a second world that addresses itself to sense and spirit. Fusing matter and form into a perfect whole, the poet satisfies our demand for both completeness and concreteness as even God's creation cannot, for its order, although perfect, is infinitely complex and thus incommensurable with our finite faculties. To be sure, the poet, too, has to make a sacrifice, even if, caught up in the aesthetic experience, we are allowed to forget that this sacrifice has been made. What he sacrifices is truth. In its place he offers us a self-sufficient presence, strong enough to lead us to accept it instead of referring us to something beyond the poem.

The pursuit of presence is inseparable from the aesthetic approach. It finds characteristic expression in Susan Sontag's claim that "transparence is the highest, most liberating value in art—and in criticism—today," where "transparence means experiencing the luminousness of the thing in itself, of things being what they are."[9] It may be that this value is realized more readily in the visual arts than in poetry, where the referentiality of language poses a greater obstacle than paint and canvas. Frank Stella's description of his artistic goals can stand for other similar statements:

> I always get into arguments with people who want to retain the old values in painting—the humanistic values that they always find on

9. Susan Sontag, *Against Interpretation* (New York, 1967), p. 13.

the canvas. If you pin them down, they always end up asserting that there is something there besides the paint on the canvas. My painting is based on the fact that only what can be seen there *is* there. It really is an object. Any painting is an object and anyone who gets involved in this finally has to face up to the objectness of whatever it is that he's doing. He is making a thing. All that should be taken for granted. If the painting were lean enough, accurate enough, or right enough, you would be able to just look at it. All I want anyone to get out of my paintings, and all that I ever get out of them, is the fact that you see the whole idea without any confusion. . . . What you see is what you see.[10]

Stella projects the ideal of an art that would not allow us to "avoid the fact that it's supposed to be entirely visual."[11] The spectator is to be reduced to a pure eye, the painting to a pure visual presence. It is significant, however, that Stella does not claim his art succeeds in being entirely visual. What he hopes is only that it would force us to acknowledge that it is *supposed to be* entirely visual. What the work of art is, is not what it is supposed to be. Instead of being fully present, it is only a metaphor of presence. Transparence remains an unrealized ideal. Presence remains absent. The work of art does not grant us immediacy of vision but communicates only the dream of such vision. Stella thus fails to get beyond what he calls the old humanistic values. There *is* something beyond the paint on the canvas.

Stella's statements are hardly isolated remarks, just as his art is not an effort in isolation but has its firm place in a development that has its roots in the eighteenth century and receives its direction from the aesthetic approach to art. Nor is this development confined to painting or sculpture. Stella's dream of creating a work that in its simple presence would discourage interpretation has its counterpart in Archibald MacLeish's much quoted "A poem should not mean / but be." MacLeish, too, knows that the poet cannot get away from meaning. Like Stella's "is supposed to be," the poet's "should" speaks of an ideal that remains unrealized, that cannot be realized. No matter how radical the pursuit of presence, the work of art will always fall short of that purer art that is its telos. It points beyond itself and lacks the plenitude it demands. We find that recognition already in Kant's *Critique of Judgment.* In spite of such examples of pure beauty as wallpaper, musical phantasies, and ornament, in the end Kant is forced to acknowledge that we approach every work of art as pointing beyond itself, as having a meaning. And yet, art should have the presence of a thing of nature.[12] This tension between

10. Frank Stella, quoted by Bruce Glaser, "Questions to Stella and Judd," in *Minimal Art: A Critical Anthology,* ed. Gregory Battcock (New York, 1968), pp. 157–58.

11. Ibid., p. 158.

12. In par. 16 of the *Critique of Judgment,* Kant suggests that not only in nature, but in art too, there can be free beauty, beauty that does not presuppose a concept of what sort of

the presence of the work of art and its meaning, made unavoidable by the aesthetic approach, offers us a key to the prevalence of metaphors of collision in modern poetry. *And in modern criticism too, I think*

3

Paul Valéry defines poetry as *"an effort by one man* to create an artificial and ideal order by means of a material of vulgar origin."[13] This definition acknowledges the poet's inevitable dependence on established discourse, even as it emphasizes that the poet must struggle against such dependence. The poem is located between ordinary language and an ideal—Valéry speaks of pure poetry—that must elude the poet. Poetry will always remain "a striving after this purely ideal state. In fact, what we call a *poem* is in practice composed of fragments of pure poetry embedded in the substance of a discourse. A very beautiful line is a very pure element of poetry."[14]

"Purity" is once again tied to presence and immediacy of vision, to a plenitude that rules out referentiality. To gain this immediacy we must take leave from the way we usually speak. The inevitable immersion of poetry in common language is seen as a contamination of its purity. One is reminded of the traditional view of man as essentially fallen. What the poet has fallen into and what estranges him from that pure realm that beckons him with its promise of self-sufficiency is the necessarily public and referential dimension of language. Poetry becomes a finally vain effort to rescue man from that dimension and to replace it with a purer environment, an environment that does not tolerate words but demands silence. The pursuit of presence has to make the poet's progress a journey towards silence. Ungaretti thus suggests that the poem should be like a brief tearing of silence, while Mallarmé writes that the poem should be silent, white.[15] This tension between desired presence and the unavoid-

silence, not solution - excellent.

---

thing the beautiful object is supposed to be. His example of ornament is particularly interesting in that it invites an interpretation of pure art as ornament become absolute, ornament that has cast off its ornamental function. But in par. 48, Kant admits that to judge a work of art one has to have a concept of what it is supposed to be, one has to presuppose a given meaning—Baumgarten would have spoken of the theme. Thus, in spite of the critique of Baumgarten's analysis of perfection offered in par. 15, Kant is forced to grant that in judging artificial beauty we have to consider the object's perfection. Baumgarten is thus vindicated although, given Kant's analysis of free beauty, this amounts to the admission that art can never be pure. To become pure it would have to negate itself as art.

13. Paul Valéry, "Pure Poetry," *The Art of Poetry,* trans. Denise Folliot (New York, 1961), p. 192.

14. Ibid., p. 185.

15. See Hugo Friedrich, *Die Struktur der modernen Lyrik* (Hamburg, 1956), pp. 90 and 131.

able referentiality of language accounts for the curious ambiguity of such poetry. We seem to know what the poet's words mean. Yet the more time we spend on his poem, the more ambiguous what at first seemed familiar becomes. Consider William Carlos Williams' "Queen-Ann's-Lace":

> Her body is not so white as
> anemone petals nor so smooth—nor
> so remote a thing. It is a field
> of the wild carrot taking
> the field by force; the grass
> does not rise above it.
> Here is no question of whiteness,
> white as can be, with a purple mole
> at the center of each flower.
> Each flower is a hand's span
> of her whiteness. Wherever
> his hand has lain there is
> a tiny purple blemish. Each part
> is a blossom under his touch
> to which the fibers of her being
> stem one by one, each to its end,
> until the whole field is a
> white desire, empty, a single stem,
> a cluster, flower by flower,
> a pious wish to whiteness gone over—
> or nothing.

Where does this metaphor lead us? What does it reveal? Reading the poem one almost sees the flower described with so much precision. But its metaphorical status invites us to pass beyond the image. The erotic theme of the poem is obvious enough. But in what sense is it illuminated by the flower metaphor? The image is so strong that the vehicle seems to emancipate itself from the tenor. Is it ever clear what is vehicle and what is tenor? Does it help to note the parallel between "a field of the wild carrot taking the field by force," only this conquest transforming the wild carrot into Queen-Ann's-lace, and the desire that loses itself in the whiteness of the body? In the end it is not only a field of wild carrot or a pious wish that goes over into whiteness, but the poem itself. And yet it continues to refer us to a very common flower.

How different is the function of metaphor in a poem like Thomas Campion's "There is a Garden in her face" (1617). The poet's roses and lilies, the "Browes like bended bowes ... Threatning with piercing frownes to kill," refer us not only to familiar things but back to traditional descriptions of the Virgin based on the Song of Songs. At the same time the "Garden in her face" is paradise, itself a common metaphor for the

Virgin, although the poem mitigates the unavailability of the garden's sacred cherries with the refrain "Till Cherry ripe themselves doe cry," the street vendor's call reducing the promise of divine grace to the promise of human surrender. That things have a spiritual significance apart from the poet's effort is taken for granted. Scripture and Nature, God's two books, furnish authoritative texts, rich with figures from which the poet can draw in his attempt to embellish or to exhibit the deeper significance of what he is celebrating.

The metaphor of "Queen-Ann's-Lace," in contrast, no longer rests on already established figures. For the modern poet there is no authoritative text, no commonly shared understanding of the spiritual significance of things that can give necessity to his metaphors. What remains are inherited ways of speaking, clichés that have grown mute in repetition. But without such a text, what gives metaphor its necessity? As the metaphorical function of the image becomes uncertain, that image gains a strangely insistent presence. The interaction of flower and body beckons us beyond this presence. But if it gestures towards a hidden meaning, it does not yield a definite insight. Perhaps we can say that the direction of traditional metaphor has been reversed. Metaphor no longer has its telos in reality. It still invites us to take leave from familiar reality but not for the sake of a more profound vision of what is. Instead metaphors become weapons directed against reality, instruments to break the referentiality of language, to deliver language from its ontological function and thus to confer on the poet's words a magical presence that lets us forget the world. As Ortega y Gasset says of such metaphor, "between the real things it lets emerge imaginary reefs, a crop of floating islands."[16] When D. H. Lawrence speaks of Bavarian gentians as "torches of darkness" spreading "the smoking blueness of Pluto's gloom" or Ezra Pound calls faces in the crowd of a subway station "Petals on a wet black bough," ordinary sensibility suffers shipwreck on the intermediate reefs of which Ortega is speaking. Or take this line from a love poem by Karl Krolow:

Dein Nacken—hörst du—ist aus Luft,
Die wie eine Taube durch die Maschen des blauen Laubes schlüpft.

[Your neck—do you hear—is of air,
That like a dove, slips through the mesh of blue leaves.]

What is the source of the undeniable strength of such metaphors? The question becomes particularly acute when lines are taken out of the context of the poem and translated into another language. In this par-

16. José Ortega y Gasset, *The Dehumanization of Art and Other Writings on Art and Culture* (Garden City, N.J., 1956), pp. 30–31.

ticular case it would not only be necessary to point back to other lines that prepare us for what taken out of context seems forced and arbitrary, but also to consider carefully the contribution made by assonance, consonance, and rhythm. A line like "Die wie eine Taube durch die Maschen des blauen Laubes schlüpft" cannot be translated, although a poet might succeed in presenting an analogous creation. The impossibility of translation points out that the collision of images is balanced by the collusion of the pattern in which these images find expression. This collusion, which has its ground not so much in a real similarity of the referents as in the flow and texture of the words themselves, gives the poem a presence that lets us accept the poet's broken metaphors.

4

Referring to Heinz Werner's theory that metaphor has one of its roots in the spirit of taboo, Ortega claims that the modern poet's use of metaphor, which disposes of an object "by having it masquerade as something else," betrays "an instinctive avoidance of certain realities. . . . The weapon of poetry turns against natural things and wounds or murders them."[17]

A poem like "There is a Garden in her face" shows that metaphors do not have to be instruments of violence. Indeed, as Ortega grants, the predominant use of poetic metaphor has been to exalt the real object, "to embellish and to throw into relief beloved reality." On the other hand, we have to admit that the aesthetic approach to art demands derealization. Ortega's claim that "an object of art is artistic only insofar as it is not real"[18] is fully in accord with what Kant has to say in the *Critique of Judgment,* although both add the qualification that a pure work of art is an impossibility. Should we then say that to the extent that art is passionately tied to reality it must fail as art? If we grant the validity of the aesthetic approach we have no choice. But that approach presupposes that we turn to art to escape from reality. Is there something about our situation that invites such escape? Why does the modern artist, more specifically the modern poet, avoid reality?

Perhaps we should not speak of *the* modern poet. Poetry continues to be many things, and poets continue to use metaphors in many ways. The modern poet of whom Ortega speaks is only a caricature. But like any good caricature, by distorting, by singling out certain features for our attention, it lets us see something essential. Perhaps "model" would be a better term; "caricature" suggests not only distortion but reliance on observation. The idea of pure art or pure poetry, however, is less the

17. Ibid., pp. 31 and 32.
18. Ibid., p. 10.

result of careful observation than it is an ideal projected by the perennial pursuit of satisfaction, plenitude, completeness. Elevating what the tradition had called pride to an ontological structure, Sartre claims that "the best way to conceive of the fundamental project of human reality is to say that man is the being whose project is to be God."[19] Sartre, too, knows that the project is vain, that reality will always transcend our grasp. In spite of the extent to which science and technology have rendered man "the master and possessor of nature," we cannot defeat the ephemeral contingency of human existence and the existence of things. This essential failure accounts for the tendency to turn away from things of nature; lacking faith, modern man seeks refuge in an unreal, aesthetic environment of his own making.

Although I would question whether all human beings desire to be God, we cannot deny the explanatory power of that conception. The search for pure poetry does indeed have its foundation in pride. To the extent that this search governs modern poetry, Harold Bloom is right to claim that Milton's Satan is the modern poet, "while God is his dead but still embarrassingly potent and present ancestor, or rather, ancestral poet."[20] Particularly suggestive in this connection is Valéry's discussion of Descartes; it is interesting not so much because of the insights it offers us into Descartes but for the way in which it presents Descartes as the precursor of the modern poet. Valéry dwells on Descartes' pride, on his egotism. He hears the *cogito* as a clarion call to the philosopher's egotistical powers.

> Therein dwells the charm—in the magical sense of the term—of this formula, which has been so endlessly written about, whereas, I believe, it is enough to feel it deeply. At the sound of these words the quiddities vanish away; the will to power invades its man, sets the hero to rights, recalls to him his uniquely personal mission, his unshared destiny—even what makes him different, his individual injustice. For, after all, it is possible that a being destined to greatness must make himself deaf, blind, unfeeling towards everything—even towards truths, even towards realities—that may cross his career, his fated achievement, his line of growth, his inner light, his orbit.[21]

Valéry misreads Descartes; he seizes just one side of his thinking. Descartes, at least, would have insisted that his turn to the *cogito* is not a turn to the isolated self but to the universal, that the turn to the clear and distinct does not replace reality with the spirit's empty constructions but helps to secure the traditional view that seeks the truth of our words and

19. Jean-Paul Sartre, *Being and Nothingness*, trans. Hazel E. Barnes (New York, 1956), p. 566.

20. Harold Bloom, *The Anxiety of Influence* (New York, 1975), p. 20.

21. Valéry, introductory essay to *The Living Thoughts of Descartes*, trans. Harry Lorrin Binsse (London, 1948), p. 31.

ideas in their correspondence with the creative words of God and makes genuine speaking a repeating after God. But if Valéry misreads Descartes, that misreading lets us see more clearly what underlies the refusal of reality that is inseparable from the aesthetic project. What makes Valéry's Descartes the precursor of the modern poet is his insistence to be the author of his own thoughts, his refusal to owe anything to the world, to others, and to God, a will to power that refuses to acknowledge its own final impotence. This refusal has to make both the things of the world and established language into obstacles that stand in the way of what is most deeply wanted. The desire for godlike self-sufficiency leads first of all to the attempt to derealize the things of nature. The collision of images helps to decompose familiar reality, to reduce it to poetic material. Out of the fragments of the world the poet creates his own poetic world.

Such appropriation still cannot satisfy the poet's pride. In Bloom's words, "If not to have conceived oneself is a burden, so for the strong poet there is also the more hidden burden: not to have brought oneself forth, not to be a god breaking one's own vessels, but to be awash in the Word not quite one's own."[22] If poetic self-sufficiency is to be preserved, the authority of the poet's poetic precursors must also be negated. The very strength of inherited metaphors becomes an obstacle that the poet seeks to remove with his own more daring combinations.

Not only the strength of earlier poems weighs on the poet but also language itself. We are always awash in words not quite our own, words that make us speak as one speaks, see as one sees. The poet, too, is forced to use a medium that is not his own, forced to begin with what has come to be established and accepted, binding him to the community and to reality. Turning against ordinary language, inviting us to take leave from familiar reality, the poet's metaphors promise a plenitude that temporal existence has to withhold. How much modern poetry longs for Byzantium, longs to journey away from nature commending "Whatever is begotten, born and dies," away from lovers, birds, and mackerel-crowded seas, to this city of artifice, where birds of gold sit on golden boughs, singing their purer songs? Yeats answers the question: Why the avoidance of natural things? Nature is not for old men! It is what Nietzsche called the spirit of revenge, the rancor against time, that lets the poet seek refuge with monuments of man's unaging intellect. And yet, these works which should transcend temporal reality depend on it for their content. This tension the poet cannot escape. His works will never be pure enough; his words will always bear traces of the sensuous music of nature that they cannot silence as they gesture towards an elusive eternity, metaphors of a transcendence that is nothing other than the place left vacant by the dead God. *But this is equally true for true place left vacant by the living God — St. Teresa Rolle John of the Cross Merton*

22. Bloom, *A Map of Misreading* (New York, 1975), pp. 15–16.

This connection between the pursuit of unity and the spirit of revenge could be developed more carefully and in greater detail by showing that completeness and presence demand that aesthetic appreciation
be disinterested, a bracketing of care and concern and their temporality.
The *Critique of Judgment* remains the most suggestive analysis of the
aesthetic sensibility that has governed the development of modern art.
Michael Fried has pushed that analysis to its last consequences: "The
authentic art of our time," he claims, aspires to "presentness." This not
only demands the rejection of all pictorial and mimetic tendencies; if the
work is to be all there, if nothing is to be lacking, it must place the
observer beyond memory and expectation, hope and fear, interest and
boredom. "It is this continuous and entire presentness, amounting, as it
were, to the perpetual creation of itself, that one experiences as a kind of
instantaneousness: as though if only one were infinitely more acute, a
single brief instant would be long enough to see everything, to experience the work in all its depth and fullness, to be forever convinced by it.
(Here it is worth noting that the concept of interest implies temporality
in the form of continuing attention directed at the object, whereas the
concept of conviction does not.)"[23] Fried points to paintings by Kenneth
Noland and Jules Olitski, to sculptures by David Smith and Anthony
Caro—once again the visual arts provide the most obvious examples—
but he also suggests that there is poetry and music that similarly lets time
stand still "because *at every moment the work itself is wholly manifest.*"[24] But
time does not stand still. Perhaps, *if* we were infinitely more acute, if like
angels we had been granted the gift of unmediated vision, we could
realize the dream that, if Fried is right, occupies "the authentic art of our
time." "Presentness," writes Fried, "is grace." But if so, grace is denied to
man. We are stuck with metaphors of eternity.

5

Metaphors speak of what remains absent. All metaphor that is more
than an abbreviation for more proper speech gestures towards what
transcends language. Thus metaphor implies lack. God knows neither
transcendence nor metaphor—nor would man, if he were truly godlike.
The refusal of metaphor is inseparably connected with the project of
pride, the dream of an unmediated vision, a vision that is not marred by
lack, that does not refer to something beyond itself that would fulfill it.
This origin ties the aesthetic approach, in spite of its willingness to surrender all claim to truth, to the Cartesian hope that the search for

23. Michael Fried, "Art and Objecthood," *Minimal Art,* p. 146.
24. Ibid., p. 145.

knowledge can come to rest in the plenitude of clear and distinct perception. It is a vain hope. We do not have an unmediated understanding of anything real, not even of our own selves. Descartes' supposedly clear and distinct idea of himself as thinking substance can be shown to rest on a quite traditional, but questionable, interpretation of being, according to which "to be" means "to be as a substance." Even though Descartes resolves to think for himself and free himself from the distorting authority of what others have said before him, from the very beginning that attempt proves impossible. No matter how hard he tries, no matter how self-consciously he goes about bracketing earlier texts, in the end he cannot cast off the burden of past writing which places itself like a veil over the evidence of intuition. Reading the *Meditations* we are led not so much to clear and distinct intuitions as back to other texts. Valéry thus suggests, with some justice, that Descartes' attempt to be purely theoretical leaves one wondering whether he does not end up being purely verbal.[25]

Should we then look at the philosopher as a curious kind of poet? Baumgarten's simile, likening the poem to the world, may suggest a more intimate connection between poet and philosopher than he had intended. Could it be that Baumgarten's simile is so successful just because the philosopher, in spite of his insistence on truth, is only a kind of poet? The metaphysician, too, replaces reality with his own airy creations. To effect such replacement he also relies on metaphors even though, if the philosopher's claim to have seized reality as it is is to be maintained, their merely metaphorical status has to be denied. Heidegger especially has alerted us to the way metaphors, their origins effaced, continue to shape philosophical discourse. His own choice of the metaphor of the clearing to describe the being of man has the virtue of making the metaphorical character of philosophical language so obvious that we have to acknowledge it. A clearing is an opening in the forest that permits light to enter. Heidegger's metaphor thus joins the distance and light metaphors that have long governed philosophical speculation, which has tended to take for granted that the model provided by vision is adequate to human understanding. But how adequate is it in fact? What is meant by "the light of the intellect" or by the distance that separates subject and object? By calling attention to its own metaphorical status, Heidegger's term "clearing" not only calls itself into question but at the same time calls attention to the metaphorical basis of traditional philosophy and makes explicit the fact that philosophical texts refer us less to reality than back to other philosophical texts. Metaphysics is, to use a term Derrida borrows from Anatole France, "white mythology" which "has effaced in itself that fabulous scene which brought it into being, and

25. Valéry, *The Living Thoughts of Descartes*, p. 19.

which yet remains, active and stirring, inscribed in white ink, an invisible drawing covered over in the palimpsest."[26] This characterization invites the attempt to return to a speaking that no longer leads us back to yet another earlier text but opens us to what transcends language. Heidegger's search for linguistic origins is part of his attempt to recall us to this dimension.

Derrida dismisses such attempts as a necessarily futile search for a saying of unveiled presence. We cannot step outside language. In his view there can be no escape from the tyranny of texts. At this point the distinction between metaphorical and proper speech, between poetry and prose, between poet and thinker, threatens to evaporate. Descartes and Freud can join Valéry and Wallace Stevens as "strong poets." What remains is a play with words, with poetic and philosophical texts, itself neither poetry nor philosophy, a metapoetry that shrugs off the demand for truth and criteria, reminiscent of Hermann Hesse's *Das Glasperlenspiel*. Its peculiar pleasures demand an aesthetic refusal of reality, where the rhetoric of deconstruction with its hermetic combinations has the derealizing function of the modern poet's metaphors of collision. That this refusal is indeed a refusal, that it is not simply the consequence of a more profound insight into the way we are imprisoned by language, is shown by the functioning of language in everyday life. The success of science and technology, which rests in good part on foundations laid by philosophers like Descartes, forces us to admit that even if the ideal of transparence, of total presence, must remain unrealized, even if there can be no fully adequate description of what is, this is not to say that we cannot distinguish between more and less proper descriptions. And in spite of the analogy between poetry and metaphysics, we should not overlook the very different way in which poetic texts, on the one hand, and philosophical texts, on the other, demand to be read.

Baumgarten's point cannot be dismissed: while the philosopher's abstractions distort ordinary language for the sake of greater objectivity and conceptual distinctness, the figures of the poet lead us in the opposite direction, restoring to language the immediacy of feeling and sensation. As Wittgenstein writes in the *Investigations:*

> We speak of understanding a sentence in the sense in which it can be replaced by another which says the same; but also in the sense in which it cannot be replaced by any other. (Any more than one musical theme can be replaced by another.)
> In the one case the thought in the sentence is something common to different sentences; in the other, something that is ex-

26. Jacques Derrida, "White Mythology: Metaphor in the Text of Philosophy," *New Literary History* 6 (Autumn 1974): 11.

pressed only by these words in these positions. (Understanding a poem.)[27]

There are situations where to understand what is meant is also to know that it can be put differently or translated into another language. Traditionally such translatability has been demanded of all discourse that claims truth. Truth demands objectivity, demands that we give our descriptions of reality a form as free as possible from the inevitable distortions imposed by one's particular point of view, including the language one happens to speak. That this is not a meaningless demand shows that our language is not a prison. As soon as we recognize a perspective as just a perspective we have already transcended its limitations, at least in thought. This power of transcendence leads inevitably to the thought of a standpoint that would allow us to see things as they are—a vision of the world that would be truly objective and transparent, free from perspectival distortion. The idea of such a vision is implicit in our experience; it can be uncovered and made the measure of what presents itself to us.

To be sure, to think an aperspectival vision of reality is not therefore to possess it. The descriptions provided by science and philosophy are not based on some aperspectival mode of vision but conjectures responsive to the ineradicably perspectival evidence furnished by the body, expressed in language that has to bend ordinary language to its demands.[28] Catachresis must help where established usage fails. But every particular occurrence of catachresis is in principle replaceable. To understand what is meant is also to know that the fact that it happens to have been expressed in just this way is inessential. This makes the metaphors of science and philosophy fundamentally different from those of poetry. The whiteness of the discourse of metaphysics is not simply the result of the fact that a richer, more fabulous scene has been forgotten and effaced; the distance that separates it from perception and feeling is an essential aspect of such discourse, demanded by the commitment to objectivity.

The power that this commitment has given man is too obvious to be denied. Our technology demonstrates that Descartes' proud hope that his method would render man the master and possessor of nature was more than the idle dream of a poet. If it had been just that, his shadow would not loom so large. We still stand in that shadow. More and more we tend to make our ability to comprehend the measure of reality. Our

27. Ludwig Wittgenstein, *Philosophical Investigations,* trans. G. E. M. Anscombe (New York, 1953), pp. 143–44.

28. For a fuller discussion see my "Descartes, Perspective, and the Angelic Eye," *Yale French Studies* 49 (1973): 28–42; and "The Infinite Sphere: Comments on the History of a Metaphor," *Journal of the History of Philosophy* 13 (January 1975): 5–15.

commitment to objectivity and transparence forces us to see the world that moves us with its sights and sounds as no more than the perspectival appearance of a reality that yields its secrets only to the dislocated spirit. So understood, reality leaves no room for genuine mysteries. Only the irreducible facticity and temporality of things remain as the last vestiges of transcendence.

In such a world we cannot feel at home. The aesthetic refusal of reality, so characteristic of our spiritual situation, is born not only of pride but also of the awareness that by making objectivity the measure of truth and reality we deny ourselves a place in the world. But perhaps this is a false problem: it has become fashionable to answer the problem of spiritual dislocation by calling for a return to the life-world or to ordinary language, suggesting that it is only the philosopher whose disengaged speculations have let him lose his place in the world. Such answers are not convincing. Descartes is too much with us. We have grown too reflective, too free in our thinking to make this return. Inseparable from this freedom is the desire to reincarnate the dislocated spirit, the longing for words that will let us rediscover where we belong and thus defeat that sense of contingency and arbitrariness which is the other side of objectivity. And yet, in spite of such longing, we find it difficult to step out of the Cartesian shadow. And when the attempt is made it seems to yield no more than poetry: we are offered a vacation from reality rather than its revelation.

6

If it is easy to show the pervasiveness of the aesthetic approach in modern art and poetry, it is equally easy to point to attempts to restore to poetry the ontological significance that is sacrificed by the aesthetic approach. Criticizing Valéry, T. S. Eliot thus insists that reading a poem should be "not merely an experience, but a serious experience."[29] Such an experience, Eliot explains, cannot have its value solely in itself; it cannot be merely aesthetic. A poem should reveal what matters and thus help the individual to determine what his place in the world is to be. The return to a more ontological approach to poetry has found its most vigorous spokesman in Heidegger. Poetry, in Heidegger's interpretation, reveals the meaning of what is as it establishes a world, where "world" does not mean the totality of facts but a space of meanings that assigns to things and to man their proper places. Following Heidegger, Paul Ricoeur claims that literary texts are about the world that is established by the work. To understand a text is to place oneself "before the world of the work," to be open to that world and to let it enlarge

29. "Introduction" to Paul Valéry, The Art of Poetry, p. xxiii.

one's own world-understanding.[30] Metaphor is discussed in the context of this ontological interpretation. Measured by established and accepted language, the collisions of poetic metaphor have no proper sense. They cannot be drawn from what has already been established. A novel metaphor is "a semantic innovation which has no status in language, as already established, neither as designation nor as connotation."[31] Precisely because it has no such status, it can help to let a new world emerge.

It should be noted how close we still are to the aesthetic view of poetry. The view that poetic metaphor lets us take leave from the already established world and carries us to the new world established by the poem is, as we have seen, quite compatible with the aesthetic approach. We escape from this approach only if we can recognize in the world established by the poem the world that assigns us our place. If it is to allow for such recognition, poetry cannot have its sole foundation in the poet's subjectivity. The poet cannot be seen as a godlike creator. This is acknowledged by the traditional emphasis on inspiration. Just as the prophet's speech gains its authority from its divine origin, so the poet's words can have ontological significance only to the extent that they are uttered in response to a reality that not only claims the poet but also his listeners so that they can recognize what his words seek to name. Heidegger calls this transcendent aspect of being the earth; poetry is as much a gift of the earth as it is the poet's own work. Thus both he and his listeners have to remain open to what lies outside and surpasses language. And there is nothing that can guarantee that such openness will be rewarded, that what transcends us will speak to us and in a way that will illuminate and allow us to gather together all the facets of our existence—and only in that case could the poet be said to establish the world in a nonaesthetic sense.[32]

We demand too much when we ask that the poet establish a new world. First we have to learn to listen more attentively to the many voices of the earth. What makes such listening difficult is the fact that as members of a community we are necessarily caught up in already-established and taken-for-granted ways of speaking and seeing. We understand things without having made them our own. The adequacy of words is taken for granted, their origin forgotten. There are moments when the inadequacy of our language seizes us, when language seems to fall apart and falling apart opens us to what transcends it. Hugo von Hofmannsthal describes such a moment in his "Lord Chandos Letter." At first it is only abstract words like "spirit," "soul," or "body" which crumble in the lord's mouth like moldy mushrooms. But like a corroding rust this in-

30. Paul Ricoeur, "Metaphor and the Main Problem of Hermeneutics," *New Literary History* 6 (Autumn 1974): 107.

31. Ibid., p. 103.

32. See my "Language and Silence: Heidegger's Dialogue with Georg Trakl," *Boundary 2* 4 (Winter 1976): 495–509.

ability to use words spreads to ordinary language until in the end all language is seen as no more than idle chatter. Sentences fall apart into words, words congeal into eyes that stare at the poet, the eyes force him to stare back at them and become whirlpools that lead into the void. And yet this disintegration of language does not lead to silence. Against the background of silence the presence of things manifests itself. As language falls apart, contact with being is reestablished. Something as simple as a half-filled pitcher, darkened by the shadow of a nut tree, becomes an epiphany of transcendence. A longing remains to find words that would capture this mystery, words which, as the poet writes, were he to find them would force to their knees the cherubim in which he does not believe. And indeed they would. For such words would close the gap between language and reality. They would be the creative words of God. Measured by the idea of that divine language, our language must seem totally inadequate. And yet Hofmannsthal succeeds in saying a great deal not only about the inadequacy of language but also about a pitcher, half-filled with water, left lying beneath some nut tree. Similarly, in "Queen-Ann's-Lace," William Carlos Williams offers us a metaphor that by letting established meanings collide gestures towards silence, and that silence lets a very common flower become a strangely moving presence. Rendering language questionable, the poet's metaphor succeeds in gesturing towards a language that shall never be ours in which, as Hofmannsthal writes, things speak to us.

Things speak to us. Is that more than a metaphor that betrays man's incurable tendency to project himself into the things of the world rather than describes these things? To answer this challenge one would have to show that such talk about projection rests on an inadequate analysis of man's being in the world. Things speak to us, although our subjection to the rule of the letter, to what has already been said and written down, may make it difficult for us to hear and, even if stuttering, interpret that usually-passed-over speech. A conception of poetry emerges that takes leave from aestheticism and its ideal of aesthetic self-sufficiency and completeness, a conception that seeks to recover the traditional view of genuine discourse as a more or less inadequate and fragmentary repetition of that speech in which nature, or perhaps God, addresses us.

Metaphor and Religion: The Test Case of Christian Texts

David Tracy

1. State of the Question in Religious Studies and Theology

That all major religions are grounded in certain root metaphors has become a commonplace in modern religious studies. In a particular religion root metaphors form a cluster or network in which certain sustained metaphors both organize subsidiary metaphors and diffuse new ones. These networks describe the enigma and promise of the human situation and prescribe certain remedies for that situation. Hence theologies from the logos theologies of Philo and Origen to the modern period have found their most natural conversation partners in philosophy, especially in metaphysics and ethics. As the long tradition of Western Jewish, Christian, and Islamic theologies testifies and as the major work of most contemporary theologians continues to witness, the prevalent theological concern has been with the truth status of religious cognitive claims in relation to various scientific, ethical, and sometimes metaphysical theories of meaning and truth. This concern may now be recognized as a necessary but not sufficient condition for intelligent, rational, and responsible reflection upon the phenomenon of religion.

An impartial observer of the history of theology cannot but be struck by the relative inattention accorded the relationship between the poetic and religious functions of the human spirit. With some notable exceptions (Santayana, Maritain, and Hans urs van Baltasar come readily to mind) Western theology has paid scant attention to the cultural intuition that art and religion have much to offer one another. In Christianity, if the theology is Catholic (for example, Neo-Thomist), one may note the extensive series of studies on the relationship of the religious object to the traditional Aristotelian and Thomist "transcendentals"—the "good," the "true" and, with relatively little attention, the "beautiful." If the theology is modern Protestant, the formulations are likely to move away from Aristotelian and Thomist categories into some form of post-Kantian philosophical concern with the problems of either the first or second *Critiques* but rarely with the problem of art and the imagination in the third *Critique.* In either case, a concern with the complex relationships between art and religion is likely to find its home solely among those brave and, one surmises, somewhat lonely practitioners of the scholarly discipline most commonly called "Religion and Literature." In the wider context of scholarship on religion, the study of metaphor—more specifically of the religious and theological use of metaphor—is likely to receive scant attention from most scholars in either religious studies or theology.

However, sustained study of the religious phenomenon seems to demand a recognition that the claims of metaphor are central to these fields. For not only is every major religion grounded in certain root metaphors, but Western religions are also "religions of the book"—books which codify root metaphors through various linguistic and generic strategies. For Judaism, Christianity, and Islam certain texts serve not only as charter documents for the religion but as "scripture" in the strict sense: that is, as *normative* for the religious community's basic understanding and control of its root metaphors and thereby its vision of reality. In the Christian religion, this common situation is intensified. The earliest Christian texts (the parables of Jesus), as recent scriptural scholarship has clarified through the use of modern literary-critical modes of analysis, achieve their parabolic status as conjunctions of a narrative genre and a metaphorical process. And yet, as the history of both Christian preaching and exegetical and theological reflection upon the parables demonstrate, parabolic metaphors have often been considered mere substitutions for some literal (ethical, conceptual, dogmatic, or political) meaning. The preacher, exegete, or theologian feels free to speak or write all too plainly about the "real" meaning of these regrettably unsophisticated first Christian scriptural texts—the parables of Jesus or such later scriptural formulations as the Johannine root metaphor "God is love"—and to note only in passing the "mere metaphors," the "decorative ornaments," or "images" which cloak the doctrinal or ethical "idea." *Mark's root metaphor is Jesus is death & life.*

David Tracy, author of *Blessed Rage for Order: The New Pluralism in Theology* and *The Analogical Imagination in Contemporary Theology,* is professor of theology at the University of Chicago Divinity School.

2. *Theological and Religious Uses of Metaphor: The Concept of Limit-Language*

Two logically prior issues demand some clarification before I discuss the theological and religious uses of metaphor. The first is the character of theology itself as a discipline; the second is a properly theological understanding of religion.[1]

Serious conflicts exist in specifying criteria for contemporary theology. In appropriately general terms, however, one may state that theology attempts to correlate certain specified meanings and truths in our common human experience and language with the interpreted meanings and truths of a specific religious tradition. In some cases, this correlation will prove pure confrontation (recall Tertullian's famous adage, "What has Athens to do with Jerusalem?"); in others it will approach an identity model (recall John Dewey's *A Common Faith* and its influence on liberal theologians); and in most cases, it will involve an argument for the relative adequacy of a transformation model. Transformation in its theological use includes both moments of confrontation and negation and moments of identity, similarity, or analogy between the specific meanings and truths described on each side of the correlation (recall Paul Tillich's distinctive transformation model for theological correlation).

Two sets of criteria will prove necessary for this theological task. First, fundamentally hermeneutical criteria of appropriateness are used to adjudicate the conflicts of interpretation in both contemporary culture and the particular religious tradition. Second, criteria of adequacy (including distinct theories of meaning and truth) are employed to correlate the meanings and claims to truth of any theologian's interpretation of a religious tradition with those of his or her cultural interpretation of our contemporary common experience and/or language.

An illustration of this correlation process may prove more useful than further methodolgial discussion of distinct models. If one presumes that theologians are committed by the nature of their discipline to investigate critically the cognitive claims of the religious phenomenon, then the first logical question is of the need for a properly theological understanding of religion itself. In contemporary religious studies the most important distinction is that between functional definitions of religion (especially those of cultural anthropologists and sociologists of religion)[2] and substantive definitions developed by such normative disci-

---

1. For a fuller analysis and defense of the two presuppositions summarized here, see my *Blessed Rage for Order: The New Pluralism in Theology* (New York, 1975), pp. 1–146.

2. Among the most influential for theologians are those by Clifford Geertz, "Religion as a Cultural System," in *The Religious Situation: 1968*, ed. Donald Cutler (Boston, 1968), pp. 639–88; and Peter Berger, *The Scared Canopy: Elements of a Sociological Theory of Religion* (New York, 1967). Geertz's analysis is, in fact, both functional and substantive; Berger's (in this work) purely functional.

plines as theology and some forms of philosophy. The most notable substantive definitions proposed have been Friedrich Schleiermacher's definition of religion as "the feeling of absolute dependence," Rudolf Otto's phenomenology of the holy as the *mysterium fascinans et tremendum,* Paul Tillich's analysis of religion as "ultimate concern," and Bernard Lonergan's definition of religious experience as "being-in-love-in-an-unrestricted-fashion."

Since my own analysis of the religious and theological uses of metaphor will employ a substantive definition of *a* (not *the* exclusive) distinguishing characteristic of "religion," it may prove helpful to indicate that definition at the outset. I have argued for this position at some length in work published elsewhere; here I will summarize only those conclusions relevant to the present question. In extending the analytical philosophy of Ian Ramsey and his successors on the "odd logic" of religious language,[3] several recent philosophers have employed the more Kantian language of "limit" (rather than oddness) in analyzing a distinguishing characteristic of religious language.[4] Summarily stated, this analysis applies to two distinct kinds of phenomena: first, the presence of an implicit religious dimension in our ordinary experience and language; second, the presence of what is called a religious-as-limit use of various language forms and genres (metaphor, narrative, myth, concept, analogy, etc.) in particular religions.

The arguments for a religious dimension in our ordinary experience and language have been formulated in existentialist, phenomenological, and analytical philosophies and theologies. Amidst a large literature on this subject, the analyses most familiar are probably Tillich's concerning the presence of an ultimate concern in all our other concerns and Karl Jaspers' concerning certain "boundary" or "limit situations," such as death, guilt, or anxiety. Both Tillich and Jaspers were of course deeply influenced by Kierkegaard's now classical analysis of the "stages of Christian existence." A phenomenological analysis of more positive limit experiences, which likewise disclose a religious dimension in our ordinary experience, may be found in Gabriel Marcel's studies of creativity, joy, and fundamental trust. In the analytical tradition, Ramsey, Frederick Ferre, and Stephen Toulmin have also argued that religious language discloses certain limit experiences and questions about the ordinary.[5] In any of the traditions, the analysis yields a description of

3. For Ian Ramsey's basic theory, see *Religious Language: An Empirical Placing of Theological Phrases* (New York, 1963); for his use of metaphor and model (influenced by the work of Max Black), see *Words about God,* ed. Ramsey (New York, 1971).

4. Paul Ricoeur, "The Specificity of Religious Language," in *Semeia: An Experimental Journal for Biblical Criticism* 4 (1975): 107–45.

5. For Ramsey, see n. 3; for Frederick Ferre, "Mapping the Logic of Models in Science and Theology," in *New Essays on Religious Language,* ed. Dallas M. High (New York, 1969), pp. 54–97; and "Metaphors, Models and Religion," *Soundings* 51 (1968): 327–45; for Stephen Toulmin's analysis of religious questions as "limiting questions," see his *An Examination of the Place of Reason in Ethics* (Cambridge, Mass., 1950), pp. 204–21.

a distinguishing characteristic of a religious dimension, an experience and language indicative of some specifiable *limit to* our common, ordinary experience and language. The religious dimension is most clearly recognized in such limit experiences as (negatively) anxiety or (positively) fundamental trust in the very worthwhileness of our existence.

A full discussion of the generic term "religion," therefore, includes analyses of both a religious dimension in our ordinary experience and language and of particular religions. In either case, the limiting character of a religious use of language will be formulated. In fact, a helpful study could be made of the metaphors various analysts choose ("limit," "horizon," "ultimacy," etc.) to describe the religious dimension they emphasize. However, as I have indicated, the central theological concern with metaphor is to analyze the root metaphors which disclose a distinctively religious form of life in the major religions. In descriptions of God in Judaism and Christianity, for example, one finds a whole cluster of metaphors ranging from father, lord, shepherd, and king to more elusive and subtle choices like light, truth, love, and wisdom. If metaphors are purely and simply defined as decorative substitutions for real, literal, ideational meanings, then the relative lack of concern among many theologians with most biblical metaphors for God is completely justified. If, however, metaphors are more properly understood to function by means of some theory of tension or interaction (on the three levels of the word, the phrase, and the text), then the move to replace these decorative images with concepts seems a precipitate one. Any Western theological discourse, after all, does claim hermeneutical fidelity for its concepts in relation to the originating religious language of the scriptural texts.

The question recurs: Is there a specifically religious and theological use of metaphor? If one's substantive definition of religion includes an insistence upon the limiting character of all religious language and one's definition of theology includes an insistence upon the second-order, reflective, and conceptual character of all properly theological language, then the theologian's problem becomes more clearly defined. First an analyst must study the actual religious and theological uses of metaphor in particular religions. The test case in this paper will be confined to two central Christian uses of metaphor: the parables of Jesus and the root metaphor of Christianity, "God is love."

3. *The New Testament Parables: The Conjunction of Narrative Form and Metaphorical Process*

The Christian religion shares with all major religions a vision (more exactly, a redescription) of reality informed by a specific cluster of metaphors. The Christian religion also shares with its parent religion, Judaism, and with the other major Western religion, Islam, the peculiarity that it is a religion of the book. The latter statement demands further elaboration. To speak of Western religions as religions of the book does not mean that they are *only* religions of a text; indeed, specific historical persons and events are central to all Western religions, and one need not insist upon a "theology of word" as distinct from either a "theology of events" or a "theology of sacrament" to admit scriptural normativity. In fact, not only Reformed Christianity insists that certain texts (which Christians name the Old and New Testaments) be taken as normative for interpreting Christianity's root metaphors. Whatever their hesitation over the sixteenth-century Reformer's formulation of *Sola Scriptura* and however strong their insistence upon uniting Sacrament (or manifestation) to Word (or proclamation) for a full understanding of the root metaphors of Christianity, Catholic and Orthodox Christians have joined their Protestant colleagues in insisting upon the priority of the Scriptures. Indeed, to interpret the root metaphors of the Christian religion, the Scriptures must function, in the words of the Roman Catholic theologian Karl Rahner as the *norma normans non normata* for all Christian theologies.

To understand the Christian religion's metaphorical network, therefore, one must study the major metaphorical expressions of the New Testament. The decisive events for Christianity are events codified in these texts. It is true, of course, that the sacramental redescription of reality in Orthodox, Anglican, and Roman Catholic Christianity may be expressed in the icons and cosmological theologies of Eastern Christianity or in the Christian nature-mysticism of a Francis of Assisi, as codified in the texts of Bonaventure's theology, wherein all reality as emanation and metaphor finally becomes sacrament. Yet even these sacramental forms of Christianity, by their own standards, are to be judged by their hermeneutical fidelity to the Christian vision of reality as expressed by the root metaphors codified in Christian Scriptures.

Granted this common Christian insistence upon texts, what specific cluster of metaphors in the New Testament should be taken as central or normative for Christian self-interpretation? As is well known, Christians remain divided on this question. One need not return to such famous intra-Christian disputes as Luther's dismissal of the Epistle of James as sub-Christian—indeed as "that right strawy epistle"—to witness the debate over *the* normative Christian root metaphors. In twentieth-century scriptural scholarship alone, a whole range of candidates have been proposed. Shall we choose the apocalyptic metaphors of Mark 13 or of the Book of Revelation? The metaphors which disclose more humanist, more liberal forms of Christianity in Luke, Acts, or James? The metaphors in the Pastoral Epistles which disclose the phenomenon of "early Catholicism"? The charged and tensive series of metaphors employed by Paul in Romans to disclose the scandal and paradox of Christian understanding? The metaphors of the Johannine literature which implicitly encourage developing metaphysical understandings of Christianity? The metaphors of Ephesians and Colossians so beloved by Eastern Christians or by Westerners like Teilhard de Chardin as scriptural backing for their sweeping poetic cosmologies?

The list of possible candidates can be expanded almost indefinitely in proportion to the two-thousand-year-old series of Christian interpretations of the distinct and contrary, if not contradictory, metaphors employed in various New Testament texts. Some contemporary New Testament scholars, like Rudolf Bultmann and Ernst Kasemann, have attempted to resolve this problem by formulating the notion of "a canon within the canon." Others, however, are approaching the problem in new ways, and a consensus seems to be emerging. First, influenced, perhaps, by the more ecumenical character of most major forms of contemporary Christianity, scholars now recognize, accept, and sometimes even delight in the pluralism of possible Christian modes of being-in-the-world disclosed by the different metaphors of the New Testament.[6]

Second, New Testament scholars and theologians are beginning to study literary genres not merely as classificatory or taxonomic devices but as genuinely productive of meaning. There follows a widespread distrust, therefore, of traditional theological and exegetical interpretations of metaphor understood on the rhetorical model of decorative device or substitution.

Third, even the most influential and distinguished hermeneutical method of contemporary Christian theology, that of Rudolf Bultmann and his followers, is coming to be recognized as still too determined by the Schleiermacher-Dilthey Romantic hermeneutical tradition's concern to find the meaning of the text behind the text (in the mind of the author, in the *sitz-im-leben* of either the early Christian community or the life of Jesus, in the reaction of the original addressee). On the contrary, for the post-Romantic understanding of hermeneutics, meaning (in the shift of metaphors employed implicitly by Hans-Georg Gadamer and explicitly by Paul Ricoeur) is located not *behind* but *in front of* the text.[7]

Fourth, the shift in interpretation theory has freed scriptural interpreters to insist upon the greater need for semiotic, structuralist, semantic, and literary-critical analyses of the production of the sense of the text and, *through* that sense, the production of the referent of the text. Ordinarily that referent is described in this theory of interpretation as a possible mode of being-in-the-world or a form of life. An analysis of metaphor in terms of a theory of substitution has also shifted to a theory of tension or interaction and, following this shift, to an analysis of the

6. See Norman Perrin, *The New Testament: An Introduction* (New York, 1974), esp. pp. 277–303.

7. Hans-Georg Gadamer, *Truth and Method* (New York, 1974), and Paul Ricoeur, *Interpretation Theory* (Fort Worth, Tex., 1975).

tension present on the level of word, the statement, and finally the text itself with all its referents.

Fifth, some interpreters of the New Testament argue that the group of stories known as the parables of Jesus is the major candidate for the kind of literary-critical and hermeneutical analysis suggested above, and for locating the most central root metaphors of Christianity.[8] In fact, the parables are the best texts we possess for understanding the actual discourse of the historical Jesus; they most clearly approximate the Jesuanic vision and, thereby, the originating root metaphors of the founder of the Christian religion. If the metaphorical character of the parables of Jesus can be properly reinterpreted in keeping with modern theories of metaphor and then related to such nonmetaphorical Jesuanic texts as Jesus' proverbs and proclamatory sayings, then the parables' candidacy can be persuasively established. Moreover, the analyses of the parables can also be related to similar analyses of other and later classical New Testament uses of metaphor to yield surprising results. My own candidate for this latter task, as I said, will be the classical Christian Johannine metaphorical statement, "God is love."

I would like, first, to summarize recent literary-critical work on the metaphors of the New Testament parables as an illustration of how a theory of metaphor functions in the interpretation of any religion. Most of the major New Testament parables are introduced by the words "The kingdom of God is like. . . ." If the interpreter of the parables is a philosophical theologian who is largely influenced by a rhetorical understanding of metaphor as a classificatory trope, then she or he will search— often using some classical theory of allegory—for *the* clear and distinct *idea* to express the "real" (i.e., spiritual, many times Neoplatonic) meaning of the "kingdom of God" lurking behind the decorative metaphors and images employed by Jesus. Various candidates have been proposed for that idea ranging from those in Augustine's *City of God* through Albrecht Ritschl's progressivist and somewhat promethean liberal kingdom of God to modern social gospel Christianity's political redefinition of that kingdom.

If the interpreter is a modern exegete employing historico-critical methods but rarely literary criticism in other than a classificatory sense, then the real meaning of the parable will be found elsewhere than in its metaphorical structure: first, *behind* the present parabolic text, in the *sitz-im-leben* of either the early Church or Jesus as these are recovered by modern historical methods; second, in the exegete's reexpression of the parable in modern theological form. For the latter, one may recall the liberal Protestant ethical interpretations of the parables by the great exegete, Adolf Jülicher, the eschatologically restrained Anglican inter-

8. The magisterial work here on reconstruction of the New Testament parabolic texts as the parables of Jesus is Joachim Jeremias' *The Parables of Jesus* (New York, 1963).

pretations of C. H. Dodd, or the German Lutheran interpretations of Joachim Jeremias.[9]

Without abandoning the historical researches of their scholarly predecessors (and thereby accepting the reconstruction of the present texts into the parables of Jesus), a number of New Testament scholars now employ a tensive or interaction theory of metaphor (ordinarily united to a related theory of narrative) to interpret the narrative and metaphorical elements in the parables. One may cite, for example, Norman Perrin's use of Philip Wheelwright's "steno" and "tensive" language, Dan O. Via's use of Neoaristotelian and, more recently, structuralist literary-critical methods, Robert Funk's use of German hermeneutical resources, or Dominic Crossman's use of several literary-critical resources.[10]

In line with this new scriptural scholarship and in keeping with his own philosophical analysis of metaphor, Paul Ricoeur has proposed an interpretation of the sense and the referent of the parables that commands the attention of many New Testament scholars and theologians. As the most developed position to date on this question, Ricoeur's analysis is worth noting at greater length. In properly summary terms, Ricoeur's interpretation of the parables proceeds along the following steps:[11]

1. Initially in general terms, a parable may be described as the conjunction of a narrative form and a metaphorical process.
2. The modern interaction theory of metaphor makes the functioning of the metaphors in the parables far more understandable by noting the inner tensions which are solved by the twist of a semantic impertinence become a genuinely informative semantic innovation.
3. When the interpreter of the parables moves from the level of the statement to the level of the discourse, with a composition of its own higher than that of the sentence, then one may relate the theory of models developed by Max Black and Mary Hesse to the interaction theory of metaphor. Hesse interprets scientific heuristic models as heuristic fictions which serve as a means of redescribing reality. In a

9. Adolf Jülicher, *Die Gleichnisreden Jesu* (Tübingen, 1888); C. H. Dodd, *The Parables of the Kingdom*, rev. ed. (New York, 1961); and Jeremias, *The Parables of Jesus*.

10. Perrin, "The Parables of Jesus as Parables, as Metaphors, and as Aesthetic Objects: A Review Article," *Journal of Religion* 47 (1967): 340–47; Dan O. Via, *The Parables* (Philadelphia, 1967); Robert W. Funk, *Language, Hermeneutics and Word of God* (New York, 1966); John Dominic Crossman, *In Parables* (New York, 1973). It might be noted that my examples are to full-fledged poetic and religious metaphors rather than to trivial or dead ones: hence the appeal to theories of metaphor that start from the poetic paradigm.

11. See Ricoeur, "Specificity of Religious Language," pp. 1–145 for his full position; for his own summary, pp. 29–36; Ricoeur's position on individual issues and thinkers (e.g., Black and Hesse) may also be found here.

parallel manner, the metaphor in parables may be said to work like a model whenever the metaphor is mediated by a literary genre. Therefore the major referent of the parable (produced by the fiction of the parable) will prove to be a redescription of human possibility. In more familiar Aristotelian language, the parable is a *mythos* (a heuristic fiction) which has the *mimetic* power of redescribing human existence. The metaphorical *process,* therefore, is the *epiphor* or the *diaphor* which transfers the meaning of the story from fiction to redescribed reality.

4. The religious use of the parable form may be stated, in general terms, as in keeping with that limit use of all language proper to its religious use (outlined in part 2 of this essay). In the more specific terms of an interpretation of the New Testament parables, that limit use of metaphor may be noted in two ways: (*a*) In a manner directly analogous to the intensification process via hyperbole and paradox present in the New Testament use of proverbs, the New Testament use of parable includes its own analogous intensification process. The most important clues in the parables for that process are found in the clash between the realism of the narrative (e.g., in the parable of the laborers in the vineyard or in the prodigal son) and the actual extravagance of the dénouement of the story. For the latter, recall the father's extravagant feast for the irresponsible returned prodigal and the relative lack of celebration the father accords the responsible elder son. In the vineyard parable, recall the extravagance—and seeming flouting of simple justice—in the way the employer pays the laborers who were hired late in the day the same wage as those who labored all day. These extravagant actions in these realistic narratives are, in fact, disorienting to the reader. Yet that strategy of disorientation may serve the function of reorienting the reader by disclosing a new religious possibility: a way of being-in-the-world not based on the ethics of justice and merit but of pure gift, pure graciousness, indeed, in Wesley's famous phrase, of "pure unbounded love." (*b*) The phrase "The kingdom of God is like . . ." performs a similar limit function by serving as a radical qualifier upon the whole model (the kingdom *of God*). That qualifier radicalizes the model (i.e., the metaphor mediated through the narrative) and relates the entire parable to the similarly radicalized possibilities expressed in the proverbs of Jesus, his proclamatory sayings, and his deeds.

5. The referents of the parables are, therefore, certain specifically Christian religious-as-limit experiences: a style of life formed by what Christians call radical faith, fundamental trust, and agapic, non-self-serving, unsentimental love. Those possibilities are disclosed by the redescription of human possibility in a metaphor which uses a narrative form to serve as a model (a heuristic fiction). Then that model is joined to a strong qualifier ("The kingdom *of God* is like . . .") to

disclose a limit use of the original metaphor, a use backed by the clues in the story itself of extravagant actions set into a realistic narrative.

This interpretation of Ricoeur's basic position on the parables should not be taken as suggesting that all the necessary warrants and backings for its acceptance have been provided. In fact, the argument is dependent upon Ricoeur's own complex position on metaphor argued, on general grounds, in *The Rule of Metaphor*[12] and, on more specific grounds for the parables, in his *Semeia* articles. However, one may observe that, whatever the particularities of Ricoeur's own position, he represents the emerging consensus in New Testament scholarship cited earlier. For however the parabolic metaphors are interpreted, the exegete must employ some theory of tension or interaction, not a theory of substitution, to understand fully what "The kingdom of God is like." When the interpreter applies a theory of substitution to the parables, she or he will inevitably either remove the limiting character of the mode of life disclosed by these heuristic fictions or will replace it with an alternative of her or his own theological or ethical choosing. Either the limit experience may be replaced by some ethical or aesthetic or pseudoscientific "real" but absent meaning; or it may well be maintained through some specific (ordinarily second-order theological) limit language. Yet the exact hermeneutical dependence of later theological languages (e.g., "justification through grace by faith," or "the divinization of humanity through incarnation," or "a sacramental vision of all reality," to recall the classical Reformed, Orthodox, and Catholic theological limit languages respectively) on the originating language of Jesus is difficult to establish. In neither case can the interpreter claim intrinsic hermeneutical fidelity to Jesus' originating root metaphors concerning what "The kingdom of God is like."

What, in the earliest Christian language, is the kingdom of God like? It is like what happens in the story; it is a metaphor become a heuristic fiction redescribing human possibility through stories qualified by the radical disclaimer "The kingdom *of God* is like. . . ." The root metaphors of the Christian religion are themselves rooted first in these metaphors and narratives of the parables of Jesus.

There is no need to hold that this interpretation of the metaphorical character of the parables of Jesus makes it impossible to employ conceptual, theological language that does maintain hermeneutical fidelity to the originating Christian root metaphors.[13] Indeed, strictly theologi-

---

12. Ricoeur, *The Rule of Metaphor: Multi-disciplinary Studies of the Creation of Meaning in Language* (Toronto, 1978).

13. I attempt to show how this is the case in relation to the classical postbiblical Christian theological languages of analogy and dialectics in *The Analogical Imagination in Modern Theology* (forthcoming).

cal discourse of the later New Testament language does maintain that hermeneutical fidelity.

4. From Religious to Theological Discourse; The Johannine Metaphor "God is Love"

If the parables represent the earliest Christian religious language, the most influential New Testament theological uses of metaphor are Paul's of the "justice of God" and John's that "God is love" (1 John 4:7). Eberhard Jungel, in fidelity to the Reformation and Pauline insistence upon justification through grace by faith, has provided an analysis of the parallelism of the logic of the parabolic language of "The kingdom of God is like . . ." and Paul's logic of superabundance—in present categories Paul's limit-language use of the metaphor of "justice" within the theological analysis of Romans.[14] Still, in the entire New Testament perhaps the most influential candidate for Christianity's root metaphor for redescribing the relationship of God and the self is the elusive statement "God is love." Unlike parabolic discourse, the Johannine metaphor is set in the context of a second-order conceptual and reflective theological discourse. Like parabolic discourse, however, this Johannine theological language demonstrates a religious-as-limit language use of metaphor. Where the parables of Jesus redescribe human possibility by telling the reader that "The kingdom of God is like" what happens in the story, John and Paul will use metaphors like justice and love to redescribe that same possibility in more strictly conceptual, second-order theological language.

Moreover, John's letter genre is directly related to the religious and theological vision of the Gospel of John. This relationship is worth noting. For amidst debates on the genre of the gospels, one point stands out clearly: they include both narrative as well as more strictly conceptual-theological discourse. In the Gospel of Mark, narrative is more prominent than conceptual-theological discourse; in John, the theological language is more prominent though still related to the narrative, especially the controlling narrative of all the gospels, the passion narrative.

At the level of discourse, therefore, the single metaphorical statement "God is love" is set within the context of the letter genre. Yet John's letter is itself intrinsically related by its Johannine character to the gospel genre and thereby to both the narrative and the entire theology of concepts and signs of the Gospel of John. This generic complexity in fact influences the interpretation of the referent of the metaphorical statement. But before moving to the level of discourse via genre, it is impor-

14. Eberhard Jüngel, *Paulus und Jesus* (Tübingen, 1972).

tant first to analyze the metaphorical tension at the level of the word and the statement.

Although metaphor is produced at the level of the statement as a whole, it focuses on the word.[15] Granted this principle, it is understandable that the theological and exegetical scholarship of the last thirty-five years has largely concentrated on the word "love" as *the* root metaphor for the Christian understanding of God and humankind. Both the famous word studies of Kittel and the most influential work on Christian love in the twentieth century, Anders Nygren's *Agape and Eros,* have signaled the tension in the Christian use of the word "love." More specifically, Nygren's famous study clarifies the central tensions between the two *words* for love employed in the New Testament period, *agape* and *eros:*[16]

1. *Eros* is acquisitive desire and longing.
   Agape is sacrificial giving.
2. *Eros* is upward movement.
   Agape "comes down."
3. *Eros* is egocentric love, a form of self-assertion of the highest, noblest, sublimest kind.
   Agape is unselfish love, it "seeks not its own," it gives itself away.
4. *Eros* is primarily man's love; God is the *object* of *eros.* Even when attributed to God, *eros* is *patterned* on human love.
   Agape is primarily *God's* love; God *is agape.* Even when attributed to man, *agape* is patterned on the divine love.
5. *Eros* is determined by the quality, beauty, worth of its object; it is not spontaneous, but "evoked," "motivated," and *recognizes* value (and then loves).
   Agape is sovereign in relation to its object and is directed to both "the evil and the good"; it is spontaneous, "overflowing," "unmotivated" and, in loving, *creates* value in the object.

One need not accept all the details of Nygren's analysis nor its application to later Christian theological understandings of love as *caritas* (i.e., the proposed syntheses of *eros* and *agape* in Augustine and Aquinas) in order to note the built-in tension in the New Testament word "love." Nygren's analysis warns the interpreter not to *substitute* some form of *eros* for *agape* in describing the Christian understanding of God's reality and the gift-command to be loving "as God has first loved us." This remains

15. For an extended treatment of these connections, see Ricoeur's "Study 4: Metaphor and the Semantics of the Word," in his *The Rule of Metaphor,* pp. 101–34, esp. pp. 125–34.

16. Anders Nygren, *Agape and Eros* (New York, 1969); for Nygren's own list, which I have abridged here, see p. 210.

the case whether *eros* is understood as the high *eros* doctrine of Plato, as Aristotle's friendship-love, as courtly and romantic love, as Freudian *eros* or, more commonly, as some sentimental version of love. Yet the linguistic limitations of Nygren's word-analysis (and similar analyses) also become evident in his own language: the metaphorical character of the word *agape* is not in fact analyzed. Rather one finds Nygren appealing to such substitute *concepts* as "value-creating" or "value-recognizing" for understanding that tension, or to such substitute metaphors as *"eros'* upward movement," *"agape* comes down" and "overflows." The pattern and attribution language indicates that the character of *agape* as a religious tensive metaphor has been overlooked. The use of such Lutheran theological language as "without merit" indicates that Nygren's own "value-free," "scientific" interpretation is not as theologically value-free as he believes.[17] Yet the route to take beyond Nygren's now classical analysis of Christian love does not lie solely through further studies of the metaphorical product, *the words* for love (or God) in the New Testament, but at the level of *statement* where the metaphor is produced.

Christian thinkers since the time of John have often chosen "love" as the most distinctively Christian root metaphor for both the reality of God and for the reality of that mode of being-in-the-world which seems distinctively Christian (namely, agapic love). A study of the word *agape* shows that an interpreter cannot understand Christian love by substituting some more familiar notion of *eros*-love for that Christian religious metaphor. The metaphorical statement "God is love," furthermore, insists that God is whatever this reality, *agape,* may be. Several clues emerge here. First, the very use of the word "God" in this statement (like the expression "The kingdom *of God*" in the parables) serves as a radicalizing qualifier upon the entire statement. In sum, the use of the expression "God" signals the presence of a religious-as-limit use of language and alerts the interpreter not to substitute some more familiar expression for love in place of this "love" which God, in some sense, *is.* Second, the metaphorical statement "God is love" must itself be understood in the context of the wide spectrum of alternative metaphors for "God" employed in the Old and New Testaments: from king, shepherd, rock, lord to light, truth, and wisdom. Moreover, the scriptural accounts also employ the metaphor "wrath" to qualify any sentimental understanding of God's "love."

One can note how easily the tension in the statement "God is love" is lost if the interpreter fails to note either the limit use or the metaphorical character of both "God" and "love." The temptation is to find or develop some seemingly more manageable *concept* to replace these elusive metaphors (e.g., Being-Itself for God; Platonic spiritual *eros* for love). However, if one allows the tension between such scriptural metaphorical

---

17. For Nygren's claims for his scientific "motif-research," see ibid., pp. 27–41.

statements as "the wrath of God" and "God is love" full play, one must discourage interpretations which head in the direction of sentimentalizing and/or literalizing the entire metaphorical statement. Just as the word "love" when used of "God" bears literal falsity but metaphorical truth, so too the copula in the statement "God *is* love" has its own tensions from the metaphorical character of the truth produced.[18]

A first tension was found within the words "God" and "love" and, thereby, *between* the words "God" and "love." That tension itself was a clue to the tension between a deceptively literal interpretation of the statement "God is love" (e.g., "The First Cause of all reality is our loving friend") and a metaphorical interpretation (e.g., "God, a God of mercy and justice, of love and wrath, *is like* agapic love"). Moreover, the "is like" is clearly a metaphorical "is like": the resemblance is *produced by* the redescriptive power of the metaphorical language; the resemblance is not simply a descriptive account of an observed empirical reality. Indeed the inclusion of the metaphor "wrath" along with the tension within the word "love" (*eros* and *agape*) already indicates that in a straightforward "literal" relational sense "God" *is not* "love." To shift the tensive redescriptive metaphorical truth of "is like" to a substituted literal description of what God "is" or "is like" is to remove the metaphorical character of John's language in exactly the same manner as a theory of substitution removes the need for parable in Jesus' kingdom-of-God language. The statement "God is love" does not say literally what God is but *produces* a metaphorical meaning for what God is like. In this redescriptive sense, the statement defines who, for the Christian, God *is*.[19]

Within the larger discourse comprising the Johannine corpus (comprised of the genres of gospel narrative, theological second-order language, and letter), the referent of all this "love" language is also redescribed in a manner directly analogous to the parabolic redescription of what "The kingdom of God is like," for Christians are said by these texts to be both enabled (gifted) and commanded to love as they have first been loved by God.[20] In the parables, the redescriptive force of the heuristic fiction discloses a religious mode of being-in-the-world like that which happens in the story. In the more theological, second-order language of John, the same kind of limit possibility is disclosed by the metaphorical production of an indicative "God is (like) love" and an imperative "and you must and are enabled to love like God." No more

18. Ricoeur, "Specificity of Religious Language," pp. 84–88; *Rule of Metaphor*, pp. 239–47.

19. I am applying Ricoeur's notion of "metaphorical truth" to these scriptural passages. For the notion itself, see *Rule of Metaphor*, pp. 247–57.

20. For the command language, 1 John 3:22–24; for gift language, 1 John 3:1–3 and 4:7–21. The tensions between the universality and sectarianism of the Johannine theology as well as the tensions in the Johannine understanding of "world" are also relevant to a full treatment of the final Johannine vision.

than the religious discourse of the parables does the theological discourse of John (or Paul) presume to describe literally either God or that
Christian mode of being-in-the-world called *agapic* love. If one removes
the tensive character of the metaphors, at any level (word, statement, or
text), one imposes—through substitution—various descriptive and pre-
scriptive candidates for the "real" meaning of these redescriptive
metaphorical statements.

This analysis has been confined to the test case of Christian religious
language. However, the same metaphorical character of Buddhist
understandings of "compassion" or Jewish understandings of "cove-
nant" would, I believe, yield the same hermeneutical results. To end
where I began: if it is true that every major religion's vision of human
reality is grounded in certain root metaphors that redescribe the human
situation, then an elimination of the metaphorical character of religious
language is effectively a substitution of one set of meanings for another.
If this is the case, then the study of metaphor in religious studies is
hardly the luxury item which many theologians and historians of religion seem to believe it. In fact, more highly developed theological languages exist which can legitimately claim hermeneutical fidelity to the
metaphorical language of the parables of Jesus and the metaphorical
statement of John that "God is love." Still, before investigating these
theological languages on their own (for example, the analogical language of Aquinas, the hidden and revealed God-language of Luther, the
sovereignty-of-God-language of Calvin), it seems more fitting to note how
these later, more strictly theological languages relate in their logic and
meaning to the normative Christian religious language of the parables of
Jesus and the theologies of John and Paul. Once that hermeneutical
admission occurs, then the study of metaphor moves to the very center
of contemporary theological studies. If, however, metaphor is finally to
be understood by means of some theory of substitution, then work in
scriptural exegesis, religious studies, and theology can proceed very
much along traditional lines, by and large oblivious to the import of
literary-critical studies. Yet through an analysis of the single test case of
Christian religious language plausible reasons have emerged to suggest
that recent theories of metaphor challenge that conventional wisdom. In
that sense, the study of metaphor may well provide *a* central clue to a
better understanding of that elusive and perplexing phenomenon our
culture calls religion.

Art and Life: A Metaphoric Relationship

Richard Shiff

The contemporary artist Robert Rauschenberg remarked that he attempts to act in the "gap" between art and life. For Rauschenberg and many others who have intentionally sought to subvert established artistic conventions, "art" itself has been associated with the construction of a fixed, external public world, a world perhaps perfected but also bounded and restrictive. Life, in contrast to art, has been conceived as immediate personal experience, never adequately captured in a reflective artistic image. The ideal of immediate experience denies the desire for reflection, tradition, and cumulative knowledge, while the ideal of a world established and made fully comprehensible through art denies the need to grow and change. Modern artists like Rauschenberg, serving as models for all members of their society, have attempted to occupy the middle ground, often producing works which, although permanent, make reference to change.

When the modern artist is seen as moving about in a nebulous area between two opposing worlds, that of life or immediate experience and that of art or established truth, I think it is appropriate to discuss this activity in terms of metaphor. Indeed the present concern for metaphor in the academic and artistic communities is but one of many reflections of our sense that life is a process of the gradual attainment of knowledge through experience, whether sensuous or intellectual. Like our artists, we strive to create a picture of our world, yet that picture is never complete; for we continually pass on to new experiences and new images of reality. Not only do we grow and change but our world seems to change with us. Although the truths revealed through our art are founded in our experience, they seem more permanent and public than the acts of discovery leading to them. A principle once established and integrated with a body of other established truths enters into recorded history perhaps to be revered, disputed, or reinterpreted, but nevertheless to remain. The individual experience or discovery, however, passes; with the individual, only the sense of the continuing search for knowledge remains, and the particularity of that search yields personal identity. In a changing world, metaphor renders the truth of experience as the truth of knowledge, for it is the means of passing from individual immediacy to an established public world; the new must be linked to the old, and the experience of any individual must be connected with that of his society. Excluding the possibility of the creation of entirely new worlds and the resultant transformation of all personal identities, acts of genius or dramatic breakthroughs in fields of study can affect our present world order only if they are joined to it by means of a powerful metaphor. Indeed establishing the metaphoric bridge itself may be considered the act of genius, and the entry into new areas of knowledge is its consequence.

I choose not to speak of metaphor as a "leap" but rather as a bridge enabling passage from one world to another, for I wish to emphasize the sense of continuity and gradual change which seems to be fundamental to the relationship between modern art and life. I will come to speak of death, as well as life, in relation to art and want to give some initial perspective on my use of that concept. Most often, I believe, we think of art as expanding our world rather than destroying it or causing us to abandon it. Art, regarded as expression or communication, functions as metaphor, linking the individual to this expanding world. There is a sense, however, that the ultimate work of art, applying its metaphoric power to its limit, would indeed cause a leap rather than a gradual passage from one level of reality to another. The experience of such a work of art would be analogous to the revelation of absolute truth, as opposed to the attainment of relativistic knowledge which further experience might modify; transported to an entirely new reality, our old identities would die with our old world. Our current values do not lead us to expect to attain absolute truth through art or any other means; at its best we hope for a life characterized by a cumulative richness, a passage from birth to death marked by a succession of rewarding experiences. In order to give positive significance to death, it is often said that at the moment of death true enlightenment comes to the individual

---

Richard Shiff is associate professor of art at the University of North Carolina at Chapel Hill.

and the meaning of his life becomes clear—with the end of life, then, comes its satisfying completion, and one discovers truth at the finish of a lifelong search, an exploration conducted by means of metaphor. Thus we may say that the experience of life, expressed or given public meaning through works of art, leads ultimately to complete comprehension or the death of the individual, the same "death" that would be brought about by the experience of the ultimate, perfected work of art. Our concept of life, then, seems to demand that our works of art be incomplete, flawed, or imperfect; otherwise death will result. In other words, we continue to live because we remain ignorant of the absolute truth which would end our passage through the experience of life.

In addition to locating artistic activity on a metaphoric bridge between a perfected art and an evolving life, I wish to demonstrate that the work of art itself has been considered by modern critics and scholars both to embody the *new* truth of immediate experience, altering and extending the known world of the past, and, alternatively, to exhibit the *established* truth, the ideal or external standard to which ongoing life experience must be related. Art in the first sense has commonly been described as generated by the life of the individual, while art in the second sense has been conceived as defining a culture or social group and as ultimately linked to the death of the individual.

Although the general remarks of this paper may apply to art of all forms, I am most familiar with the visual arts and will confine my specific references to artists working within the traditions of painting and sculpture.

It has never been conclusively argued that the various visual means of human expression, often called "visual language," have a potential for reasoned communication as precise as that of verbal language; in fact, the modern visual arts have been associated repeatedly with the attempt to suggest the immediacy and idiosyncrasy of life. We often think of productivity in the visual arts as paradigmatic creativity, a spontaneous welling forth of imaginative and emotional energy only minimally constrained by reason, planning, and social purpose. While nineteenth-century psychologists sought to demonstrate that the style of a painter must depend upon his racial, environmental, and historical situation, nineteenth-century art critics often insisted that the artist was defined instead by his isolation; he was the one individual liberated from social or historical constraints, and consequently his works might appear incomprehensible to his public. Today we find, indeed, that visitors to museums of contemporary art claim not to "understand" the works displayed yet often express no great disconcertion, for they do not *expect* to understand the works. For many, art is a mere curiosity. As Edgar Wind noted, it has become "marginal," set apart from ordinary social life.[1]

But in an era in which life's meaning seems to be found in the individual's search for an unattainable truth, when one seeks new truths rather than the reaffirmation of accepted models of reality, we might indeed expect the appreciation and evaluation of works of art to become especially problematic. This must be so if the work of art is thought to provide an ideal model either of the individual's life or of the external world. When both individual and world are conceived as evolving and hence incomplete or unresolved, it does not seem sufficient that works of painting or sculpture resemble and stand comparison with accepted great works of the past, nor is it enough that a work of art treat a traditional theme in an accomplished or refined manner; for the truth of the past is not necessarily the truth of the present, and the work of art may succeed to the extent that it diverges from past models rather than resembling them.

We have, in fact, come to expect and demand novelty from our art; we associate artistic genius and creativity with originality and invention rather than with excellence and distinction. We choose as artistic heroes those like Cézanne and Van Gogh known for an unresolved, even awkward, art but an art clearly departing from accepted norms. The ultimate work of art, perhaps more confusing than Cézanne's, more frenzied than Van Gogh's, would seem to bear us so far beyond our present reality that we could form no judgment of it in comparison with accepted masterpieces. Indeed works of art are often now evaluated not in terms of comparison but, negatively, in terms of contrast; we praise breaking a tradition or convention, establishing a new medium or technique, redefining art itself by way of the new work of art. Harold Rosenberg wrote in 1952 that the American "action painters" conceived their art as marking a liberation from past goals and values; when asked what their art was, they explained what it was not.[2] More recently, painters have created three-dimensional objects which seem to have the properties of sculptures; sculptors have advocated a new environmental art without traditional bounds; and painters, sculptors, dancers, and musicians have regrouped to create new works called "happenings" and "performances" which evade the conventions of the theater and appear to be events in life rather than objects of art.

Critics and theorists have appealed to two alternative definitions of the work of art in order to meet the challenge of an art born out of a concern for individuality and the immediate experience of a world conceived as evolving. On the one hand, relying upon metaphors of organic

1. Edgar Wind, *Art and Anarchy* (New York, 1965), pp. 12–13. Wind cites Hegel on this issue.

2. Harold Rosenberg, "The American Action Painters," *The Tradition of the New* (New York, 1959), pp. 29–32.

growth and change, they have defined art in terms of the experience of the individual artist or viewer; on the other hand, in a more conservative manner, employing metaphors of stasis, they have defined art in terms of an external object of fixed properties. When art is conceived as experience, the work of art is seen as revealing reality from the inside by serving as a comprehensible model for life's persistent immediacy, a fixed image of flux; when art is conceived as an object, the work of art seems to reveal reality as an external world, a reality against which the life of the individual is thrown in relief and gains definition.

If art is found in personal experience, the world of art may seem to be idiosyncratic, mysterious, and private. Visual artists commonly maintain that they cannot explain the meaning of their own art in words; this is not so much a claim that the visual experience cannot be translated into a verbal mode but that verbalization is usually not poetry and words with their fixed dictionary definitions belong to the public domain, while the visual image must always retain its private mystery. This visual image, the argument goes, was born in the intensity of individual experience and it directs its speech confidentially to each individual who encounters it. The painter or sculptor often admonishes the critic to "let the work speak for itself."

The experience associated with the work of art may be that of the artist or that of the audience. In either case the work is commonly regarded as living. It seems alive both because it presents the life or experience of the artist and because it may induce an empathetic response in the viewer which causes him to sense the living force that lies within the work itself.

The notion that the work of art embodies the experience of the artist, in effect preserving that transient experience in permanent form, gives rise to the modern art history monograph, the study of the works of an individual artist. Characteristically the paintings or sculptures are discussed in chronological sequence, and attention is given to corresponding biographical data, as if the works themselves defined a biography. In the monographic study the historian usually considers the artist's own genuine emotion, rather than the sentiment attributed to characters represented in the work, as the source of expressive content. It thus becomes logical to speak of expression in works of pure abstraction, even in the grids of a geometric painter. The identification of the character of the works with the life and personality of the artist (as opposed to, say, his technical capacities) makes possible the kind of psychoanalytic interpretation of abstract art which Peter Gay, for example, has recently applied to Mondrian.[3]

3. Peter Gay, *Art and Act* (New York, 1976), pp. 175–226.

In the typical monograph the historian describes the general style of the works as belonging to the artist himself and only secondarily to his period. In fact, the degree to which the artist's personal style diverges from that of his period is often taken as an indication of the extent of his achievement. The more personal the art, the more meaningful is the model of reality it provides. In the evaluation of an individual artist, it might often be said that the later works, especially those of an artist of advanced years such as Monet or Picasso, fail to meet the standard of excellence established by the earlier works. But the author of a monograph rarely takes this approach, for he assumes that the later works reflect later, more mature experience, and as the artist's life evolves, so must his style. Here, for example, is a passage from a monograph on Rembrandt by Jakob Rosenberg in which the artist's late work is given special praise; it was first published in 1948:

> A deep feeling of humility penetrates the gloom of [Rembrandt's] late works and raises his art to a spiritual level in which individual experience takes on universal significance.
> Rembrandt, in reaching this phase, went far beyond the bounds of ordinary Dutch realism. His contemporaries described the life and the world around them, but Rembrandt mirrored the world within himself.[4]

What Rosenberg calls the "gloom" of Rembrandt's late works was regarded by some of the artist's contemporary viewers as an excessive darkness, a technical or stylistic failing; but for the writer of the monograph, external standards and comparisons have become irrelevant—the gloom is not a visual effect but a psychological state. Rosenberg indicates that Rembrandt's art of individual experience is superior to that of "ordinary Dutch realism," an art of an accepted external reality; yet he also implies that Rembrandt's greatest achievement is to link his own individuality to a higher spirituality to which all of us may respond with sympathetic understanding.

In the monograph, works of art do not stand alone as distinct monuments but are linked together as the record of a lifelong search; the artist's style is never fully defined, nor is his achievement fully revealed, until the activity ceases, until death limits his life of experience. This sense of artistic activity as an unending or even undirected search is revealed not only in the sketchlike quality of many modern works but in the repetition of motifs. Cézanne paints a sequence of views of Mont Sainte-Victoire which reveals no clear, deliberate pattern of investigation; Picasso paints great numbers of similar, anonymous female figures, often identified only by a signature and date, references to the life of the artist, not to his subject; and Rothko paints rectangles of brilliant colors

4. Jakob Rosenberg, *Rembrandt, Life and Work* (Greenwich, Conn., 1964), p. 35.

in similar configurations over a period of twenty-five years. In all three cases critics hesitate to pass judgment on individual paintings but regard the entire oeuvre, once limited by the artist's death, as an organic whole.

When artistic style is so closely linked to the personality of the individual and when style gains its value from the exemplary manner in which it reveals the world of that individual, evaluation by means of comparison with an external standard foreign to the artist may seem inappropriate. In such cases modern critics have evaluated the artist himself by judging the degree of his "sincerity." Zola found Manet's idiosyncratic works acceptable because, as he put it, they revealed the world with the truth of an individual "original language." "We are not accustomed," Zola wrote, "to seeing such simple and sincere translations of nature."[5] The critic implied that Manet could be trusted to paint what he knew through personal experience and nothing more. In this sense his vision was authentic and his paintings conveyed his personality as if he himself were present.

The critic who wishes to evaluate the sincerity of a work risks being duped; he may mistake a conventional sign of sincerity or individuality for the mark of authenticity. The sketchlike brushstroke or the unusual, even disturbing, color may have been calculated to imitate the look of another's individuality rather than being the mark of one's own. Nevertheless, modern critics have insisted on the validity of their own judgments of quality, as if the work of art, like a living person, could be looked in the eye to establish the sense of its sincerity or deceit. Albert Aurier, the first to give a comprehensive evaluation of Van Gogh's art, admitted that there could be no objective judgment of the desired authenticity of expression, yet he insisted that a genuine personality was revealed in Van Gogh's paintings. For Aurier these works gave off "the indefinable scent of sincerity."[6] This critic, then, did even more than evaluate the look of the paintings; he responded to their "smell." In a characteristic manner, he leaves his reader with little to debate and only the desire to experience the paintings' perfume of truth for himself. With a similar reliance on personal conviction, Harold Rosenberg has defined "serious" painting as the record of an action related to "a transforming process in the artist . . . the artist's total effort to make over his experience." Rosenberg follows with a description of "easy" painting, "the tremors produced by a few expanses of tone or by the juxtaposition of colors and shapes purposely brought to the verge of bad taste."[7] The latter work will reveal itself as inauthentic. We must take this on faith,

5. Emile Zola, "Edouard Manet" (1867), *Mon salon, Manet, écrits sur l'art*, ed. Antoinette Ehrard (Paris, 1970), p. 102; here and elsewhere, unless otherwise cited, my translation.

6. Albert Aurier, "Les Isolés: Vincent Van Gogh" (1891), *Oeuvres posthumes* (Paris, 1893), p. 260.

7. Harold Rosenberg, pp. 33–34.

however, for we are offered no objective standards by which to distinguish the record of a genuine personal act from its facile imitation, the truth from the lie. Significantly, Rosenberg describes authentic art in terms of experience—this is a living art, part of a vital process—while its imitation is seen as an object, a still-born art of the contrived arrangement of colors and shapes.

At times the work of art has been described not so much as having its own life but as instilling life or vital sensation in its observer. Around the turn of the century the vitally generative work of art was called "life-enhancing," and one responded to it by means of the process of empathy. The work of art, although an external object, seemed to generate activity in the viewer, to set him in correspondence with the work's metaphoric rhythm or dynamism. The viewer might sense movement or actually find himself moving before a work which only seemed to move. The German critic Julius Meier-Graefe, for example, wrote of a still life by Cézanne: "There is no movement [in the painting]; the subject before me is a simple still life; and yet I feel something in the pupil of my eye quivering, as if set in motion by some movement taking place in a higher dimension."[8]

If the movement which Meier-Graefe experienced were taken as a sign of the authenticity or success of the work of art, critical judgment would depend on a direct personal encounter with the work. A description of the object would not seem adequate to convey its merit, and the popular notion that seeing—and, in this case, feeling—is believing would be reinforced. But if the value of the work of art is to be found only in its immediate experience, an experience each viewer must have for himself, and if the authenticity of a work, the sincerity of its creator, can only be sensed in its immediate presence and cannot be attributed to a specific describable property, what can we learn from the work? What generalizations can be made, other than that works of art stimulate us, that in their presence we feel alive?

A work of art can establish standards of excellence to be applied in many areas of social endeavor as long as the sense of the work can be externalized, as long as the work becomes or remains a fixed object rather than one altered or consumed through the experience of life. Such a work may express a theme that can be conveyed in other media, a theme known not only through a particular work but in its translations. The work of art regarded as a fixed object may be evaluated with reference to its technique, the manner in which it reveals a truth that may be known in other forms. Metaphors of stasis or completion—balance, harmony, structure, composition, logic—are used to describe the charac-

8. Julius Meier-Graefe, *The Development of Modern Art* (1904), trans. Florence Simmonds and George W. Chrystal, 2 vols. (New York, 1908), 1:267.

ter of such a work; one even speaks of tension, the tension of an equilibrium established among a number of forces. It is appropriate that works of art considered as external objects be seen as permanent, for such works reveal accepted truths, aspects of experience which are common to the members of a society. The technique or language of the work of art is itself the bridge or link between the world of the experience of the individual and the world of "shared" experience or culture. In their different personal styles individual artists who are members of the same society may seem to discover common truths; they express the same content. This view is implicit in the type of art historical study—the study of the art of a particular period or nation—which is as common as the monograph. We think, for example, of French art, Russian art, or the art of the early Middle Ages as appropriate topics for scholarly research and assume that although the extroverted Renoir and the reclusive Cézanne may have had very different experiences of life, their art will reveal a similar world view. Moreover, the connoisseur attempting to determine whether a drawing attributed to Rubens is genuine might compare it to the work of other Flemish baroque artists but not to the work of Delacroix or Manet, painters sharing aspects of Rubens' temperament but living in a different age. The external qualities of an artist's work, those readily subject to evaluation, relate most clearly to his period and culture, not to his innermost personal experience.

According to the arguments set forth in Heinrich Wölfflin's influential *Principles of Art History* (1915), the bounds established by national and period styles limit individual artistic expression. The period style itself is formed independently of any particular human effort; it is the reflection of historical time alone. Wölfflin writes: "Every artist finds certain visual possibilities before him, to which he is bound. Not everything is possible at all times. . . . one could envisage a history of the development of occidental seeing, for which the variations in individual and national characteristics would cease to have any importance."[9] In other words, at any given time all artistic expression is governed by a particular mode of vision or constellation of visual forms, as if the world were seen through a single grand metaphor. Thus, as Wölfflin argued, the Gothic cathedral and the Gothic shoe will exhibit the same formal principles.

According to this reasoning any linguistic utterance or formalized communication, as well as any artifact, might be regarded as a work of art to the extent that it conveys "objective" meaning to all members of a society; the fundamental measure of the success of the work of art would be its capacity to provide a stable reference, a picture of the world we can convincingly conceive as real, a world seeming to conform to that of our own experience. For Wölfflin the accessibility of the work within its own

9. Heinrich Wölfflin, *Principles of Art History* (New York, 1932), pp. 11–12.

period would seem assured by the necessity that it exhibit its own period style. The most serious threat to comprehension becomes the eccentricity of individual emotional expression. The work of art, conceived as an object of specific historical style, comes to represent an arrested life, reflected, fixed, and given an interpretation or meaning. Thus, the meaning of life's major and minor experiences—its cathedrals and its shoes, so to speak—is conveyed through a publicly accessible means of communication, an artistic technique, and is available to all who can interpret the work of art. The work becomes an object of shared experience, a cultural artifact, making the life of its creator available to all others in a form that is theirs. By such means the individual overcomes his isolation, cultural bonds are established, and we speak of art as representing an ordered, ideal world.

But the link between the concept of the individual and that of experience is a strong one, and the notion of shared experience seems contradictory. The meaning of life must remain particularized; we might lose our true individual identities in accepting any universal truth or generalized picture of reality. As the surrealist André Breton argued, even the most commonplace conversation, an exchange of the simplest sentences, is a work of art—not in the sense of being an object of consistent form and interpretation, a source of shared experience, but in the sense that a conversation is a unique, spontaneous sequence of expressive utterances, each incomprehensible to the other party and even to its author.[10] Each remark is itself a mysterious, immediate life experience; the speakers are incapable of translating their own sentences, and the entire exchange comes to represent the life process. The meaning of this life experience may be known directly through internal sensation but not external formulation. Such isolation of the individual is revealed in the common remark, "I know what I mean, but I can't put it into words." It is a strange kind of knowledge that cannot be expressed, yet its public expression, the verbal statement or visual representation, would seem to render the truth of immediate experience fixed and lifeless, cut off from the living source.

Such public representation of private experience must depend on a medium or metaphor; a public art is never the equivalent of individual experience but aspires to attain that status through the perfection of its technique. As the medium which separates art from life experience is perfected, it becomes transparent: we see through it as if it were not there; we pass immediately from life to art, art to life. The ultimately successful work of art would employ a metaphor not recognizable as such; the passage from the world of life to the world of art would seem to occupy neither space nor time, and the two realms would coalesce. Paul

10. André Breton, "Manifesto of Surrealism" (1924), in *Manifestoes of Surrealism*, trans. Richard Seaver and Helen R. Lane (Ann Arbor, Mich., 1969), pp. 32–47.

Gauguin, who wished to move from a highly differentiated civilized state to a unified primitive one, sought to reduce his medium, his technical language, to elementary forms immediately comprehensible so that the truth of his art would seem not to depend on a particularized metaphor but would be recognized universally. In order to explain his work to August Strindberg, he compared his style to a primitive Oceanic tongue in which the elements common to all languages are apparent.[11] Similarly, when Mondrian related his opposing vertical and horizontal lines to primordial male and female principles, the connection was not intended to depend on the interpretation of a symbolic representation, for the association of these fundamental directional and genetic forces would be universal and immediate both in art and in life. The many arguments given in support of arts of simplified abstraction—such as Gauguin's, Mondrian's, or Kandinsky's—reflect the general concern for the immediacy of the link between the emotions or sensations of life and the representations of art. Roger Fry, for example, spoke of the "emotional elements of design"—line, color, space, and so forth—and of their capacity to induce specific emotional states in any viewer; particularlized naturalistic representation should not be allowed to interfere with this fundamental communication of emotion.[12]

The possibility of the identity of art and life is a myth which guides the modern artist. We find the union of art and life expressed as an ideal in the criticism and poetry of Baudelaire and the theories of the symbolists and surrealists. The desired identity of art and life has given direction to the careers of artists as diverse as Marcel Duchamp, Jackson Pollock, Joseph Beuys, and Chris Burden, who all seem to have acted out their art. Pollock, for example, was praised for taking risks in his art because he was, as Clement Greenberg wrote, "not afraid to look ugly." Pollock's personal life, too, was reckless and precarious; with his heavy drinking and bursts of violence, he often appeared an ugly outcast to those around him.[13] With Pollock and many others an individualistic, iconoclastic art seems to be linked to wildness and antisocial behavior.

In order to draw art and life together artists have often assumed the personal manner of those deemed uncivilized, unsophisticated, and "naturally" creative, children and primitives, for whom, supposedly, the distinction between art and life, dream and reality, does not exist. In his study of the depiction of nature in early Greek art, Emanuel Loewy argued in 1900 that the child and the primitive establish an identity between two fundamental groups of images: those derived from sensory contact with the external environment and those generated from within

11. Paul Gauguin, letter of 5 February 1895, published in *L'Ermitage* 15 (January 1904): 79–80.

12. Roger Fry, "An Essay in Aesthetics" (1909), *Vision and Design* (New York, 1956), pp. 33–38.

13. Clement Greenberg, "Art," *Nation*, 7 April 1945, p. 397.

as dreams or fantasies, metaphoric representations of reality.[14] The world of art or metaphoric representation is for them indistinguishable from reality; an externalized public world is experienced with the immediacy of private mental life. The world of art, although shared with others, is known not through a common metaphor but directly, as if in the possession of the individual. Picasso, among others, reflected this association of an ideal union of art and life in the person of the child or primitive through his interest in the same early Greek and non-Western arts which fascinated Loewy. He allowed himself to be pictured before his public not as a sophisticated master of refined technique but half-naked, like a child playing with his sculptures as if they were toys; and he delighted in making and wearing masks, in passing between art and life repeatedly.

We know that the identity of art and life is an ideal, not a reality. Neither an art possessing the immediacy of life's experience nor a life having the fixed formal structure of art would seem to belong to the world as we know it. Art seems to depend upon its distinction from life, and vice versa, just as objects and subjects depend upon each other. If our lives had the form of works of art, experience of the most intimate sort would seem to be shared by all members of the culture, all whose lives took on the same externalized artistic style. Individual identity would be lost unless the idiosyncrasy of lived experience were re-incorporated into the work of art, but such idiosyncrasy would seem a flaw when applying a standard of critical judgment. A life perfected in art could not be experienced, could not be lived, for it would exist in a state of absolute knowledge: all would be comprehensible form; nothing would be in process; nothing could change.

The architect Adolph Loos once told the story of a "poor rich man" who had everything in his life but art, so he hired a famous architect to provide him with the ultimate artistic environment; every aspect of the world he experienced was to be designed, to be given fixed form. The rich man, of course, became a prisoner of this world within which nothing could be altered. As Loos wrote, "He was excluded for the future from living and striving, becoming and wishing. He felt: Now I have to learn to live within my own corpse. Yes. I am finished. *I am complete!*"[15] For Loos, a life preserved in an art of an imposed order is a living death.

I do not wish to put art in such a negative light, for only in its extreme perfection does it become dangerous to life. Baudelaire, who spoke provocatively of life and death, wished as a critic to consider art

14. Emanuel Loewy, *The Rendering of Nature in Early Greek Art*, trans. John Fothergill (London, 1907), p. 18.

15. Adolph Loos, "The Story of a Poor Rich Man" (1900), rpt. in Ludwig Munz and Gustav Kunstler, *Adolph Loos, Pioneer of Modern Architecture* (London, 1966), pp. 223–25.

vital rather than dead, and he concerned himself with the distinction between a perfected academic art, the kind Loos' rich man had encountered, and a flawed but beautiful art. For Baudelaire beauty was found in the idiosyncratic, the bizarre, that which could not be measured against any established standard, that which resisted translation into the terms of the known. Any foreign object of artistic expression established its own identity and reinforced that of the critic through its stubborn opposition to his appreciation, evaluation, and assimilation.

An artist, according to Baudelaire, might actively seek out the critical disorientation resulting from an encounter with the new, the foreign, or the bizarre. In such a situation, as art and life seem to merge, life does not become ordered and predictable like art but art becomes novel and unpredictable like life. The vital spontaneity of life is in this case not threatened by the formulizations of art (as Loos' rich man's life was indeed threatened), but now art itself comes under attack and stands to be rendered incoherent through its immediate response to life's vagaries. Baudelaire's rational system for judging art never, as he stated, "stopped chasing after multiform and multi-colored Beauty as it moved in the infinite spirals of life."[16] Although Baudelaire moderated his position by stating that the painter of modern life must capture elements of both classical eternal beauty and the fleeting beauty of the bizarre, his suggestion that this may be facilitated through the willful application of a childlike naiveté, a kind of drunken disorientation, is a dangerous one. Much of the art to which the Baudelairean position has given rise has remained incomprehensible to many members of its general audience. Perhaps the science and rationality of the adult, which Baudelaire argued must accompany the immediacy and openness of the child, failed to provide an adequate technical metaphor, failed to induce the mass of the audience to relate the new work of art convincingly to their established world of beliefs and values. Tolstoy recognized the problem in his essay "What is Art?" where he included Baudelaire's poems among those failing as art because they appealed only to an educated elite; they lacked universal accessibility.

Indeed an art accessible to all, an art of perfect communicative powers, has often been envisaged as a goal toward which modern artists must strive. Such art has been associated with the primitive roots of a society—its myths, folk songs, dances, costumes, and other ritualistic imagery. Tolstoy attributed the increasingly elite and alien character of modern art to its divorce from fundamental Christian values; art, like religious ceremony, must appeal to faith and a spirit of brotherhood. The world of art that captures the universal communicative power of religious faith has the capacity to give the individual events of life a

---

16. Charles Baudelaire, "The Exposition Universelle, 1855," *Art in Paris: 1845–1862*, ed. Jonathan Mayne (London, 1965), p. 123.

socially acceptable meaning, no matter how challenging to comprehension those events may be.

This point can be illustrated by a parable taken from Kafka:

> Leopards break into the temple and drink up the sacrificial wine; this is repeated over and over again; eventually it becomes predictable, and is incorporated into the ceremony.[17]

Here an immediate, unpredictable element in the life of the society, the leopards, is given purpose and meaning; their act of incomprehensible disruption is "incorporated into the ceremony," and the leopards themselves become part of the society. Once the ceremony includes the leopards, it is not even necessary that they actually behave predictably; they might even disappear. They will, nevertheless, exist as a meaningful part of the society's world.

A ceremony is a work of art conveying meaning, yet it need not be understood analytically; its sense is comprehended directly and universally. A ceremony is not reality but a representation of it, apparently dependent on a metaphor so natural that it escapes attention and investigation. The truth of ceremony or ritual, like the truth of a perfected art, is universally accessible and acceptable; it forms the foundation of a culture. A challenge to the metaphor of the ceremony or to the universally valid work of art challenges the stability of the entire society. Yet the society may change and grow while maintaining its standard metaphors, for the metaphor of the ceremony recognizes the leopards' identity. This foreign element is given meaning and assimilated but is not completely lost within the culture. The entire society seems to grow and gain new knowledge as a result.

While the society may grow, however, it seems to extend itself only in one direction. It gains more knowledge, but of a familiar type. Religious doctrine, a body of ritual, or a tradition of works of fine art may appear academic and confining. Like timeless rituals which provide standards for behavior in unusual circumstances—such as marriage ceremonies, funerals, or religious initiations—great works of art establish standards of excellence and define certain metaphoric techniques, or means of expression, as acceptable approaches to truth. Unless the artistic metaphors themselves change, further knowledge does not lead to absolute truth but becomes a mere material accretion to be added to an already bulging storehouse. The danger inherent in establishing rational academic formulizations for artistic procedure and critical evaluation, as Baudelaire knew, is artistic impotence, the incapacity to extend art further into life, to recognize new experience or allow for the possibility of yet other wild beasts breaking into the temple.

17. Franz Kafka, "Leopards in the Temple," *Parables and Paradoxes* (New York, 1961), p. 93. I have slightly altered the translation by Ernst Kaiser and Eithne Wilkins.

The threat posed to liberated artistic expression by established convention has preoccupied many modern artists. They have responded by seeking ways of linking their art to the immediacy of life's experience. In the painting and sculpture of the nineteenth century, the subjects represented often came from the artist's immediate environment; he was praised for depicting "what he saw." In addition, he left references to his technical procedure, signs of the movement of his hand, so that the finished work might appear as a sketch, a tentative and continuing expressive gesture. In the twentieth century, Marcel Duchamp called still more attention to the immediate circumstances in which art is created by producing works whose meaning seems to depend upon the context for viewing them; his snow shovel, when titled and placed in a gallery, is seen as a work of art. Similarly, surrealists have allowed art to "happen" as life happens; they "find" art rather than make it as they discover the so-called found object of art, an unimagined form of compelling interest, often something very ordinary seen in unusual surroundings. Furthermore, many recent works of art seem to change and grow like forms of life; sculptors have produced so-called environmental works which may employ impermanent media such as grass, water, or decaying organic matter. In addition, they have hung themselves in galleries, acted out special roles in the living performance of art, and sometimes even rented themselves out to carry on conversations at parties. The professional title of "artist" has itself become suspect since it implies that artistic activity is specialized and therefore subject to specific restrictions. Joseph Beuys has said that "every man is an artist." With a similar disdain for professional specialization, Allan Kaprow has noted that escape from artistic convention is now advocated in academic circles and has itself become a cliché of modern art; he argues not for the iconoclastic "anti-artist" but for the "un-artist," a person content to live ignoring all professional art, even refusing to regard it as a foil against which to react.[18]

In our extreme moments of fear of the academic, when we suspect that our reason may hide from us a desired new truth, we often seek from the work of art a nonrational sense of conviction. Like the surrealists with their dream images and found objects, we expect the true experience of art to be overwhelming and as convincingly real as that of our life, yet apart from us, revealing a world beyond that which we know. But if the ultimate work of art would transport us to a new world, one with no rational link to the old, there could be no return; the old individual identity would be lost and a kind of "death" would occur. Art possessing the ultimate immediacy of life and its convincing reality can have no meaning, for it cannot be questioned.

18. Allan Kaprow, "The Education of the Un-Artist," *Art News* (February 1971): 28–31, 66–68; (May 1972): 34–39, 62–63.

Neither a life perfected as art nor an art perfected as life seems possible for us; both lead to death. Life as art allows neither change nor growth; art as life conveys no meaning. Our world lies between the two extremes. In effect we shift back and forth along the metaphoric bridge; our life is modeled upon our art, and our art is modeled upon our life. In this way we maintain ourselves as individuals in a state of doubt; we seek knowledge by means of experience, we discover new truths. Our present interest in metaphor seems appropriate to our intermediary position; we see ourselves in transit between life and art, or life and death.

The Development of Metaphoric Competence: Implications for Humanistic Disciplines

Howard Gardner and Ellen Winner

1. The Relationship between Psychological and Humanistic Studies of Metaphor

To present psychological research to a distinguished group of philosophers, linguists, and literary critics is to place oneself at risk, to court misunderstanding if not total noncommunication. For, despite their superficially common concerns, there remains widespread feeling today that psychologists and humanistically oriented scholars are embarked on fundamentally different ventures. The conceptual distinctions and theoretical concerns of humanists are perceived by many psychologists as endless "common room talk" which can never decisively settle anything; while these individuals are speculating, psychologists want to find out "the facts." Conversely, the tests, experiments, and laboratory apparatus of psychologists are perceived by many humanists as possibly ill-conceived yet harmless paraphernalia. Occasionally, interesting phenomena will surface (although most of these discoveries could have been made simply by using common sense); rarely, however, will demonstrations by a psychologist interestingly constrain the vexing issues with which philosophers, linguists, and literary critics are grappling.

Of course, we are caricaturing here, and our remarks would not

The research in this paper was supported by the National Science Foundation (BNS 77-13699), the National Institute of Neurological Disease, Communication Disorders and Stroke (NS 11408), the National Institute of Education (G78-00319), and the Spencer Foundation. We wish to thank Robin Bechhofer, Margaret McCarthy, and Wendy Wapner for help in the design and implementation of these studies.

apply to the reasonable individuals gathered at this conference. And yet, one does not have to search far for intimations of these uncompromising attitudes. For instance, in a recent conference on metaphor, the philosopher Jonathan Cohen had this to say on the invention and comprehension of metaphors: "It is reasonable to suppose that, until the linguistic problem has a definite solution, the psychological one cannot be adequately articulated."[1] Lifting the gauntlet for the linguists, Roman Jakobson has described a straightforward relationship between the disciplines of linguistics and psychology.[2] Analogizing the situation to the study of traffic patterns, he indicates that the linguist must discern the rules of the traffic code (its language); only then can psychologists enter the fray, their task being principally to specify the conditions under which these rules are honored by the average "subject." And, representing literary critics, René Wellek remarked at an interdisciplinary conference on style some years ago:

> From the point of view of the literary critic, the psychological papers were of least immediate interest. To my mind, they established nothing that could not be predicted from common observation . . . I recognize of course that psychologists consider their task as that of quantification, that they believe nothing to be objectively ascertained and verified before it has been reduced to some quantitative ratio. I, as every humanist must, however, argue that this is a false epistemology based on the superstition of behaviorism. It denies the evidence of introspection and empathy, the two main sources of human and humane knowledge.[3]

Nor have psychologists hesitated to register their impatience with humanistic endeavors. Jean Piaget has devoted an entire book to the

1. Jonathan Cohen, "The Semantics of Metaphor" (paper presented at the Conference on Metaphor and Thought, University of Illinois, Urbana, Ill., September 1977), p. 23.
2. Roman Jakobson, Lectures on Language and Poetics (Cambridge, Mass., 1969).
3. René Wellek, "Closing Statement from the Viewpoint of Literary Criticism," in *Style in Language*, ed. Thomas A. Sebeok (Cambridge, Mass., 1960), p. 409.

Howard Gardner, a developmental psychologist, is codirector of Harvard Project Zero and a clinical investigator at the Boston Veterans Administration Hospital. His books include *The Quest for Mind, The Arts and Human Development,* and *Developmental Psychology: An Introduction.* **Ellen Winner** teaches in the psychology department of Boston College and is a research associate at Harvard Project Zero. A developmental psychologist, she has conducted research on the development and breakdown of metaphoric language capacities and on the emergence of metaphoric capacities in very young children.

"illusions" of philosophers,[4] those hermitic scholars who rely entirely on personal introspection and who never have to compete in the marketplace of hypothesis stating, verification, and disproof. From his vantage point, the classic issues of philosophy have remained in limbo until psychologists (and particularly genetic epistemologists) have fashioned ways to test the rival points of view. An analogous kind of impatience has recently been voiced by several psycholinguists who find current discussions in the field of linguistics increasingly remote from verifiability. And, while literary critics have rarely been singled out for attack (or praise) by contemporary psychologists, the very fact that their writings are so widely ignored signals the adjudged relevance to empirically oriented psychologists of this brand of humanistic scholarship.

Our own view is that these various scholars are embarked on separate but related inquiries. Initially stimulated by many of the same broad concerns, these researchers proceed, on the basis of training and orientation, to tackle such issues in quite different ways. Sometimes, in fact, the concerns of one group have little interest for those in a rival discipline. At other times, however, these concerns tend to converge, and the practice of one researcher can be significantly enhanced by contact with workers in the neighboring disciplines. Certainly this conference has been conceived in the hope that this point of view has some validity.

In lieu of hand-waving, let us begin our treatment of psychological research on metaphor by considering some common interests shared by psychologists, on the one hand, and by philosophically oriented humanists, on the other. At least four areas have proved sufficiently central to both groups to merit extensive discussion in the respective literatures. A first issue centers on the specificity of the processes involved in metaphor: Is metaphoric skill a capacity especially intertwined with linguistic skills, or is it a much broader human capacity, one identified with general perceptual and conceptual processes? A related question has arisen within the area of language: Is metaphor a special kind of trope, with its own rules, properties, and applications, or should it be closely allied (or even collapsed) with such other tropes as similies, analogies, or hyperbole? The third issue moves yet further within the circle of metaphor to treat the question of whether all metaphors are of a piece, or whether various types of metaphor (cross-sensory, perceptual, psychological-physical, predicative, etc.) each require their own analysis. And a final issue of concern to both groups is the question of whether metaphoric usage is better illuminated by probing the structure of language (for instance, the semantic features of the topic and vehicle) or by considering its pragmatic aspects—the various speech acts employed within a community.[5] One could go on to state other issues, but this

4. Jean Piaget, *Insights and Illusions of Philosophy* (New York, 1971).
5. Cf. Cohen, "The Semantics of Metaphor" and John Searle, "Presentation on Metaphor and Pragmatics" (Conference on Metaphor and Thought).

tetrad should suffice to indicate the common body of concerns addressed by experimental and humanistic researchers.

It goes without saying, of course, that philosophers and psychologists address these issues in quite different ways, with analysis dominating the approach of the philosopher, experimentation paving the way for the psychologist. And, partially for this reason, neither discipline can supplant the other. Psychologists will make additional discoveries germane to philosophical debates and will continue to sort out the regular, the replicable, and the reliable from the subjective and solipsistic. By the same token, philosophers will continue to sharpen conceptual distinctions and offer alternative interpretations for psychological work: they can be relied upon not only to poke holes and offer counterexamples but also to suggest fertile hypotheses.

Even within the field of psychology, rather separate investigative approaches can be taken and different dividends secured.[6] One distinction of importance for the present effort is that obtaining between experimental-cognitive psychologists, who work primarily with adults (read "college sophomores"), and developmental psychologists, whose subjects are children of various ages. Reflecting their different populations, these psychologists characteristically focus on different issues. Because adult subjects can almost always understand, paraphrase, and produce metaphors, the interest of experimental-cognitive psychologists has centered upon the covert processes utilized in such activity. Students of metaphoric competence, like Samuel Glucksberg, George Miller, Andrew Ortony, and Robert Verbrugge, seek to build models of the processes involved in metaphoric behaviors: they attempt to identify the steps taken, the order in which they are taken, the possibility of alternative routes, all in an effort to build an information-flow model of what is going on in the brain (or at least the mind) of a metaphorizing subject.[7]

Developmental psychologists, on the other hand, confront a population whose metaphoric competence is at least open to debate and whose striking lack of competence can frequently be demonstrated. Accordingly, developmentalists seek to trace the course of acquisition of various metaphoric abilities: they attempt to identify the features which aid in

6. For some recent reviews of these alternative approaches within the area of metaphor, see Richard Billow, "Metaphor: A Review of the Psychological Literature," *Psychological Bulletin* 84, no. 1 (1977): 81–92; Robert Hoffman and Richard Honeck, "Figurative Language: Recent Psycholinguistic Theory and Research" (unpublished paper, Westfield State College, Westfield, Mass., 1978); and Andrew Ortony, Ralph Reynolds, and Judith Arter, "Metaphor: Theoretical and Empirical Research," *Psychological Bulletin*, forthcoming.

7. Samuel Glucksberg, David Hartman, and Ronald Stack, "Metaphor Comprehension Is an Automatic and Parallel Process" (paper presented to the Psychonomic Science Society, Washington, D.C., November 1977); George A. Miller, "Closing Address" (Conference on Metaphor and Thought); Ortony et al., "Metaphor"; and Robert Verbrugge, "The Comprehension of Analogy" (Ph.D. diss., University of Minnesota, 1974).

metaphoric behaviors, those which thwart or prevent their appearance, the capacities which correlate with metaphoric competence, and at times the conditions under which various metaphoric abilities may break down. Both of these bodies of information—the findings of "adult psychologists" and the results of "child psychologists"—can contribute to any consideration of metaphor. But for the remainder of this paper we will concentrate on the developmental enterprise; we will cite some recent findings from our own laboratory on the development and breakdown of metaphoric competence and offer some concluding comments about the possible relevance of this work for the broader issues under review at this conference.

2. A Developmental Approach to Metaphoric Competence

The developmental approach in psychology, rooted in the mid-nineteenth-century writings of Charles Darwin, Herbert Spencer, and other students of evolution, entails the assumption that any behavior can exist in more or less "developed," "mature," or "perfect forms."[8] Generally speaking, the most developed form is found in normal (or gifted) adults; and so a developmental inquiry characteristically begins with a study of the "end state" of competence in the chosen realm (of course, the way one characterizes the end state reflects one's theory and thus ought not be seen as separable from the philosophic enterprise). Once the defining features of this competence have been isolated, the next steps are to outline various immature forms of skill, to order them in some way, and to consider the means by which the organism may "move" from a less to a more developed form. Theoretically, this entire enterprise can be carried out at one's own desk; and, indeed, early developmental analyses were little more than mental exercises by evolutionarily minded scholars. But, at least since the advent of Piaget's work, developmental studies have become doggedly empiricist. The "stages" of development, their order of appearance, their conditions of emergence are now discovered in the real world, most often through observations and experiments with children. In some quarters, moreover, developmental psychology has been viewed more broadly as considering not only the steps of acquisition but also the way in which competences may break down under various pathological states. Indeed, to the committed developmentalist, the multifarious ways in which developmental stages may be realized "in the real world" are all equally germane to any treatment of development in a given domain of behavior and knowledge. And, correlatively, the link between age and devel-

---

8. See Bernard Kaplan, "Meditations on Genesis," *Human Development* 10 (1967): 65–87; and Heinz Werner, *Comparative Psychology of Mental Development* (New York, 1948).

opmental stage is only a coincidence: one can discover a range of stages at the same age, as well as an array of individuals from different cultures and age cohorts, all at the same stage of competence.

Because the basic techniques and rationale for developmental studies are now widely familiar,[9] it will not be necessary to review the assumptions and methodology here. But in view of our opening intimation of tensions between the experimental and humanistic camps, it is worth noting recent claims about the centrality of developmental studies. Researchers working with infants have provided data, said to bear decisively on the age-old debates about the origins of knowledge, which challenge the traditional empiricist accounts. Bornstein, Kessen, and Weiskopf, and Bower, on the one hand, have documented that newborn infants possess certain perceptual capacities of a high order; in contrast, Fraiberg, modulating the competing nativist case, has documented the importance of specific sensory systems in determining how blind children come to organize their world.[10] Studies with somewhat older children have provided persuasive evidence that human conceptualization is organized around more and less prototypical category members rather than by virtue of lists of defining features.[11] And investigations with brain-damaged patients have challenged a number of entrenched philosophical distinctions; these studies suggest, for example, that different cerebral processes are involved in the decoding of such seemingly similar symbols as letters and numbers, that consciousness may not be a unitary phenomenon, and that various forms of thought and praxis can function at a high level even in the absence of linguistic capability.[12] While some of these demonstrations and interpretations remain controversial, the relevance of these findings to certain long-standing philosophical dilemmas is becoming increasingly well established.[13]

An inquiry undertaken by developmental psychologists in the realm of metaphor can be expected to follow the pattern sketched above. That is, researchers should begin by defining a set of competences—say, the

9. See Howard Gardner, *Developmental Psychology* (Boston, 1978); Paul Mussen, *Handbook of Research Methods in Child Development* (New York, 1960); *Carmichael's Manual of Child Psychology*, ed. Mussen (New York, 1970); and Werner, *Comparative Psychology*.

10. Marc Bornstein, William Kessen, and Sally Weiskopf, "The Categories of Hue in Infancy," *Science* 191 (1976): 201–2; T. G. R. Bower, *Development in Infancy* (San Francisco, 1974); Selma Fraiberg, *Insights from the Blind* (New York, 1977).

11. Eleanor Rosch et al., "Basic Objects in Natural Categories," *Cognitive Psychology* 8 (1976): 382–439.

12. See Gardner, *The Shattered Mind* (New York, 1975); Michael S. Gazzaniga, *The Bisected Brain* (New York, 1970); and Aleksandr R. Luria, *Higher Cortical Functions in Man* (New York, 1966).

13. See Daniel Dennett, "Current Issues in the Philosophy of Mind" (unpublished paper, Tufts University, Medford, Mass., 1976); and Jerry A. Fodor, *The Language of Thought* (New York, 1975).

capacity to paraphrase a metaphor, to explain the rationale for the metaphor's effectiveness, to produce a metaphor appropriate to a given context, to evaluate the appropriateness of several competing metaphoric expressions. Once these competences are defined, and their existence demonstrated in a relevant population, the search for their developmental course can proceed. This procedure generally entails the devising of simple tasks whose requirements young children can grasp, the devising of a scoring system, and the securing of normative performances from subjects at a range of ages and putative developmental stages. Often the "objective" facets of such a task or test battery will be supplemented by open-ended clinical interviews in which further "qualitative" evidence is sought on the way in which the realm is construed (or misconstrued) by the subject.[14] Related tasks may be administered to various populations in an effort to determine how the skill breaks down under conditions of pathology. Finally, utilizing the accumulated evidence from a variety of studies gauging a variety of competences, researchers will postulate a model of metaphoric development. Then, armed with a description of some power and generality, they can go on to focus on the more process-oriented issues of concern to researchers who work with "competent" adult metaphorizers.

Interest among developmental psychologists has, in the past, centered largely on the development of scientific reasoning capacities and, within the study of language, on the more conventional aspects of syntax and semantics. Metaphor has been perceived as a frill or ornament, one marginal to a treatment of the human mind.[15] For these reasons, there is but a small body of research on metaphoric capacities in children.[16] Some of this research will be touched upon in the following pages, but for the most part we will focus on three separate bodies of data which we and our colleagues have accumulated over the past few years. This review should, on the one hand, provide a summary picture of what has thus far been established about the development of metaphoric competences in children; at the same time, we hope to suggest some ways in which these findings—and the numerous questions they raise—can contribute to discussions among scholars who have never "run a subject," performed an analysis of variance, or normalized a task with relevant control groups.

14. Piaget, *The Child's Conception of the World* (London, 1929).

15. See Ted Cohen, "Metaphor and the Cultivation of Intimacy," pp. 1–10 in this volume.

16. See Billow, "Metaphor"; Gardner, "Children's Literary Development," in *Children's Humor*, ed. Tony Chapman and Paul McGhee (London, 1978); Gardner, Ellen Winner, Robin Bechhofer, and Dennie Wolf, "The Development of Figurative Language," in *Children's Language,* ed. Keith Nelson (New York, 1978); and Ortony et al., "Metaphor."

3. Three Studies of Metaphoric Competence

A. The Development of Metaphoric Comprehension

One important facet of metaphoric competence is the ability to paraphrase a figure of speech of the type encountered in everyday conversation or in writing. To secure information on how children acquire this ability, we presented subjects ranging in age from six to twelve with a number of predicative metaphors in sentence form and asked for their meaning.[17] Subjects were also given a series of paraphrases which we ourselves had devised and asked to select the one which they felt offered the most cogent interpretation of the figurative sentence. Thus, given the sentence "After many years of working at the jail, the prison guard had become a hard rock that could not be moved," one group of subjects had to offer their own interpretation, while a second group had to select from multiple choices the "best" paraphrase.

Both of these measures yielded a similar, converging portrait of the development of capacities crucial for metaphoric comprehension. The youngest subjects, aged six or seven, sometimes embraced a totally literal version of the statement. Accepting it at face value, they magically transformed the world to fit the sentence, invoking, for example, a king who turned the guard into a rock. An even more common practice among the youngest subjects was to alter the connection between the topic and the vehicle. Changing the relation of identity to one of contiguity, the children suggested the prison guard worked in a prison with hard rock walls or that he happened to like rocks.

At a somewhat older age, around eight or so, children came to realize that the prison guard was in some sense *like* a rock. Yet, still unable to discern a connection between domains as remote from one another as physical objects and psychological states, they tended to treat both terms as belonging to the physical domain. Thus they would speak of a prison guard with muscles as hard as a rock.

Finally, by about the age of ten, subjects came to realize that some aspect of the guard's personality or character was being described: they were able to make the bridge from the physical to the psychological realm. Still, they would often select a personality trait which was somewhat at odds with what was intended; for instance, they would treat the guard as bad, or fussy, or furious. Only at a somewhat later age did children consistently hit upon the appropriate psychological trait that constituted the ground of the metaphor.

Once such a developmental sequence has been proposed, an essential first step is replication. We have confirmed our findings with other

17. Winner, Anne Rosentiel, and Gardner, "The Development of Metaphoric Understanding," *Developmental Psychology* 12 (1976): 289–97.

kinds of metaphors (for example, cross-sensory metaphors—"The smell of her perfume was bright sunshine") and with a variety of school populations (drawn from different social classes and communities). A next step is to ensure that the findings are not an artifact of testing conditions. This we have done by asking subjects to match a metaphor to its appropriate illustration in a set of pictures. The demonstration that young subjects continue to favor "literal" depictions indicates that it is not simply a metalinguistic obstacle which produces the apparent incapacity to understand metaphors.

Having established that children do, indeed, interpret metaphors in a concrete manner until middle childhood, we have now turned our attention to the issue of what it is that prevents an appropriate interpretation or, to put it more positively, which factors may facilitate comprehension. This research, although still very much in progress, bears on some of the issues raised above, and thus it is worth mentioning briefly our preliminary results.

Our analysis suggests that two forms of information might aid in the comprehension and paraphrase of metaphor. On the one hand, it is possible that children become capable of understanding a metaphor once they have mastered those features of word meaning which are relevant to the linking of the topic with the vehicle. Thus a child may understand the statement "A pond is a mirror" once he appreciates the property of reflection common to both; or he may understand "The pebble was wearing a green coat" once he understands that coat can refer to any kind of covering.

It is also possible, however, that such lexical knowledge is neither necessary nor sufficient for accurate paraphrase. As Max Black has suggested, "dictionary definitions" may be unnecessary for the comprehension of metaphor.[18] Indeed, individuals may ferret out the meanings of metaphor not primarily by drawing upon lexical knowledge but rather by virtue of their sensitivity to the surrounding linguistic, visual, or situational context. On this latter account, our prison guard would be more likely to be seen as stubborn if he was so described in the presence of a picture of a stern looking guard or in the course of a story about life in the prison. Of course, in the latter case, one must ensure that the metaphors are not being interpreted simply by attending to the context, in which case the metaphor is actually ignored. And so, our test of this hypothesis involves presentation of the same picture, or the same linguistic context, with two opposing sentences: the prison guard as a "hard rock" and the prison guard as a "bendable blade of grass." In such cases only attention to the actual wording of the metaphor can result in a successful response.

While it is premature to report a decisive result with respect to these

18. Max Black, *Models and Metaphors* (Ithaca, N.Y., 1962).

competing explanations, it seems fair at this point to say that our various efforts have failed to indicate that lexical knowledge (in the sense of "core meanings" or knowledge of features) figures prominently in the paraphrase of metaphor;[19] in contrast, our attempts to document the power of context have been largely successful. We also are accumulating suggestive evidence that the central relations underlying predicative metaphors are more readily grasped when these relations are presented in simile, riddle, or analogy forms. These findings suggest that children are much more likely to decode metaphors successfully if they encounter them in some kind of a situational context than if they have to draw, in isolation, upon their knowledge of the meanings of the words which constitute the trope.

B. *The Development of Metaphoric Production*

Most authorities consider the development of the capacity to understand metaphors to be a lengthy process, one which lags well behind the comprehension of "literal language," and one which calls upon a variety of skills.[20] Considerably more dispute surrounds developmental descriptions of the capacity to invent metaphors. Some individuals, particularly those who emphasize the importance of overriding tension in the production of metaphor, see this ability as a late developing one, as a capacity which awaits considerable linguistic and metalinguistic knowledge.[21] Other equally vocal analysts, however, deem metaphor as part of the birthright of the very young. These scholars, who tend to stress the daringness, spontaneity, and invention involved in the creation of tropes, see the years of early childhood as a time of poetic genius.[22] Indeed, in their admiring eyes, the process of metaphoric development is often marred by dissolution, with the older child straining to recapture what was effortlessly available to the innocent young.

In an effort to adjudicate among these opposing stances, we devised a simple simile-production test.[23] Children were given a short vignette and asked to produce an ending which "sounded right" and which "fit

19. Winner and Gardner, "What Does It Take to Understand a Metaphor?" (paper presented to the Society for Research in Child Development, New Orleans, La., March 1977).

20. See Solomon E. Asch and Harriet Nerlove, "The Development of Double-Function Terms in Children: An Exploratory Investigation," in *Perspectives in Psychological Theory: Essays in Honor of Heinz Werner*, ed. Kaplan and Heinz Werner (New York, 1960); David Elkind, "Piagetian and Psychometric Conceptions of Intelligence," *Harvard Educational Review* 39 (1969): 319–37; and Bärbel Inhelder and Piaget, *The Growth of Logical Thinking from Childhood to Adolescence* (New York, 1958). For a contrasting view see Ortony et al., "Metaphor."

21. See Elkind, "Piagetian and Psychometric Conceptions of Intelligence."

22. Kornei Chukovsky, *From Two to Five* (Berkeley, 1968).

23. Gardner et al., "Children's Metaphoric Productions and Preferences," *Journal of Child Language* 2 (1975): 125–41.

the story." For instance, one of the sixteen stories had the following form:

> Things don't have to be huge in size to look that way. Look at that boy standing over there. He looks as gigantic as . . .

The endings contrived by children were scored according to a set of criteria as being either literal (e.g., "as gigantic as the most gigantic person in the whole world"); trite or conventional (e.g., "as gigantic as a skyscraper in the center of town"); appropriately metaphoric (involving a radical shift across domains which nonetheless made sense in the context; e.g., "as gigantic as a double-decker ice cream cone in a baby's hand"); or metaphorically inappropriate (a shift in domains judged inappropriate in the context; e.g., "as gigantic as a clock from a department store").

Not surprisingly, there was a paucity of appropriate metaphoric productions at every age: conventional and literal responses predominated. Intriguing support, however, was gained for the "child-as-poet" position. The highest number of appropriate metaphors was secured from the preschool children, who even exceeded college students; moreover, these three- and four-year-olds fashioned significantly more appropriate metaphors than did children aged seven or eleven. These latter children, mired in what we have come to term the "literal" stage, actively reject invitations to metaphorize and cling instead to the most literal modes of language use. To be sure, there was another, less happy facet to the performance of the preschoolers. In addition to producing a greater number of appropriate metaphors, they also produced many more inappropriate metaphors. Indeed, their performance reflected an insensitivity to (or a willingness to disregard or cut across) conventional boundaries of experience and language. They willingly made outrageous comparisons (e.g., "quiet as a nose," "sad as a shirt"), only some of which made sense to others (e.g., "quiet as a magic marker," "sad as a pimple"). They lacked the "blue-pencilling" and "decentering" capacity to reject those metaphors which, while appealing to them, would not make sense to other individuals.

The performance of the young children raises sharply the question of what ought to count as a metaphor. If one takes a purely inscriptional approach, one would have to conclude that even (or especially) preschoolers are capable of metaphoric production. On the other hand, once one invokes subtler psychological distinctions—are children *conscious* of the effect, are they *aware* of the tension, do they seek to *override* this tension, are they simply ignorant of the conventional extensions of the words—then the relation of such "early metaphor" to the work of the adult poet becomes much more problematic—yet also, perhaps, more intriguing.

We are currently engaged in an effort to study this early form of metaphor. Our procedure involves administering a large number of "renaming" tasks to children. Subjects are presented with diverse stimuli (e.g., familiar and unfamiliar objects, line drawings, and color swatches) and engaged in a game where their puppets have either to make up "pretend names," to select the best pretend name from multiple choices, or to correct another puppet (held by the experimenter) when that second puppet produces "pretend names" that are "silly" rather than "good." By varying the child's interaction with the object (whether the object may be actively manipulated) and the acceptability (as plausible metaphors) of pretend names devised by the experimenter-puppet, we are gaining considerable detailed information about the metaphor-making capacities of young children and the grounds on which they make their metaphors. And, by studying their actions and reactions both in these games and in spontaneous conversation (their laughter, teasing, signalling, playfulness, etc.), we are gaining textured information about the extent to which children appear cognizant of their nonconventional word use. After considerable piloting, we are gaining some confidence that we can distinguish intentional wordplay from simple over-generalization, misperception of objects, or inadequate linguistic resources.

Once again, the final results are not yet in, and so any generalizations we share with you must be seen as tentative. It seems reasonable to say at this point that "early metaphor" follows a predictable course. Youngest subjects, aged two and one-half to three, are unable to play this game and seem tied either to literal naming or to over-generalization. By the age of about three and one-half, children can readily enter into the puppetry; their renamings are more successful from a metaphoric point of view when they have the opportunity to handle the objects, with renamings customarily arising after the action has taken place. Four- and five-year-olds also prefer to name after handling but prove more successful at naming in the "hands-off" conditions; like the younger subjects, their renamings focus on potential actions of the stimuli and on the most salient perceptual features (which happen to be shape and size rather than color). In virtually no cases do renamings seem to have any psychological (expressive or characterological) impact or flavor. While we are being careful not to prejudge the issue of amount of awareness, intention, or tension on the part of the children, we feel comfortable in saying that the children seem quite aware that they are overriding usual names (they often tell us that they are); they differ from the somewhat older children, those in the literal stage, in that they appear not to be bothered by such transgression of customary boundaries. They find the wordplay enjoyable rather than tension-arousing.

Quite possibly, the most intriguing phenomenon uncovered so far in this study of early metaphor is the capacity of at least some young children to perform this game at an astonishingly high level. Not only do such youngsters frequently contrive clever names for the very objects which have stumped our adult pilot subjects; more dramatically, some of them can nearly effortlessly come up with a whole series of appropriate and appealing metaphoric renamings. Thus, in the course of a few minutes, one subject looked inside a paper towel roller and called it a tunnel; picked up a ring-shaped block and termed it a donut; tore up some paper and christened the pieces dollars; put a bucket on his head and labelled it a hat; held a strip of paper with a scissors and described it as a flag; pretended to play piano on the arm of his mother and announced that she was a piano; termed a piece of a jigsaw puzzle a boot and another one a gun; spoke into the plug of an extension cord and declared it a microphone; unrolled a roll of film and proclaimed it a ribbon; tied this film around a microphone and said it was a bib for the microphone; and termed a crayon lying by itself "a lonely crayon." Another subject in our studies in short order renamed a flashlight battery, "a sleeping bag all rolled up and ready to go over to a friend's house"; a hairbrush, "a park with grass"; a spotted rubber ball, "a big fat lady bug"; a puppet placed on top of a block, "a statue"; and when the puppet was moved past it, a red block was labelled "a thing to show where the rocks are . . . he's sailing in a boat."

These remarkable behaviors have suggested to us that objects and actions may be organized in the mind of the preschool child in a manner rather different from that usually described with older subjects. Specifically, while the "mature" classification usually is based on membership in the same taxonomic class (e.g., furniture, clothing, vehicle) and while free associates are almost invariably paradigmatic in nature (e.g., table—chair; coat—hat), the conceptual world of the young child may well be organized in a fundamentally different way. Our attempts to describe this mode of classification highlight the role of physiognomic and synesthetic features in the conceptual organization of the young child; such youngsters seem to respond readily to these more expressive features of objects, features which—when exploited by adults—often produce fresh and unexpected comparisons, renamings, and predications. Should children be able to classify objects only on these bases, it would be unreasonable to consider them metaphorically competent; after all, they would only be organizing things differently, not overriding a customary mode of organization. But if, as appears to be the case, children have available to them both this mode of organization and the more typical superordinate taxonomic classes, then their early language can justifiably be termed metaphoric.

Yet another possibility merits brief mention. It may be that the child's early metaphoric behavior has both strong parallels and interesting divergences from the more mature metaphoric competence found in some adults, and especially in literary artists. At an early stage, the properties of the "new name" may be inextricably fused with the object: at such a time, the pencil may *become* a rocket ship, with pretense overriding reality, and no metaphoric competence can be deduced. At a somewhat later stage, about the age of four or five, the child is aware that the pencil "isn't really a rocket ship," but because the boundaries of these concepts have not yet been firmly fixed, this "overriding" of ordinary concepts does not assume great moment. Moving up the developmental scale, children of elementary school age become upset by such categorical transgressions, so much so, in fact, that they may resist any engagement whatsoever in various metaphoric games. Only in the years preceding adolescence, when the categorical practices of the culture have been well consolidated, is the child once again willing to undertake metaphoric language use. At such time, children newly allow a metaphoric renaming but they differ from the preschoolers in their greater awareness that tension has been overridden. Should one hold (with some authorities) that the greater the overriding of tension, the greater the achievement, then the metaphoric competence of the adolescent bears but a family resemblance to the earlier, more carefree linguistic experimentation of the preschool child.

C. The Breakdown of Metaphoric Capacities

The preceding sketches have provided at least a glimpse of standard developmental research: we have beheld a plausible progression of steps in the realm of metaphoric understanding, and a somewhat more mysterious and controversial array of possibilities in the domain of metaphoric production. And we have noted the puzzling appearance, during middle childhood, of a penchant for literalness. This penchant realizes itself in a reluctance on the part of such youngsters to produce metaphors on request as well as a tendency to provide literal or narrational paraphrases for these figures of speech. Though possibly a culturally motivated phenomenon, this stage may well be a necessary and even an important one: perhaps the capacity to appreciate the overriding of tension inherent in mature metaphor presupposes the establishment of clear-cut meanings and categorical boundaries, a task customarily confronted during the first years of schooling. Yet even so, it seems clear that this literalism has its less beneficent aspects and that the "metaphoric flowering" of early childhood must somehow be kept alive if later unambiguous forms of metaphor are to be fully realized.

Shifting our perspective radically, let us now suppose that we have a fully mature adult, one competent in the range of metaphoric behaviors. And suppose, further, that this individual suffers a stroke which destroys part of the brain and leaves him to some extent incapacitated both physically and mentally. What happens to his metaphoric capacity? Is metaphor a basic and robust capacity, one likely to remain relatively intact even in the face of considerable injury to the brain? Or is it rather a highly elaborated and consequently brittle capacity, one likely to be rapidly undermined in the wake of brain damage? And what of the variety of metaphoric competences? Do they all break down together? Or can they be considered "localized" in some sense, with one form (and its underlying psychological process) linked to one site—the other forms associated with other sites and other processes?

It must be said at the outset that we do not have the answers to these intriguing questions. A recent study, however, has at least indicated that aspects of metaphoric competence can be studied in the light of data from pathology. Such an approach, considered in the light of more standard developmental studies, may contribute to our understanding of the various forms of metaphorizing.

This study was actually framed in an effort to gain information on a currently popular (and perhaps excessively popular) issue: the division of labor between the two halves of the brain. It is well established that the left half of the brain is dominant for language; on this account, individuals with injury to the left hemisphere (hereafter, left-hemisphere or aphasic subjects) should lose their metaphoric capacities, while those with injury to the right hemisphere (hereafter, right-hemisphere subjects) should remain capable of metaphoric activities. A more recent account of the division of labor between the hemispheres, however, would offer a different set of predictions. It has been suggested by some that the right half of the brain figures prominently in artistic activities and in intuitive and affective matters, while the left hemisphere is critical for abstract and logical thought.[24] On this account one might well expect impaired metaphoric capacities among right-hemisphere patients, preserved metaphorizing skills among a left-hemisphere population.

To secure information on these rival claims, we prepared two simple tasks for administration to unilaterally brain-injured patients.[25] They were first presented orally with simple figures of speech (e.g., "He wore a loud tie," or "He had a heavy heart") and asked to match them to the most appropriate picture from a set of four. The three incorrect depictions were the noun alone (a tie, a heart); the adjective alone (a loud sound emanating from a speaker, a heavy weight); and a "literal" depiction (a tie with noise coming forth from it, a man trying to lift a large heart-shaped object). The correct responses in this case were, respectively, a garish tie and a despondent-looking man. After selecting a

24. See, e.g., Joseph Bogen, "The Other Side of the Brain," pts. 1 and 2, *Bulletin of the Los Angeles Neurological Society* 34 (1970): 73–105, 135–62; David Galin, "Implications for Psychiatry of Left and Right Cerebral Specialization," *Archives of General Psychiatry* 31 (1974): 572–83; and Robert Ornstein, *The Psychology of Consciousness* (New York, 1972).

25. Winner and Gardner, "Sensitivity to Metaphor in Organic Patients," *Brain* 100 (1977): 719–27.

picture, patients were then asked to supply a verbal paraphrase of the metaphoric sentence.

Not surprisingly, the left-hemisphere patients, all of whom had language difficulties, had trouble paraphrasing the metaphors. Either they produced little language at all or they simply repeated the referents themselves (e.g., "heart," "heavy," "tie," clothing"). The right-hemisphere patients showed some reluctance to paraphrase the metaphor but, when encouraged to do so, usually offered an appropriate, more abstract characterization (he's sad; the tie is very colorful).

Results in the picture condition were quite unexpected, however. Despite their aphasia, most of the left-hemisphere patients made the correct selection of the sad man or the garish tie. They rarely selected the literal depictions and, like normal control subjects, usually found them amusing. In sharp contrast to both aphasics and normal control subjects, the right-hemisphere patients were attracted to the literal depictions, choosing them as often as the metaphoric depictions, even when they themselves had offered the appropriate verbal paraphrase. Moreover, they never found the literal depictions amusing and seemed to feel that either depiction was equally plausible.

We have pondered these enigmatic findings for some time without arriving at an interpretation with which we are completely satisfied. Whatever is going on is very complicated and will require a further program of research. For our purposes here, it may suffice to make the following points. First of all, the results clearly indicate that metaphoric competence is not of a single piece. It is possible to be metaphorically competent in one modality or with one type of stimulus while appearing relatively incompetent (or primitive) when the same metaphor is presented in another modality or when another modality of response is required.

These results suggest two dissociable aspects of metaphoric competence in normal individuals. On the one hand, there is the capacity—preserved in the right hemisphere–injured patients—to provide a linguistic paraphrase of a frozen figure of speech. Such patients have apparently retained appropriate lexical markers for the terms "heavy" or "loud": they can use these "dual function" adjectives appropriately when interrogated in the linguistic sphere.

At the same time there seems to exist a rather different capacity, this one preserved in the left hemisphere–injured patients. What is entailed here, we believe, is the capacity to map a particular figure of speech onto a situation in which it is likely to be uttered. Even in the face of marked difficulties in both language production and comprehension, aphasic patients seem to appreciate the kind of situation in which a certain statement is likely to be made, even as their laughter designates the situation which they (rightly) believe is unlikely to prompt such a remark. To rephrase this point in terms of the distinction introduced earlier, these patients seem to have retained sensitivity to the pragmatics, or the context, of metaphoric utterances: they have a sense of the occasion on which a given figure of speech is likely to be uttered even though, in contradistinction to the right-hemisphere patients, they cannot themselves put into words the precise lexical meaning of that utterance. Conversely, the right-hemisphere patients are clearly responsive to the literal meanings of the words and can even paraphrase a metaphor appropriately. Where they seem deficient is in detecting the situation in which a given statement might be uttered, in discerning the intention of the speaker.[26]

4. Conclusion

In our review we have clearly been all over the map: the treatment of the misinterpretations of psychological-physical metaphors, the discussion of the attributes of early child metaphors, the account of various behavioral profiles exhibited by unilaterally brain-injured patients— have each raised a host of issues, some methodological, others entailing deep questions of interpretation. Indeed, so slippery and unmanageable do the issues of metaphor become once one commences work with the populations of normal children or brain-injured patients that humanistically oriented scholars might seem well advised to return at once to their book-lined studies, and even to lock their doors!

Ultimately, the individual humanists to whom we have addressed our remarks must determine their usefulness, and we will not be surprised (although we will be disappointed) if you decide that the findings we have reported and the interpretations we have offered seem quite remote from the workaday concerns of most philosophers, linguists, literary critics, and other humanistically oriented scholars. Moreover, we are all too painfully aware of the limitations of these studies: the colorless and often frozen nature of the stimulus materials, the need to regularize items and to eliminate their surrounding context, even at the cost of destroying their poetic flavor, the difficulty of inferring the intent and the tension experienced by the subject, and a host of other equally troublesome issues. Nonetheless, we would like to conclude by touching briefly on certain points made above and by suggesting how they might inform future discussions about metaphor, even as we indicate in brief compass how those same points might be further illuminated by individuals skilled in the analysis of concepts, verbal statements, and literary texts.

To begin with—and at the very least—we hope we have described some phenomena of interest in their own right, ones which call for

26. See Donald Davidson, "What Metaphors Mean," pp. 29–45 in this volume.

further investigation and interpretation and ones which might challenge some conventional categories and distinctions in the area of metaphor. Findings concerning the development of metaphoric comprehension suggest a wide range of possible misconstruals of even the simplest metaphors, and they raise the possibility that, given more difficult tropes, analogous misconstruals might be found across a range of populations and a number of kinds of metaphors;[27] the role of particular wording, and of surrounding context, in the comprehensibility of metaphoric relations has also been well documented in our studies. The findings on the development of metaphoric production suggest a sharp distinction between those metaphors based on perceptual and functional aspects, which are readily fashioned, and those based on psychological properties, which do not announce themselves to young subjects. Finally, the findings on the breakdown of metaphoric competence offer critical evidence on the existence of a set of metaphoric competences which may be mediated by different psychological processes and have different practical significance.

While we are pleased to offer food for thought, we also hope to provide data relevant to current philosophical debates. In our view, the findings concerning metaphoric comprehension support those analysts who stress the importance of pragmatic and contextual considerations in metaphoric behavior. Yet the results on metaphoric breakdown suggest an even more complicated picture. Our brain-damaged patients offer evidence for the existence of one neural "center" housing knowledge of linguistic features and a second "center" which judges the situational appropriateness of linguistic figures.

The neuropsychological evidence suggests that both the pragmatic and the "featural" perspectives, taken together, have some validity, with the crucial variable being the kinds of tasks posed and responses required. Indeed, if this finding proves robust, it would reinforce our view of the most important contribution made by developmental psychology to philosophical debates: not to prove that one side is wholly "right" or wholly "wrong" but rather to delineate the conditions under which each position possesses validity. We would stress in this connection that no single study, nor even a small set of studies, can ever decisively adjudicate among rival positions; if anything, it is too easy for psychologists to conjure up a study which will support (or refute) one or the other of two opposed views. Nonetheless, over a period of time, evidence generally accrues to indicate *which* of the rival positions is more reasonable and, more especially, the conditions under which each position is relatively plausible.

Finally, and ecumenically, we join this conference in the hope of receiving some skilled aid in the interpretation (or reinterpretation) of

27. See I. A. Richards, *Practical Criticism: A Study of Literary Judgment* (New York, 1935).

our findings, and in the formulation (or reformulation) of our basic concepts and our experimental procedures. Numerous issues raised in our studies cry out for further analysis: the adequacy of paraphrase as a test for metaphoric competence; the use of "normal control" subjects from one's cultural subgroup as a baseline for adequate metaphoric competence; the ontological status of "early metaphor" and the kinds of evidence on which one would want to make inferences about the "awareness," "intention," and "consciousness" of young subjects; the possible nature and meaning of a "literal" stage; the relationship of our simple paper and pencil and picture tests to the more elaborate forms of figurative language found in great literature; and, perhaps most intriguingly, the optimal way to describe those processes of the two halves of the brain which have announced themselves in our studies of the breakdown of metaphoric competence. If humanistically oriented scholars will add to their judicious consideration of texts an equally critical attitude toward the findings reported by psychologists of various stripes, future treatments of figurative language should be significantly enriched.

The Metaphorical Process as Cognition, Imagination, and Feeling

Paul Ricoeur

This paper will focus on a specific problem in the somewhat boundless field of metaphor theory. Although this problem may sound merely psychological, insofar as it includes such terms as "image" and "feeling," I would rather characterize it as a problem arising on the boundary between a *semantic* theory of metaphor and a *psychological* theory of imagination and feeling. By a semantic theory, I mean an inquiry into the capacity of metaphor to provide untranslatable information and, accordingly, into metaphor's claim to yield some true insight about reality. The question to which I will address myself is whether such an inquiry may be completed without including as a necessary component a psychological moment of the kind usually described as "image" or "feeling."

At first glance, it seems that it is only in theories in which metaphorical phrases have no informative value and consequently no truth claim that the so-called images or feelings are advocated as substitutive explanatory factors. By substitutive explanation I mean the attempt to derive the alleged significance of metaphorical phrases from their capacity to display streams of images and to elicit feelings that we mistakenly hold for genuine information and for fresh insight into reality. My thesis is that it is not only for theories which deny metaphors any informative value and any truth claim that images and feelings have a *constitutive* function. I want instead to show that the kind of theory of metaphor initiated by I. A. Richards in *Philosophy of Rhetoric,* Max Black in *Models and Metaphors,* Beardsley, Berggren, and others cannot achieve its own goal without including imagining and feeling, that is, without assigning a *semantic* function to what seems to be mere *psychological* features and without, therefore, concerning itself with some accompanying factors extrinsic to the informative kernel of metaphor. This contention seems to run against a well-established—at least since Frege's famous article "Sinn und Bedeutung" and Husserl's *Logical Investigations*—dichotomy, that between *Sinn* or sense and *Vorstellung* or representation, if we understand "sense" as the objective content of an expression and "representation" as its mental actualization, precisely in the form of image and feeling. But the question is whether the functioning of metaphorical sense does not put to the test and even hold at bay this very dichotomy.

The first articulate account of metaphor, that of Aristotle, already provides some hints concerning what I will call the semantic role of imagination (and by implication, feeling) in the establishment of metaphorical sense. Aristotle says of the *lexis* in general—that is, of diction, elocution, and style, of which metaphor is one of the figures—that it makes discourse (*logos*) *appear* as such and such. He also says that the gift of making good metaphors relies on the capacity to contemplate similarities. Moreover, the vividness of such good metaphors consists in their ability to "set before the eyes" the sense that they display. What is suggested here is a kind of pictorial dimension, which can be called the *picturing function* of metaphorical meaning.

The tradition of rhetoric confirms that hint beyond any specific theory concerning the semantic status of metaphor. The very expression "figure of speech" implies that in metaphor, as in the other tropes or turns, discourse assumes the nature of a body by displaying forms and traits which usually characterize the human face, man's "figure"; it is as though the tropes gave to discourse a quasi-bodily externalization. By providing a kind of figurability to the message, the tropes make discourse appear.

Roman Jakobson suggests a similar interpretation when he characterizes the "poetic" function in his general model of communication as the valorization of the message *for its own sake*. In the same way, Tzvetan Todorov, the Bulgarian theoretician of neo-rhetorics, defines "figure" as the visibility of discourse. Gérard Genette, in *Figures I,* speaks of deviance as an "inner space of language." "Simple and common expressions," he says, "have no form, figures [of speech] have some."

I am quite aware that these are only hints which point toward a problem rather than toward a statement. Furthermore, I am quite aware

---

Paul Ricoeur is professor of philosophy at the Université de Paris (Nanterre) and John Nuveen Professor at the University of Chicago. He is editor of *Revue de métaphysique et de morale* and the author of many influential works on phenomenology, hermeneutics, and the philosophy of language, including *The Rule of Metaphor: Multi-disciplinary Studies of the Creation of Meaning in Language.*

that they add to this difficulty the fact that they tend to speak metaphorically about metaphor and thus introduce a kind of circularity which obscures the issue. But is not the word "metaphor" itself a metaphor, the metaphor of a displacement and therefore of a transfer in a kind of space? What is at stake is precisely the necessity of these *spatial* metaphors about metaphor included in our talk about "figures" of speech.

Such being the problem, in what direction are we to look for a correct assessment of the *semantic* role of imagination and eventually of feeling? It seems that it is in the *work of resemblance* that a pictorial or iconic moment is implied, as Aristotle suggests when he says that to make good metaphors is to contemplate similarities or (according to some other translations) to have an insight into likeness.

But in order to understand correctly the work of resemblance in metaphor and to introduce the pictorial or iconic moment at the right place, it is necessary briefly to recall the mutation undergone by the theory of metaphor at the level of semantics by contrast with the tradition of classical rhetoric. In this tradition, metaphor was correctly described in terms of *deviance,* but this deviance was mistakenly ascribed to denomination only. Instead of giving a thing its usual common *name,* one designates it by means of a borrowed name, a "foreign" name in Aristotle's terminology. The rationale of this transfer of name was understood as the objective similarity between the things themselves or the subjective similarity between the attitudes linked to the grasping of these things. As concerns the goal of this transfer, it was supposed either to fill up a lexical lacuna, and therefore to serve the principle of economy which rules the endeavor of giving appropriate names to new things, new ideas, or new experiences, or to decorate discourse, and therefore to serve the main purpose of rhetorical discourse, which is to persuade and to please.

The problem of resemblance receives a new articulation in the semantic theory characterized by Max Black as an interaction theory (as opposed to a substitutive theory). The bearer of the metaphorical meaning is no longer the word but the sentence as a whole. The interaction process does not merely consist of the substitution of a word for a word, of a name for a name—which, strictly speaking, defines only metonymy—but in an interaction between a logical subject and a predicate. If metaphor consists in some deviance—this feature is not denied but is described and explained in a new way—this deviance concerns the predicative structure itself. Metaphor, then, has to be described as a deviant predication rather than a deviant denomination. We come closer to what I called the work of resemblance if we ask *how* this deviant predication obtains. A French theoretician in the field of poetics, Jean Cohen, in *Structure du langage poétique,* speaks of this deviance in terms of a semantic impertinence, meaning by that the violation of the code of pertinence or relevance which rules the ascription of predicates in ordinary use.[1] The metaphorical statement works as the reduction of this syntagmatic deviance by the establishment of a new semantic pertinence. This new pertinence in turn is secured by the production of a lexical deviance, which is therefore a paradigmatic deviance, that is, precisely the kind of deviance described by classical rhetoricians. Classical rhetoric, in that sense, was not wrong, but it only described the "effect of sense" at the level of the word while it overlooked the production of this semantic twist at the level of sense. While it is true that the effect of sense is focused on the word, the production of sense is borne by the whole utterance. It is in that way that the theory of metaphor hinges on a semantics of the sentence.

Such is the main presupposition of the following analysis. The first question is to understand *how* resemblance works in this production of meaning. The next step will be to connect in the right way the pictorial or iconic moment to this work of resemblance.

As concerns the first step, the work of resemblance as such, it seems to me that we are still only halfway to a full understanding of the semantic innovation which characterizes metaphorical phrases or sentences if we underline only the aspect of deviance in metaphor, even if we distinguish the semantic impertinence which requires the lexical deviance from this lexical deviance itself, as described by Aristotle and all classical rhetoricians. The decisive feature is the semantic innovation, thanks to which a new pertinence, a new congruence, is established in such a way that the utterance "makes sense" as a whole. The *maker* of metaphors is this craftsman with verbal skill *who,* from an inconsistent utterance for a literal interpretation, draws a significant utterance for a new interpretation which deserves to be called metaphorical because it generates the metaphor not only as deviant but as acceptable. In other words, metaphorical meaning does not merely consist of a semantic clash but of the *new* predicative meaning which emerges from the collapse of the literal meaning, that is, from the collapse of the meaning which obtains if we rely only on the common or usual lexical values of our words. The metaphor is not the enigma but the solution of the enigma.

It is here, in the mutation characteristic of the semantic innovation, that similarity and accordingly imagination play a role. But which role? I think that this role cannot be but misunderstood as long as one has in mind the Humean theory of image as a faint impression, that is, as a perceptual residue. It is no better understood if one shifts to the other tradition, according to which imagination can be reduced to the alternation between two modalities of association, either by contiguity or by similarity. Unfortunately, this prejudice has been assumed by such important theoreticians as Jakobson, for whom the metaphoric process is

1. Jean Cohen, *Structure du langage poétique* (Paris, 1966).

opposed to the metonymic process in the same way as the substitution of one sign for another within a sphere of similarity is opposed to the concatenation between signs along a string of contiguity. What must be understood and underscored is a mode of functioning of similarity and accordingly of imagination which is immanent—that is, nonextrinsic—to the predicative process itself. In other words, the work of resemblance has to be appropriate and homogeneous to the deviance and the oddness and the freshness of the semantic innovation itself.

How is this possible? I think that the decisive problem that an interaction theory of metaphor has helped to delineate but not to solve is the transition from literal incongruence to metaphorical congruence between two semantic fields. Here the metaphor of space is useful. It is as though a change of distance between meanings occurred within a logical space. The *new* pertinence or congruence proper to a meaningful metaphoric utterance proceeds from the kind of semantic proximity which suddenly obtains between terms in spite of their distance. Things or ideas which were remote appear now as close. Resemblance ultimately is nothing else than this rapprochement which reveals a generic kinship between heterogeneous ideas. What Aristotle called the *epiphora* of the metaphor, that is, the transfer of meaning, is nothing else than this move or shift in the logical distance, from the far to the near. The lacuna of some recent theories of metaphor, including Max Black's, concerns precisely the innovation proper to this shift.[2]

It is the first task of an appropriate theory of imagination to plug this hole. But this theory of imagination must deliberately break with Hume and draw on Kant, specifically on Kant's concept of productive imagination *as schematizing a synthetic operation*. This will provide us with the first step in our attempt to adjust a psychology of imagination to a semantics of metaphor or, if you prefer, to complete a semantics of metaphor by having recourse to a psychology of imagination. There will be three steps in this attempt of adjustment and of completion.

In the first step, imagination is understood as the "seeing," still homogeneous to discourse itself, which effects the shift in logical distance, the rapprochement itself. The place and the role of productive imagination is there, in the *insight*, to which Aristotle alluded when he said that to make good metaphors is to contemplate likeness—*theorein to omoion*. This insight into likeness is both a thinking and a seeing. It is a

2. Black's explanation of the metaphorical process by the "system of associated commonplaces" leaves unsolved the problem of innovation, as the following reservations and qualifications suggest: "Metaphors," he says, "can be supported by specifically constructed systems of implications as well as by accepted commonplaces" (*Models and Metaphors* [Ithaca, N.Y., 1962], p. 43). And further: "These implications usually consist of commonplaces about the subsidiary subject, but may, in suitable cases, consist of deviant implications established *ad hoc* by the writer" (p. 44). How are we to think of these implications that are created on the spot?

thinking to the extent that it effects a restructuration of semantic fields; it is transcategorical because it is categorical. This can be shown on the basis of the kind of metaphor in which the logical aspect of this re-structuration is the most conspicuous, the metaphor which Aristotle called metaphor by analogy, that is, the proportional metaphor: A is to B what C is to D. The cup is to Dionysus what the shield is to Ares. There-fore we may say, by shifting terms, Dionysus' shield or Ares' cup. But this thinking is a seeing, to the extent that the insight consists of the in-stantaneous grasping of the combinatory possibilities offered by the proportionality and consequently the establishment of the propor-tionality by the rapprochement between the two ratios. I suggest we call this *productive* character of the insight *predicative assimilation.* But we miss entirely its semantic role if we interpret it in terms of the old association by resemblance. A kind of mechanical attraction between mental atoms is thereby substituted for an operation homogeneous to language and to its nuclear act, the predication act. The assimilation consists precisely in *making* similar, that is, semantically proximate, the terms that the metaphorical utterance brings together.

Some will probably object to my ascribing to the imagination this predicative assimilation. Without returning to my earlier critique of the prejudices concerning the imagination itself which may prevent the analysts from doing justice to productive imagination, I want to under-score a trait of predicative assimilation which may support my conten-tion that the rapprochement characteristic of the metaphorical process offers a typical kinship to Kant's *schematism.* I mean the *paradoxical* character of the predicative assimilation which has been compared by some authors to Ryle's concept of "category mistake," which consists in presenting the facts pertaining to one category in the terms appropriate to another. All new rapprochement runs against a previous categorization which resists, or rather which yields while resisting, as Nelson Goodman says. This is what the idea of a semantic impertinence or incongruence preserves. In order that a metaphor obtains, one must continue to iden-tify the previous incompatibility *through* the new compatibility. The pred-icative assimilation involves, in that way, a specific kind of tension which is not so much between a subject and a predicate as between semantic incongruence and congruence. The insight into likeness is the percep-tion of the conflict between the previous incompatibility and the new compatibility. "Remoteness" is preserved within "proximity." To see *the like* is to see the same in spite of, and through, the different. This tension between sameness and difference characterizes the logical structure of likeness. Imagination, accordingly, is this *ability* to produce new kinds by assimilation and to produce them not *above* the differences, as in the concept, but in spite of and through the differences. Imagination is this stage in the production of genres where generic kinship has not reached the level of conceptual peace and rest but remains caught in the war between distance and proximity, between remoteness and nearness. In that sense, we may speak with Gadamer of the fundamental metaphoricity of thought to the extent that the figure of speech that we call "metaphor" allows us a glance at the general procedure by which we produce concepts. This is because in the metaphoric process the movement toward the genus is arrested by the resistance of the difference and, as it were, intercepted by the figure of rhetoric.

Such is the first function of imagination in the process of semantic innovation. Imagination has not yet been considered under its sensible, quasi-optic aspect but under its quasi-verbal aspect. However, the latter is the condition of the former. We first have to understand an image, according to Bachelard's remark in the *Poetics of Space,* as "a being pertaining to language."[3] Before being a fading perception, the image is an emerging meaning. Such is, in fact, the tradition of Kant's productive imagination and schematism. What we have above described is nothing else than the schematism of metaphorical attribution.

The next step will be to incorporate into the semantics of metaphor the second aspect of imagination, its *pictorial* dimension. It is this aspect which is at stake in the *figurative* character of metaphor. It is also this aspect which was intended by I. A. Richards' distinction between tenor and vehicle. This distinction is not entirely absorbed in the one Black makes between frame and focus. Frame and focus designate only the contextual setting—say, the sentence as a whole—and the term which is the bearer of the shift of meaning, whereas tenor and vehicle designate the conceptual import and its pictorial envelope. The first function of imagination was to give an account of the frame/focus interplay; its second function is to give an account of the difference of level between tenor and vehicle or, in other words, of the way in which a semantic innovation is not only schematized but pictured. Paul Henle borrows from Charles Sanders Peirce the distinction between sign and icon and speaks of the *iconic* aspect of metaphor.[4] If there are two thoughts in one in a metaphor, there is one which is intended; the other is the concrete aspect *under* which the first one is presented. In Keats' verse "When by my solitary hearth I sit / And hateful thoughts enwrap my soul in gloom," the metaphorical expression "enwrap" consists in presenting sorrow as if it were capable of enveloping the soul in a cloak. Henle comments: "We are led [by figurative discourse] to think of something by a consideration of something like it, and this is what constitutes the iconic mode of signifying."

Someone might object at this point that we are in danger of reintroducing an obsolete theory of the image, in the Humean sense of a weakened sensorial impression. This is therefore the place to recall a

3. Gaston Bachelard, *The Poetics of Space,* trans. Maria Jolas (New York, 1964).
4. Paul Henle, "Metaphor," in *Language, Thought, and Culture,* ed. Henle (Ann Arbor, Mich., 1958).

remark made by Kant that one of the functions of the schema is to provide images for a concept. In the same vein, Henle writes: "If there is an iconic element in metaphor it is equally clear that the icon is not presented, but merely described." And further: "What is presented is a formula for the construction of icons." What we have therefore to show is that if this new extension of the role of imagination is not exactly included in the previous one, it makes sense for a semantic theory only to the extent that it is controlled by it. What is at issue is the development from schematization to iconic presentation.

The enigma of iconic presentation is the way in which depiction occurs in predicative assimilation: something appears on which we read the new connection. The enigma remains unsolved as long as we treat the image as a mental picture, that is, as the replica of an absent thing. Then the image must remain foreign to the process, extrinsic to predicative assimilation.

We have to understand the process by which a certain production of images channels the schematization of predicative assimilation. By displaying a flow of images, discourse initiates changes of logical distance, generates rapprochement. Imaging or imagining, thus, is the concrete milieu in which and through which we see similarities. To imagine, then, is not to have a mental picture of something but to display relations in a depicting mode. Whether this depiction concerns unsaid and unheard similarities or refers to qualities, structures, localizations, situations, attitudes, or feelings, each time the new intended connection is grasped as what the icon describes or depicts.

It is in this way, I think, that one can do justice within a semantic theory of metaphor to the Wittgensteinian concept of "seeing as." Wittgenstein himself did not extend this analysis beyond the field of perception and beyond the process of interpretation made obvious by the case of ambiguous "Gestalten," as in the famous duck/rabbit drawing. Marcus B. Hester, in his *The Meaning of Poetic Metaphor,* has attempted to extend the concept of "seeing as" to the functioning of poetic images.[5] Describing the experience of *reading,* he shows that the kind of images which are interesting for a theory of poetic language are not those that interrupt reading and distort or divert it. These images—these "wild" images, if I may say so—are properly extrinsic to the fabric of sense. They induce the reader, who has become a dreamer rather than a reader, to indulge himself in the delusive attempt, described by Sartre as fascination, to possess magically the absent thing, body, or person. The kind of images which still belong to the production of sense are rather what Hester calls "bound" images, that is, concrete representations aroused by the verbal element and controlled by it. Poetic

5. Marcus B. Hester, *The Meaning of Poetic Metaphor* (The Hague, 1967).

language, says Hester, is this language which not only merges sense and sound, as many theoreticians have said, but sense and senses, meaning by that the flow of bound images displayed by the sense. We are not very far from what Bachelard called *retentissement* [reverberation]. In reading, Bachelard says, the verbal meaning generates images which, so to speak, rejuvenate and reenact the traces of sensorial experience. Yet it is not the process of reverberation which expands the schematization and, in Kant's words, provides a concept with an image. In fact, as the experience of reading shows, this display of images ranges from schematization without full-blown images to wild images which distract thought more than they instruct it. The kind of images which are relevant for a semantics of the poetic image are those which belong to the intermediary range of the scale, which are, therefore, the bound images of Hester's theory. These images bring to concrete completion the metaphorical process. The meaning is then depicted under the features of ellipsis. Through this depiction, the meaning is not only schematized but lets itself be read *on* the image in which it is inverted. Or, to put it another way, the metaphorical sense is generated in the thickness of the imagining scene displayed by the verbal structure of the poem. Such is, to my mind, the functioning of the intuitive grasp of a predicative connection.

I do not deny that this second stage of our theory of imagination has brought us to the borderline between pure semantics and psychology or, more precisely, to the borderline between a semantics of productive imagination and a psychology of reproductive imagination. But the metaphorical meaning, as I said in the introduction, is precisely this kind of meaning which denies the well-established distinction between sense and representation, to evoke once more Frege's opposition between *Sinn* and *Vorstellung*. By blurring this distinction, the metaphorical meaning compels us to explore the borderline between the verbal and the nonverbal. The process of schematization and that of the bound images aroused and controlled by schematization obtain precisely on that borderline between a semantics of metaphorical utterances and a psychology of imagination.

The third and final step in our attempt to complete a semantic theory of metaphor with a proper consideration of the role of imagination concerns what I shall call the "suspension" or, if you prefer, the moment of negativity brought by the image in the metaphorical process.

In order to understand this new contribution of the image to this process, we have to come back to the basic notion of meaning as applied to a metaphorical expression. By meaning we may understand—as we have in the preceding as well—the inner functioning of the proposition as a predicative operation, for example, in Black's vocabulary, the "filter" or the "screen" effect of the subsidiary subject on the main subject. Meaning, then, is nothing else than what Frege called *Sinn* [sense], in ·

contradistinction to *Bedeutung* [reference or denotation]. But to ask *about what* a metaphorical statement is, is something other and something more than to ask *what* it says.

The question of reference in metaphor is a particular case of the more general question of the truth claim of poetic language. As Goodman says in *Languages of Art,* all symbolic systems are denotative in the sense that they "make" and "remake" reality. To raise the question of the referential value of poetic language is to try to show how symbolic systems *reorganize* "the world in terms of works and works in terms of the world."[6] At that point the theory of metaphor tends to merge with that of models to the extent that a metaphor may be seen as a model for changing our way of looking at things, of perceiving the world. The word "insight," very often applied to the *cognitive* import of metaphor, conveys in a very appropriate manner this move from sense to reference which is no less obvious in poetic discourse than in so-called descriptive discourse. Here, too, we do not restrict ourselves to talking about ideas nor, as Frege says of proper names, "are we satisfied with the sense alone." "We presuppose besides a reference," the "striving for truth," which prompts "our intention in speaking or thinking" and "drives us always to advance from the sense of the reference."[7]

But the paradox of metaphorical reference is that its functioning is as odd as that of the metaphorical sense. At first glance, poetic language refers to nothing but itself. In a classic essay entitled "Word and Language," which defines the poetic function of language in relation to the other functions implied in any communicative transaction, Jakobson bluntly opposes the poetic function of the message to its referential function. On the contrary, the referential function prevails in descriptive language, be it ordinary or scientific. Descriptive language, he says, is not about itself, not inwardly oriented, but outwardly directed. Here language, so to speak, effaces itself for the sake of what is said about reality. "The poetic function—which is more than mere poetry—lays the stress on the palpable side of the signs, underscores the message for its own sake and deepens the fundamental dichotomy between signs and objects."[8] The poetic function and the referential function, accordingly, seem to be polar opposites. The latter directs language toward the non-linguistic context, the former directs message toward itself.

This analysis seems to strengthen some other classical arguments among literary critics and more specifically in the structuralist camp according to which not only poetry but literature in general implies a mutation in the use of language. This redirects language toward itself to

6. Nelson Goodman, *Languages of Art* (Indianapolis, Ind., 1968), p. 241.

7. As quoted from Frege's "Sense and Reference" in my *The Rule of Metaphor: Multidisciplinary Studies of the Creation of Meaning in Language* (Toronto, 1978), pp. 217–18.

8. Jakobson, *Selected Writings,* 2 vols. (The Hague, 1962), 2:356.

the point that language may be said, in Roland Barthes' words, to "celebrate itself" rather than to celebrate the world.

My contention is that these arguments are not false but give an incomplete picture of the whole process of reference in poetic discourse. Jakobson himself acknowledged that what happens in poetry is not the suppression of the referential function but its profound alteration by the workings of the ambiguity of the message itself. "The supremacy of poetic function over referential function," he says, "does not obliterate the reference but makes it ambiguous. The double-sensed message finds correspondence in a split addresser, in a split addressee, and what is more, in a split reference, as is cogently exposed in the preambles to fairy tales of various people, for instance, in the usual exortation of the Majorca story tellers: *Aixo era y no era* (it was and it was not)."[9]

I suggest that we take the expression "split reference" as our leading line in our discussion of the referential function of the metaphorical statement. This expression, as well as the wonderful "it was and it was not," contains *in nuce* all that can be said about metaphorical reference. To summarize, poetic language is no less *about* reality than any other use of language but refers to it by the means of a complex strategy which implies, as an essential component, a suspension and seemingly an abolition of the ordinary reference attached to descriptive language. This suspension, however, is only the negative condition of a second-order reference, of an indirect reference built on the ruins of the direct reference. This reference is called second-order reference only with respect to the primacy of the reference of ordinary language. For, in another respect, it constitutes the primordial reference to the extent that it suggests, reveals, unconceals—or whatever you say—the deep structures of reality to which we are related as mortals who are born into this world and who *dwell* in it for a while.

This is not the place to discuss the ontological implications of this contention nor to ascertain its similarities and dissimilarities with Husserl's concept of *Lebenswelt* or with Heidegger's concept of *In-der-Welt-Sein*. I want to emphasize, for the sake of our further discussion of the role of imagination in the completion of the *meaning* of metaphor, the mediating role of the *suspension*—or *epoché*—of ordinary descriptive reference in connection with the ontological claims of poetic discourse. This mediating role of the *epoché* in the functioning of the reference in metaphor is in complete agreement with the interpretation we have given to the functioning of sense. The sense of a novel metaphor, we said, is the emergence of a new semantic congruence or pertinence from the ruins of the literal sense shattered by semantic incompatibility or absurdity. In the same way as the self-abolition of literal sense is the

9. As found in my *The Rule of Metaphor*, p. 224.

negative condition for the emergence of the metaphorical sense, the
suspension of the reference proper to ordinary descriptive language is
the negative condition for the emergence of a more radical way of looking at things, whether it is akin or not to the unconcealing of that layer of
reality which phenomenology calls preobjective and which, according to
Heidegger, constitutes the horizon of all our modes of dwelling in the
world. Once more, what interests me here is the parallelism between the
suspension of literal sense and the suspension of ordinary descriptive
reference. This parallelism goes very far. In the same way as the
metaphorical sense not only abolishes but preserves the literal sense, the
metaphorical reference maintains the ordinary vision in tension with the
new one it suggests. As Berggren says in "The Use and Abuse of
Metaphor": "The possibility or comprehension of metaphorical construing requires, therefore, a peculiar and rather sophisticated intellectual
ability which W. Bedell Stanford metaphorically labels 'stereoscopic vision': the ability to entertain two different points of view at the same
time. That is to say, the perspective prior to and subsequent to the
transformation of the metaphor's principle and subsidiary subjects must
both be conjointly maintained."[10]

But what Bedell Stanford called stereoscopic vision is nothing else
than what Jakobson called split reference: ambiguity in reference.

My contention now is that one of the functions of imagination is to
give a concrete dimension to the suspension or *epoché* proper to split
reference. Imagination does not merely *schematize* the predicative assimilation between terms by its synthetic insight into similarities nor does it
merely *picture* the sense thanks to the display of images aroused and
controlled by the cognitive process. Rather, it contributes concretely to
the *epoché* of ordinary reference and to the *projection* of new possibilities
of redescribing the world.

In a sense, all *epoché* is the work of the imagination. Imagination *is*
epoché. As Sartre emphasized, to imagine is to address oneself to what is
not. More radically, to imagine is to make oneself absent to the whole of
things. Yet I do not want to elaborate further this thesis of the negativity
proper to the image. What I do want to underscore is the solidarity
between the *epoché* and the capacity to project new possibilities. Image as
absence is the negative side of image as fiction. It is to this aspect of the
image as fiction that is attached the power of symbolic systems to "remake" reality, to return to Goodman's idiom. But this productive and
projective function of fiction can only be acknowledged if one sharply
distinguishes it from the reproductive role of the so-called mental image
which merely provides us with a re-presentation of things already perceived. *Fiction* addresses itself to deeply rooted potentialities of reality to

10. Douglas Berggren, "The Use and Abuse of Metaphor," *Review of Metaphysics* 16
(December 1962): 243.

the extent that they are absent from the actualities with which we deal in everyday life under the mode of empirical control and manipulation. In that sense, fiction presents under a concrete mode the split structure of the reference pertaining to the metaphorical statement. It both reflects and completes it. It reflects it in the sense that the mediating role of the *epoché* proper to the image is homogeneous to the paradoxical structure of the cognitive process of reference. The "it was and it was not" of the Majorca storytellers rules both the split reference of the metaphorical statement and the contradictory structure of fiction. Yet, we may say as well that the structure of the fiction not only reflects but completes the logical structure of the split reference. The poet is this genius who generates split references *by* creating fictions. It is in fiction that the "absence" proper to the power of suspending what we call "reality" in ordinary language concretely coalesces and fuses with the *positive insight* into the potentialities of our being in the world which our everyday transactions with manipulatable objects tend to conceal.

You may have noticed that until now I have said nothing concerning feelings in spite of the commitment implied in this paper's title to deal with the problem of the connection between cognition, imagination, *and* feeling. I have no intention to elude this problem.

Imagination and feeling have always been closely linked in classical theories of metaphor. We cannot forget that rhetoric has always been defined as a strategy of discourse aiming at persuading and pleasing. And we know the central role played by pleasure in the aesthetics of Kant. A theory of metaphor, therefore, is not complete if it does not give an account of the place and role of feeling in the metaphorical process.

My contention is that feeling has a place not just in theories of metaphor which deny the *cognitive* import of metaphor. These theories ascribe a substitutive role to image and feeling due to the metaphor's lack of informative value. In addition, I claim that feeling as well as imagination are genuine components in the process described in an interaction theory of metaphor. They both *achieve* the semantic bearing of metaphor.

I have already tried to show the way in which a *psychology* of imagination has to be integrated into a semantics of metaphor. I will now try to extend the same kind of description to feeling. A bad psychology of imagination in which imagination is conceived as a residue of perception prevents us from acknowledging the constructive role of imagination. In the same way, a bad psychology of feeling is responsible for a similar misunderstanding. Indeed, our natural inclination is to speak of feeling in terms appropriate to emotion, that is, to affections conceived as (1) inwardly directed states of mind, and (2) mental experiences closely tied to bodily disturbances, as is the case in fear, anger, pleasure, and pain. In fact both traits come together. To the extent that in emotion we are, so to speak, under the spell of our body, we are delivered to mental states with little intentionality, as though in emotion we "lived" our body in a more intense way.

Genuine feelings are not emotions, as may be shown by feelings which are rightly called *poetic feelings*. Just like the corresponding images which they reverberate, they enjoy a specific kinship with language. They are properly displayed by the poem as a verbal texture. But how are they linked to its meaning?

I suggest that we construe the role of feeling according to the three similar moments which provided an articulation to my theory of imagination.

Feelings, first, accompany and complete imagination in its function of *schematization* of the new predicative congruence. This schematization, as I said, is a kind of insight into the mixture of "like" and "unlike" proper to similarity. Now we may say that this instantaneous grasping of the new congruence is "felt" as well as "seen." By saying that it is felt, we underscore the fact that we are included in the process as knowing subjects. If the process can be called, as I called it, predicative *assimilation*, it is true that *we* are assimilated, that is, made similar, to what is seen as similar. This self-assimilation is a part of the commitment proper to the "illocutionary" force of the metaphor as speech act. We feel *like* what we see *like*.

If we are somewhat reluctant to acknowledge this contribution of feeling to the illocutionary act of metaphorical statements, it is because we keep applying to feeling our usual interpretation of emotion as both inner and bodily states. We then miss the specific structure of feeling. As Stephan Strasser shows in *Das Gemut* [The heart], a feeling is a second-order intentional structure.[11] It is a process of interiorization succeeding a movement of intentional transcendence directed toward some objective state of affairs. To *feel*, in the emotional sense of the word, is to make ours what has been put at a distance by thought in its objectifying phase. Feelings, therefore, have a very complex kind of intentionality. They are not merely inner states but interiorized thoughts. It is as such that they accompany and complete the work of imagination as schematizing a synthetic operation: they make the schematized thought ours. Feeling, then, is a case of *Selbst-Affektion,* in the sense Kant used it in the second edition of the *Critique*. This *Selbst-Affektion,* in turn, is a part of what we call poetic feeling. Its function is to abolish the distance between knower and known without canceling the cognitive structure of thought and the intentional distance which it implies. Feeling is not contrary to thought. It is thought made ours. This felt participation is a part of its complete meaning as poem.

Feelings, furthermore, accompany and complete imagination as *picturing* relationships. This aspect of feeling has been emphasized by

11. Stephan Strasser, *Das Gemut* (Freiberg, 1956).

Northrop Frye in *Anatomy of Criticism* under the designation of "mood."
Each poem, he says, structures a mood which is *this* unique mood generated by *this* unique string of words. In that sense, it is coextensive to the
verbal structure itself. The mood is nothing other than the way in which
the poem affects us as an *icon*. Frye offers strong expression here: "The
unity of a poem is the unity of a mood"; the poetic images "express or
articulate this mood. This mood is the poem and nothing else behind
it."[12] In my own terms, I would say, in a tentative way, that the mood is
the iconic as felt. Perhaps we could arrive at the same assumption by
starting from Goodman's concept of *dense* vs. *discrete* symbols. Dense
symbols are felt as dense. That does not mean, once more, that feelings
are radically opaque and ineffable. "Density" is a mode of articulation
just as discreteness is. Or, to speak in Pascal's terms, the "esprit de
finesse" is no less thought than the "esprit géometrique." However, I
leave these suggestions open to discussion.

Finally, the most important function of feelings can be construed
according to the third feature of imagination, that is, its contribution to
the split reference of poetic discourse. The imagination contributes to it,
as I said, owing to its own split structure. On the one hand, imagination
entails the *epoché,* the suspension, of the direct reference of thought to
the objects of our ordinary discourse. On the other hand, imagination
provides *models for* reading reality in a new way. This split structure is the
structure of imagination as fiction.

What could be the counterpart and the complement of this split
structure at the level of feelings? My contention is that feelings, too,
display a split structure which completes the split structure pertaining to
the cognitive component of metaphor.

On the one hand, feelings—I mean poetic feelings—imply a kind of
epoché of our bodily emotions. Feelings are negative, suspensive experiences in relation to the literal emotions of everyday life. When we read,
we do not literally feel fear or anger. Just as poetic language denies the
first-order reference of descriptive discourse to ordinary objects of our
concern, feelings deny the first-order feelings which tie us to these first-
order objects of reference.

But this denial, too, is only the reverse side of a more deeply rooted
operation of feeling which is to insert us within the world in a nonobjec-
tifying manner. That feelings are not merely the denial of emotions but
their metamorphosis has been explicitly asserted by Aristotle in his
analysis of catharsis. But this analysis remains trivial as long as it is not
interpreted in relation to the split reference of the cognitive and the
imaginative function of poetic discourse. It is the tragic poem itself, as
thought (*dianoia*), which displays specific feelings which are the poetic
transposition—I mean the transposition by means of poetic *language*

12. Northrop Frye, *Anatomy of Criticism: Four Essays* (Princeton, 1957).

—of fear and compassion, that is, of feelings of the first order, of emotions. The tragic *phobos* and the tragic *eleos* (terror and pity, as some translators say) are both the denial and the transfiguration of the literal feelings of fear and compassion.

On the basis of this analysis of the split structure of poetic feeling, it is possible to do justice to a certain extent to a claim of Heidegger's analytic of the *Dasein* that feelings have *ontological* bearing, that they are ways of "being-there," of "finding" ourselves within the world, to keep something of the semantic intent of the German *Befindlichkeit*. Because of feelings we are "attuned to" aspects of reality which cannot be expressed in terms of the objects referred to in ordinary language. Our entire analysis of the split reference of both language and feeling is in agreement with this claim. But it must be underscored that this analysis of *Befindlichkeit* makes sense only to the extent that it is paired with that of split reference both in verbal and imaginative structures. If we miss this fundamental connection, we are tempted to construe this concept of *Befindlichkeit* as a new kind of intuitionism—and the worst kind!—in the form of a new emotional realism. We miss, in Heidegger's *Daseinanalyse* itself, the close connections between *Befindlichkeit* and *Verstehen*, between situation and project, between anxiety and interpretation. The ontological bearing of feeling cannot be separated from the negative process applied to the first-order emotions, such as fear and sympathy, according to the Aristotelian paradigm of catharsis. With this qualification in mind, we may assume the Heideggerian thesis that it is mainly through feelings that we are attuned to reality. But this attunement is nothing else than the reverberation in terms of feelings of the split reference of both verbal and imaginative structure.

To conclude, I would like to emphasize the points which I submit to discussion:

1. There are three main *presuppositions* on which the rest of my analysis relies: (*a*) metaphor is an act of *predication* rather than of *denomination;* (*b*) a theory of deviance is not enough to give an account of the emergence of a *new congruence* at the predicative level; and (*c*) the notion of metaphorical sense is not complete without a description of the *split reference* which is specific to poetic discourse.
2. On this threefold basis, I have tried to show that imagination and feeling are not extrinsic to the emergence of the metaphorical sense and of the split reference. They are not substitutive for a lack of informative content in metaphorical statements, but they complete their full cognitive intent.
3. *But* the price to pay for the last point is a theory of imagination and of feeling which is still in infancy. The burden of my argument is that the notion of *poetic image* and of *poetic feeling* has to be construed in accordance with the cognitive component, understood itself as a ten-

sion between congruence and incongruence at the level of sense, between *epoché* and commitment at the level of reference.

4. My paper suggests that there is a *structural analogy* between the cognitive, the imaginative, and the emotional components of the complete metaphorical act and that the metaphorical process draws its concreteness and its completeness from this structural analogy and this complementary functioning.

Afterthoughts on Metaphor

I

A Postscript on Metaphor

W. V. Quine

Pleasure precedes business. The child at play is practicing for life's responsibilities. Young impalas play at fencing with one another, thrusting and parrying. Art for art's sake was the main avenue, says Cyril Smith, to ancient technological breakthroughs. Such also is the way of metaphor: it flourishes in playful prose and high poetic art, but it is vital also at the growing edges of science and philosophy.

The molecular theory of gases emerged as an ingenious metaphor: a gas was likened to a vast swarm of absurdly small bodies. So pat was the metaphor that it was declared literally true and thus became straightway a dead metaphor; the fancied miniature bodies were declared real, and the term "body" was extended to cover them all. In recent years the molecules have even been observed by means of electron microscopy; but I speak of origins.

Or consider light waves. There being no ether, there is no substance for them to be waves of. Talk of light waves is thus best understood as metaphorical, so long as "wave" is read in the time-honored way. Or we may liberalize "wave" and kill the metaphor.

Along the philosophical fringes of science we may find reasons to question basic conceptual structures and to grope for ways to refashion them. Old idioms are bound to fail us here, and only metaphor can begin to limn the new order. If the venture succeeds, the old metaphor may die and be embalmed in a newly literalistic idiom accommodating the changed perspective.

Religion, or much of it, is evidently involved in metaphor for good. The parables, according to David Tracy's paper, are the "founding language" of Christianity. Exegete succeeds exegete, ever construing metaphor in further metaphor. There are deep mysteries here. There is mystery as to the literal content, if any, that this metaphorical material is meant to convey. And there is then a second-order mystery: Why the indirection? If the message is as urgent and important as one supposes, why are we not given it straight in the first place? A partial answer to both questions may lie in the nature of mystical experience: it is without content and so resists literal communication, but one may still try to induce the feeling in others by skillful metaphor.

Besides serving us at the growing edge of science and beyond, metaphor figures even in our first learning of language; or, if not quite metaphor, something akin to it. We hear a word or phrase on some occasion, or by chance we babble a fair approximation ourselves on what happens to be a pat occasion and are applauded for it. On a later occasion, then, one that resembles that first occasion by our lights, we repeat the expression. Resemblance of occasions is what matters, here as in metaphor. We generalize our application of the expression by degrees of subjective resemblance of occasions, until we discover from other people's behavior that we have pushed analogy too far and exceeded the established usage. If the crux of metaphor is creative extension through analogy, then we have forged a metaphor at each succeeding application of that early word or phrase. These primitive metaphors differ from the deliberate and sophisticated ones, however, in that they accrete directly to our growing store of standard usage. They are metaphors stillborn.

It is a mistake, then, to think of linguistic usage as literalistic in its main body and metaphorical in its trimming. Metaphor, or something like it, governs both the growth of language and our acquisition of it. What comes as a subsequent refinement is rather cognitive discourse itself, at its most dryly literal. The neatly worked inner stretches of science are an open space in the tropical jungle, created by clearing tropes away.

W. V. Quine is the Edgar Pierce professor emeritus of philosophy at Harvard University. His many influential works include *Methods of Logic, Word and Object,* and *The Roots of Reference.*

Afterthoughts on Metaphor

II

Toward a Psychology of Metaphor

Don R. Swanson

Karl Popper takes his philosophy of scientific method as the model for a general theory of knowledge. He claims that we gain knowledge of the world by trial-and-error elimination. Theories are conjectures or hypotheses, and experience is the testing of hypotheses. We begin life with certain innate expectations—our earliest theories. Confrontations with the real world lead us to eliminate erroneous theories; we then reshape our conjectures and try again. The better theories emerge as the survivors in a process of natural selection. We approach, but never attain, a true model of objective reality by endless cycles of conjectures and refutations.[1]

In this light, how might we see a three-year-old child at play? A child is a small scientist who tries out all kinds of ways of using the world. A box or a wastebasket he might use as a boot, a plate as a hat, a ring-shaped toy as a doughnut, and a potato chip as a cowboy hat for a doll.[2] He acts and speaks in metaphors. I propose that we look upon such metaphors as partly erroneous conjectures being put to the test. One might argue against such a view by pointing out that the child knows the errors to be errors, and so not in need of testing; but the child's way of saying "I know this isn't so" might be to playfully try it out. The appeal of the metaphoric act lies both in its resemblance to the truth and in the

1. Karl Popper, *Conjectures and Refutations: The Growth of Scientific Knowledge* (London, 1963), esp. pp. 33–59; *Objective Knowledge: An Evolutionary Approach* (Oxford, 1972), esp. pp. 67–70, 112, 156, 164, 165, 256–65, and 341–61.
2. See Gardner and Winner, "The Development of Metaphoric Competence: Implications for Humanistic Disciplines," pp. 130–34 in this volume.

presence of error. It is pleasurable to master the distinction between the true and the false—between reality and fantasy—by repeatedly testing what is already known to be refuted. In any event, it is reasonable to expect the child to show some degree of tenacity for his theories or conjectures. Like the scientist, he does not, and indeed should not, lightly abandon them.

But we expect this kind of uninhibited metaphoric behavior to be phased out over the years, or moderated, or perhaps modulated beyond recognition as more realistic behavior sets in. Thus one might account for the descending left half of the U-shaped curve mentioned by Howard Gardner, a curve that describes the amount of metaphoric behavior as a function of age. That the curve should rise again as age increases suggests a new phenomenon and invites comparison of adults' metaphors with those of children.

Donald Davidson has pointed out that a metaphor is, literally, a false statement.[3] This property of being false I take now as my springboard, for it is a property common to both children's and adults' metaphors. But the two cases differ in the matter of intent. The child is displaying a characteristic disposition to explore the world and is not primarily trying to produce an effect on or in someone else. He is talking to himself and enjoying it. The adult, on the other hand, is engaging in the creation of a persuasive argument or an evocative description. He constructs a deliberate falsehood in order to allude to some underlying "truth"—or at least what he hopes will be taken as true.

How and why does a metaphor work? What happens to us when we hear or read one? My guess is that a metaphor, because it is an erroneous statement, conflicts with our expectations. It releases, triggers, and stimulates our predisposition to detect error and to take corrective action. We do not dismiss or reject a metaphor as *simply* a false statement for we recognize it *as* a metaphor and know as Davidson suggests that it alludes to something else that we might wish to notice. It preempts our attention and propels us on a quest for the underlying truth. We are launched into a creative, inventive, pleasurable act. To turn Piaget around, to invent is to understand. For the hearer or reader of a metaphor to detect, by himself, the nature of the error and to invent his own (conjectural) version of the truth entails understanding and achievement and thus pleasure. Such pleasure perhaps owes its origin to, and is enhanced by an echo from, the metaphoric playfulness of childhood.

3. Davidson, "What Metaphors Mean," pp. 29–45 in this volume.

Don R. Swanson is professor and dean of the graduate library school at the University of Chicago.

A metaphor is a peremptory invitation to discovery. What is discoverable are the various allusive ties, or common attributes, between the metaphor and the underlying truth to which it points. It is plausible to guess that the pleasure, and hence power, of the metaphor depends on two factors. It is the more powerful and effective the greater the number of allusive ties discovered and the greater the speed or suddenness with which the discoveries are made. A metaphor that packs all of its allusions into one or a few words should be more effective than a metaphor in which the same allusions are scattered throughout a long chain of words or sentences. The number of allusive ties in some sense reflects how close the metaphor approaches the truth—how near it is to being on target. Perhaps the closer it is, the more compelling the urge to correct the error—like the pull of a magnet.

It follows, if my guess is anywhere near the truth, that a simile is usually less potent than a metaphor simply because, as Davidson has observed, it is a *true* statement. It is not a provocation to correction, invention, and discovery. We hear a metaphor and become a cat after a mouse. We pounce. A simile is more like a wheelbarrow—we are carried along.

Consider Wayne Booth's catfish.[4] A small public utility is battling a giant competitor in court. The lawyer for the former accuses the latter of picking up his client by the tail, pointing a long sharp knife, and saying: "You jes set still, little catfish, we're *jes* going to *gut* ya'." Absolutely electrifying! Why? First, the metaphorical narrative carries numerous allusions to the truth the lawyer was trying to persuade the jury to construct. As Booth noted, a catfish is a perfect victim. It is not a game fish, it is easy to catch, and it is a harmless scavenger; gutting entails a profusion of allusions, and "held by the tail" poignantly points to helplessness. But the really striking force of this metaphor centers in the suddenness of the word *gut*. At that instant the leap is made, and all of these connections snap together. The mouse is caught.

Another example: nine-year-old Ivan was helping his mother clean house. Two vacuum cleaners were in his small, cluttered room—a tall upright one and a small round cannister type. Ivan said to his mother, "If you'll get Artoo Detoo out of here, I'll vacuum with C-Threepio."

The following metaphor is syntactically identical but clearly less effective: "If you'll get Costello out of here, I'll vacuum with Abbott." The suddenness of the evoked leap does not differ here from the other case. What differs is the relative richness or number of facets of the real situation that are alluded to by the metaphor. Lou Costello is short and round and has a tall partner, but his resemblance to the cannister goes no further. Artoo Detoo, the android hero of *Star Wars*, is also short and

---

4. Booth, "Metaphor as Rhetoric: The Problem of Evaluation," especially pp. 50–56.

round and has a tall partner; but he is a machine, rolls on three wheels, and pivots. Since more connections can be established for the same degree of suddenness, Artoo Detoo is the better metaphor.

In suggesting that the pleasure and power of a metaphor might be related to the number of allusive ties, I do not imply that, to understand and enjoy a metaphor, we must be explicitly aware of each of the ties discovered. But we could identify most of them if we were asked to do so. These ties or attributes, and their packing density, are objective properties of the metaphor and its situational context. A study of these—and perhaps other—objective properties might help to explain certain subjective experiences in creating and understanding metaphors. In principle, this conjecture can be put to the test—at least in the case of metaphors for which a consensus can be reached with respect to the subjective experience. We might be able to agree, for example, that certain metaphors seem more effective than others.

I have no confidence that all of these guesses come close to the truth, but I think that they have enough substance to be arguable and that such argument perhaps can lead us to see how, in the searchlight of Popperian epistemology, one might illuminate at least some aspects of the psychology of metaphors.

Afterthoughts on Metaphor

III

The Many Uses of Metaphor

Karsten Harries

The title of this symposium, "Metaphor: The Conceptual Leap," suggests that when talking about metaphor we agree on what we are talking about. The papers that were read, however, revealed disagreements that invite further discussion. One obstacle to such discussion is the tendency to think of a particular use of metaphor and to base a general theory of metaphor on an examination of that usage. Given that tendency, it may be helpful to postpone for the time being the general question What is metaphor? and to examine instead how metaphor functions in more limited contexts.

In my paper I presented a model that helps to explain a certain kind of poetic metaphor. Limited as my claims are, they are difficult to reconcile with any general theory of metaphor that maintains (1) that metaphor belongs exclusively to the domain of semantics, or (2) that metaphor belongs exclusively to the domain of pragmatics, or (3) that successful metaphors reveal reality and can thus claim to be true. Here I would like to consider briefly each of these difficulties in the hope that this will bring some of the issues raised in the course of this conference into sharper focus.

1

Some metaphorical expressions—such as, "God is love" or "The chairman plowed through the discussion"—are readily translated into other languages. In such cases I should want to agree with Max Black that "the translated sentence is a case of the *very same* metaphor." But we would be misled were we to conclude from such examples that in all cases "to call a sentence an instance of metaphor" is therefore "to say something about its *meaning,* not about its orthography, its phonetic pattern, or its grammatical form."[1] Most poetic metaphors resist translation. The "translation" I offered in my paper of two lines from Karl Krolow's "Liebesgedicht" demonstrates this resistance. If the semantic collisions are obvious, that collusion which gives the poet's metaphors their strength would seem to depend here more on consonance and assonance, on a collusion of sound rather than of meaning. This, however, may be a misleading way of putting the matter: the attempt to separate meaning from the phonetic pattern is discouraged by the way sound intimates sense. For example, it is by their sound that "Taube," "blauen," and "Laubes" evoke the absent "Frau." The poem thus forces us to question whether or to what extent an approach that insists on a sharp separation between sound and meaning can do justice to poetic metaphor.

We do not have to confine ourselves to poetry to challenge the thesis that the success of metaphor depends on meaning rather than sound. Bernard Kaplan has called our attention to the functioning of metaphor in slang. Consider his example: someone is called an AC/DC. Try to translate that metaphor into another language, into German, for example. It falls flat and loses its point, in part because "Wechselstrom" and "Gleichstrom" have a different field of associated connotations and images but more importantly because the German words have a lumbering sound. Once again we are forced to recognize the importance of sound pattern for metaphoric success.

Just as poetic metaphor tends to resist translation, so it also tends to resist paraphrase. Both are incompatible with that incarnation of meaning that is often thought characteristic of poetic discourse. Not that translation should be confused with paraphrase. I may have no difficulty translating a metaphor, for example, "God is love," into some other language, and yet I find myself unable to paraphrase what the metaphor means. The possibility of translation shows that the semantic resources on which the metaphor rests are not tied to a particular language, while the impossibility of finding an adequate paraphrase may show, as Donald Davidson suggests, that there is nothing to paraphrase. Still, I cannot agree with Davidson's more general claim that metaphorical expressions cannot be paraphrased because they do not say something, because they do not make an assertion. Consider once more Kaplan's example: someone is called an AC/DC. Literally understood the claim would have to be considered false or perhaps meaningless. Once the figurative meaning of the term has been understood, however, the ex-

1. Max Black, *Models and Metaphors* (Ithaca, N.Y., 1962), p. 28.

pression is recognized as an assertion that may be true or false. The most obvious way of finding out whether this figurative meaning has in fact been understood is to ask for a more literal paraphrase. There is, thus, nothing questionable about Howard Gardner's and Ellen Winner's decision to use the ability to paraphrase a sentence such as "After many years of working at the jail, the prison guard had become a hard rock that could not be moved" as a test of metaphoric comprehension. We would be misled only if we were to think that all metaphoric comprehension must be of this kind. Here it is important to keep in mind the many ways in which metaphors can function.

In the *Philosophical Investigations* Wittgenstein remarks that "We speak of understanding a sentence in the sense in which it can be replaced by another which says the same; but also in the sense in which it cannot be replaced by any other."[2] In the first case the sense of the sentence presents itself to us as only accidentally bound to the particular words in which it happens to be expressed and to the situation in which these words are used. Focusing on this sort of example, we are likely to insist on a separation of the semantic and phonetic aspects of language. In the second case—and Wittgenstein is thinking of poetry—sense and sound are so essentially intertwined that such separations are impossible without doing violence to what has been said or written. Similarly we have to grant that sometimes the ability to paraphrase is a good test of metaphoric comprehension, while at other times understanding a metaphor entails knowing that a paraphrase cannot be found. In the former case the metaphorical expression presents itself to us as one of several possible ways of saying something; in the latter case we are prevented from separating what has been said from how it was said—the discourse here calls attention to itself, not to some meaning or reality that lies beyond it. We can thus attempt to classify metaphors by locating them on a spectrum that has one extreme in expressions that permit the substitution of some other expression without loss of effectiveness and the other extreme in expressions that rule out such substitution. Such a classification of metaphors allows us to reestablish the distinction between literary and philosophical language that threatens to evaporate as a result of the deconstructive enterprises of Jacques Derrida and Paul de Man. I would grant that metaphors cannot be eliminated from philosophy. The philosopher's dream of a purely univocal speech has to remain a dream. But this is not to say that metaphor has the same function in philosophical and poetic texts. As I point out in my paper, the peculiar "whiteness" of philosophical (and scientific) discourse has its foundation not simply in a forgetting or a concealing of that discourse's metaphoric origins but in a commitment to objectivity, a commitment that demands that we try to

2. Ludwig Wittgenstein, *Philosophical Investigations*, trans. G. E. M. Anscombe (New York, 1953), pp. 143–44.

free ourselves from the limitations of forms of expression that would tie us to a particular perspective. As Wittgenstein observes in the *Philosophische Bemerkungen:* "Every time I say that this or that representation could be replaced with another, we take a further step toward the goal of grasping the essence of what is represented."[3] Such exercises in paraphrase let us recognize what is independent of our way of saying something. They allow us to go beyond the limitations of a particular form of description towards what is essential. The metaphors of philosophy should thus be contingent and questionable. They invite paraphrase and interpretation that has as its goal the recognition that a particular metaphor is dispensable. Poetic metaphor, too, invites interpretation. But here interpretation does not have as its goal the recognition of the metaphor's contingency but rather its necessity. The poet's incarnation of meaning forbids translation and paraphrase. In such cases we may still want to say that metaphor belongs to the domain of semantics but, if so, semantics must not be understood too narrowly. We must acknowledge, for example, the semantic function of sound and word order.

2

Pointing to certain metaphors that depend on no semantic resources beyond those provided by standard usage, Black suggests that there is "a sense of 'metaphor' that belongs to 'pragmatics' rather than to 'semantics' " and adds that "this sense may be the one most deserving of attention."[4] But even if examples supporting this claim are easily provided—Black mentions the expression "logical form"—such examples do not warrant the much more general claim made by Davidson when he introduced his paper, namely that metaphor belongs exclusively to the domain of pragmatics. This is not the place for a thorough examination of the distinction between meaning and use that is here being presupposed, a distinction that both Wittgenstein and Heidegger have taught us to challenge. Here I would only like to question the suggestion that "what distinguishes metaphor is not meaning, but use" by taking a second look at the way metaphor functions in Thomas Campion's "There is a Garden in her face."

In cases such as this the poet's achievement does seem to depend on semantic resources beyond those furnished by ordinary language; here interpretation does indeed involve something very much like decoding a message that yields its secrets only when we recognize that the things to which the poet's words refer us function themselves as signs or figures, giving these words beyond their literal meaning a figurative one. These

3. Wittgenstein, *Philosophische Bemerkungen* (Frankfurt am Main, 1964), p. 51, my translation.
4. Black, p. 30.

figurative meanings are not established by the poet but are presupposed by him and by his audience. Such meanings, part of the poet's material, were thought to be furnished by the figures found in God's two books, in Nature and in Scripture. Countless attempts were made to collect and codify these meanings. As anyone who has worked on medieval, Renaissance, or baroque art or literature knows, Davidson's claim notwithstanding, there are in fact manuals that help us to determine what certain metaphors mean. In cases such as this, the functioning of metaphor presupposes at least two quite distinct semantic domains. Semantic collision on the level of literal sense yields to semantic collusion on a higher level: the different features of "her face" are related not only to familiar flowers and fruits, not only to the heavenly paradise, but to the Virgin. Words gain a figurative meaning because the things they name are themselves figures. Alan of Lille summed up this view of things in the often-repeated lines, "Omnis mundi creatura / Quasi liber et pictura / Nobis est et speculum; / Nostrae vitae, nostrae mortis, / Nostri status, nostrae sortis /Fidele signaculum."[5]

What stands between us and such a view is the characteristically modern and, it seems to me, questionable privilege afforded to univocity, to the simple and literal sense of the text, and to an accordingly strict, or rather narrow, conception of meaning. But any general approach that reduces the meanings of words to what Philip Wheelwright called steno-signs cannot shed much light on texts that presuppose something like the medieval interpretation of the spiritual significance of things, an interpretation that shapes art and literature at least until the eighteenth century. And I would suggest that even if this particular interpretation and codification of the domain of spiritual meaning lie behind us, even if Scripture no longer furnishes us with an authoritative key to the decoding of the hidden meanings of things, these meanings still speak to us and remain active in the words that name them. By their tensions and collisions certain metaphors continue to call us beyond the literal meaning of words and let their figurative meaning become active. There are still thinkers who, like Freud or Bachelard, can help us to decode the figurative significance of things. There still is poetry that forces us to question the claim that metaphor belongs exclusively to the domain of pragmatics and, more fundamentally, the overly restricted theory of meaning on which it rests.

3

Towards the end of his paper Davidson points out that his critique of the claim that metaphor has, besides its literal meaning, a figurative

---

5. "All the world's creatures are like a book, a picture, and a mirror to us, the truthful sign of our life, death, condition, and destiny."

one does not simply urge restraint in using the word "meaning." More is at stake. What is attacked is the view that metaphors are used to communicate a cognitive content. Davidson's critique seems to me to overshoot the mark. As our slang example shows, metaphors can in fact be used to communicate such a content. Davidson's claim becomes more plausible when it is restricted to literature or perhaps just to poetry. Do poetry's metaphors communicate a cognitive content that would permit us to speak of "truth"? An affirmative answer to this question is given by Paul Ricoeur who ascribes an ontological function to metaphor. In his paper he thus insists that the metaphorical language of the poet "is no less *about* reality than any other use of language but refers to it by the means of a complex strategy which implies, as an essential component, a suspension and seemingly an abolition of the ordinary reference attached to descriptive language."[6]

How incompatible are Davidson's and Ricoeur's claims? One might understand Davidson's paper not only as a plea for restraint in using the word "meaning" but also as a plea for restraint in using expressions like "cognitive content" or "truth." Davidson grants that metaphors can provide something like a lattice or lens that lets us see things in a new and perhaps illuminating manner, that they can lead us to thoughts that may be true or false. In his view, too, it is thus possible to speak of "metaphorical truth." Still, there is a difference between providing a lattice or lens that allows us to perceive something better or at least differently and making an assertion about what is being perceived. What sense does it make to call the former true or false? How is "truth" being used in that case?

Ricoeur's use of "truth" can be traced back to Heidegger. In *Being and Time* Heidegger draws a distinction between the truth of propositions and what he considers a more original sense of truth. Propositions present something *as* something. Such presentation presupposes an already established and usually taken-for-granted domain of meaning. To present something *as* something, we can say, is to locate it in a semantic space. This space determines a manner in which things present themselves to us; it constitutes what Heidegger calls the being of these things, and it is important to keep in mind that "being" here does not refer to existence but to the way existent things can become present. All descriptions of things presuppose a disclosure of their being. It is here that we have to locate the primary sense of truth.

It is this truth that poetry serves, in Heidegger's interpretation. To claim truth for poetry is to say that poetry discloses a semantic space; given the tendency to understand "semantic" rather narrowly, however, it may be less misleading to say with Heidegger or Ricoeur that poetry

6. See Paul Ricoeur, "The Metaphorical Process as Cognition, Imagination, and Feeling," p. 151.

establishes or helps to establish a world, provided that "world" is understood to refer not to the totality of what is but to a domain of meaning. To speak with Wittgenstein, poetry—and the same can be true of slang—lets us look at things in a new way. I agree with Ricoeur when he places metaphor at the center of this process and calls attention to the essential contribution made by imagination and feeling in effecting such a change. I would only suggest that not all metaphor, not even all poetic metaphor, has this function. Thus the metaphors of collision that I discuss in my paper do not bring about semantic change; no "new semantic congruence or pertinence emerges from the ruins of the literal sense shattered by semantic incompatibility or absurdity." There are metaphors that direct us away from reality towards the aesthetic object; in such instances semantic collision weakens or breaks the referential function of language and, supported by phonetic collusion, lets us become absorbed only in the poem.

Ricoeur is of course aware of this; and he could deal with my objection as he deals with Roman Jakobson's attempt to oppose the poetic and the referential functions of language. My contention, he might say, is "not false but gives an incomplete picture of the whole process of reference in poetic discourse." Indeed, in my paper, I was forced to admit that the poet's attempt to escape from the referentiality of language finally cannot succeed. The attempt to use metaphor to establish the poem as an autonomous aesthetic object must fail, and this failure can open us to the mysterious presence of the things to which the poem obliquely refers. Nor should this reversal, which endows the aesthetic project with an ontological significance, surprise us. As members of a community we are caught up in already-established and taken-for-granted language games. We speak as one speaks, think as one thinks, see as one sees. The adequacy of words is taken for granted. Reality and language are so intimately joined that the rift that separates the two—recognition of this rift is preserved by such metaphors as "lattice" or "lens"—is covered up. Semantic collision helps to dissolve this too intimate union. As language gains a certain autonomy we are forced to recognize the usually forgotten distance that separates words and things. There is poetry that does little more than recall us to an awareness of this distance. The revelatory power of such poetry does not lie in the fact that it gives us more complete descriptions of things. That it obviously does not do. Nor does it transform our semantic space. Its power lies rather in its ability to reveal the usually-passed-over inadequacy of language, of the lattices and lenses through which we see things. Revealing this inadequacy, it reestablishes the rift between words and things, the conflict between language and what transcends it as its ground and measure.

Even when we confine ourselves to poetry, we have to agree with Ortega y Gasset's observation that "the instrument of metaphoric expression can be used for many diverse purposes." It can be used to embellish or ennoble things or persons—Campion's poem offers a good example. Such embellishment need not involve semantic innovation. Metaphors can also function as weapons turned against reality. There are metaphors that negate the referential function of language so successfully that talk about truth or, for that matter, about lattices or lenses seems inappropriate. Yet as poetry pushes towards this extreme, it may acquire a revelatory power all its own: from the ruins of literal sense emerges not a new semantic congruence but a silence that is heard as the language of transcendence. This is not to deny that metaphors can effect semantic change or help to establish a new world. As David Tracy's contribution to this symposium shows, Scripture furnishes the most obvious example. Heidegger's claim that poetry establishes the world can indeed be shown to rest on this paradigm. It is a claim that tends to ascribe something of the prophetic power of Scripture to all great poetry. But, although we may long to rediscover the prophet in the poet, to what extent does the scriptural paradigm help to illuminate poetry in general and, more especially, the poetry of this godless age? Most modern poetry has an aesthetic character that is incompatible with a religious world view. Theories of poetic metaphor cannot afford to neglect the history of poetry, just as general theories of metaphor cannot afford to neglect the many uses of metaphor.

Afterthoughts on Metaphor

IV

Ten Literal "Theses"

Wayne C. Booth

Because my paper was often metaphorical, some participants in the symposium expressed puzzlement about my literal meaning, especially about the passage from Mailer. Here are ten literal "theses" that the paper either argues for, implies, or depends on.

1. What metaphor *is* can never be determined with a single answer. Because the word has now become subject to all of the ambiguities of our notions about similarity and difference, the irreducible plurality of philosophical views of how similarities and differences relate will always produce conflicting definitions that will in turn produce different borderlines between what is metaphor and what is not. We thus need taxonomies, not frozen single definitions, of this "essentially contested concept."

2. What any metaphor *says* or *means* or *does* will always be to some degree alterable by altering its context. Every metaphor cited in any of the symposium papers could be made to communicate various shades of meaning; each of them could even be made, by employing the easy turns of irony, to say the reverse of what it seems to say.

3. Whether or not such transformations occur, the receiver's process of interpretation is itself part of what is communicated; the activity of interpretation, performed at the speaker's command, produces a "bonding" which is part of the "meaning." Thus the act of interpreting metaphor will always be more intense ("other things being equal") than engagement with whatever we take to be non-metaphoric (for some, what is *literal;* for others, what is *normal*).

173

4. The question of what a metaphor *means* is thus actually many different questions. If by "meaning" we mean "all that is effected by an utterance," or "all that is communicated by a speaker," then the meaning of most metaphors is far richer than most accounts have acknowledged, even those that claim that metaphoric meanings are mysterious or ineffable. (Note the radical difference between this notion of meaning and say, Donald Davidson's.)

5. It follows that whether any metaphor is judged to be *good* is inescapably dependent on its context: what surrounds it in the text, spoken or written, and who speaks it to whom for what purpose. But "context" is another essentially contested concept: different critical purposes will discover and impose different contexts.

6. For those who agree upon a given purpose in a given social context, judgments of value can be simple, unambiguous, and as nearly certain as anyone could reasonably ask in this vale of uncertainties. (See "catfish" above.)

7. Even such judgments are not, however, simple judgments of craft in any usual sense because the deliberate use of a recognizable metaphor (a special case of the deliberate use of any abnormality, any figuring) inevitably invites judgments of the speaker's character. No jury member can resist engagement with the character of the metaphorist. Any critic can carry the engagement to further levels of judgment by making explicit what a given metaphor implies about its maker.

8. Thus judgments of skill are always complicated, or complicatable, with questions of intent, and judgments of intent entail judgments of characters working in the cultures that both produce and are produced by them. Most of the metaphors we care about are, like Mailer's, immensely complicated, and they are embedded in contexts that force us to think about questions that go beyond matters of "craft."

9. The resources available to the critic who would judge characters and cultures are far richer than is suggested by our usual notions of "literary criticism." The best criticism of Mailer might well be another history of the same events, a history laden with alternative metaphors; or it might be a philosophical inquiry, or a religious tract, or an epic poem.

10. A good measure of our culture would be our capacity to produce such criticism, that is, to create metaphoric visions that would rival and improve on Mailer's inventive, courageous, but finally self-defeating blast.

Afterthoughts on Metaphor

V

Metaphor as Moonlighting

Nelson Goodman

1.—The present symposium is evidence of a growing sense that metaphor is both important and odd—its importance odd and its oddity important—and that its place in a general theory of language and knowledge needs study.

Metaphorical use of language differs in significant ways from literal use but is no less comprehensible, no more recondite, no less practical, and no more independent of truth and falsity than is literal use. Far from being a mere matter of ornament, it participates fully in the progress of knowledge: in replacing some stale "natural" kinds with novel and illuminating categories, in contriving facts, in revising theory, and in bringing us new worlds. The oddity is that metaphorical truth is compatible with literal falsity;[1] a sentence false when taken literally may be true when taken metaphorically, as in the case of "The joint is jumping" or "The lake is a sapphire".

The oddity vanishes upon recognition that a metaphorical application of a term is normally quite different from the literal application. Applied literally, the noun "sapphire" sorts out various things including a certain gem but no lake; applied metaphorically (in the way here in question) it sorts out various things including a certain lake but no gem. "The lake is a sapphire" is thus literally false but metaphorically true,

---

1. "Metaphorical truth" does not mean that the truth of the sentence is metaphorical but that the sentence taken metaphorically is true. The same sort of ellipsis is to be understood in many like locutions. Furthermore, in what follows I have usually avoided the confusing word "meaning"; and for readers not familiar with philosophical terminology, I have ordinarily written "application" rather than "extension" for the collection of things denoted by a word or other label. I have also often kept clear of an ambiguity of "use" by writing either "application" or "function" as the case may be.

while "Muddy Pond is a sapphire" is both literally and metaphorically false. Metaphorical truth and falsity are as distinct from—and as opposite to—each other as are literal truth and falsity. And "The lake is a sapphire" is metaphorically true if and only if "The lake is metaphorically a sapphire" is literally true.

Obviously, metaphor and ambiguity are closely akin in that ambiguous terms likewise have two or more different applications. But metaphor differs from ambiguity in that a literal application precedes and influences a correlative metaphorical application. Words often have many different metaphorical as well as many different literal applications. In an ironic metaphorical use, "Muddy Pond is a sapphire" is true while "The lake is a sapphire" is false. The two metaphorical applications here derive in different ways from the literal application of "sapphire" to gems.

2.—Donald Davidson[2] disputes this straightforward account, denying that a term may have a metaphorical application different from its literal one, and scorning the notions of metaphorical truth and falsity. A sentence is true or false, he maintains, only as taken literally; to take a literally false sentence metaphorically is not to take it as saying something else that may be true, but merely to bring out certain suggestions of that false sentence, to invite comparisons or evoke thoughts or feelings. What can be said for this position?

The acknowledged difficulty and even impossibility of finding a literal paraphrase for most metaphors is offered by Davidson as evidence that there is nothing to be paraphrased—that a sentence says nothing metaphorically that it does not say literally, but rather functions differently, inviting comparisons and stimulating thought. But paraphrase of many literal sentences also is exceedingly difficult, and indeed we may seriously question whether any sentence can be translated exactly into other words in the same or any other language. Let's agree, though, that literal paraphrase of metaphor is on the whole especially hard. That is easily understood since the metaphorical application of terms has the effect, and usually the purpose, of drawing significant boundaries that cut across ruts worn by habit, of picking out new relevant kinds for which we have no simple and familiar literal descriptions.

2. In "What Metaphors Mean", pp. 29–45 in this volume.

Nelson Goodman, emeritus professor of philosophy at Harvard University, has written *The Structure of Appearance; Fact, Fiction, and Forecast; Languages of Art: An Approach to a Theory of Symbols; Problems and Projects,* and, most recently, *Ways of Worldmaking.*

We must note in passing, though, that the metaphorical application may nevertheless be quite clear. For just as inability to define "desk" is compatible with knowing which articles are desks, so inability to paraphrase a metaphorical term is compatible with knowing what it applies to. And as I have remarked elsewhere,[3] whether a man is metaphorically a Don Quixote or a Don Juan is perhaps even easier to decide than whether he is literally a schizoid or a paranoiac.

In a second argument, Davidson considers the example of a term, "burned up", that after being used metaphorically later loses its metaphorical force through overuse. His argument runs somewhat as follows: "burned up" does not change its application when it ceases to be metaphorical; what is lost is the way it functions in inviting comparisons between angry people and things consumed by flame; and this shows that metaphor is a matter of function rather than of application. Now I agree that when a metaphor wilts, it no longer instigates such comparison—comparison, I would say, between two different applications of the term. But Davidson's argument seems at odds with his thesis that the metaphorical and literal applications of a term cannot be different. For if when "burned up" becomes a literal term for angry people, it has the same application as when metaphorical, then its metaphorical application must have been different from its other (original) literal application to things consumed by flame. When "burned up" retires as a metaphor, it becomes ambiguous; one literal application no longer suggests or is influenced by the other, but neither one is newly established.

Incidentally, if "burned up" retains its metaphorical application when its metaphorical force vanishes and is, as Davidson claims, in that application coextensive with "angry", we may well ask: Why, then, is there any difficulty about paraphrasing "burned up" when metaphorical by "angry"? I think that "burned up" was an effective metaphor in being not quite coextensive with "angry"; that, for example, "burned up" and "come to a boil" did not apply metaphorically in exactly the same cases; and that for a while after the metaphor fades, the second literal application of "burned up" still departs somewhat from that of "angry". Of course, as with words in general, such differences tend to rub off with frequent careless use.

Davidson, in a further argument, cites T. S. Eliot's "The Hippopotamus" to show that a nonmetaphorical text can invite comparison as pointedly as does a metaphor. That seems obvious enough also from simpler examples. The nonmetaphorical sentences "Compare the True Church with the hippopotamus" and "The True Church has important

3. In "Stories upon Stories; or Reality in Tiers", delivered at the conference Levels of Reality in Florence, Italy, September 1978.

features in common with the hippopotamus" are quite as explicit invitations as the metaphorical "The True Church is a hippopotamus"; and in general, metaphorical and nonmetaphorical sentences alike can be put to such uses as inviting, warning, shocking, enticing, misleading, inquiring, informing, persuading, etc. Plainly, then, no such function is peculiar to metaphor, and metaphor cannot be defined in terms of the performance of, or the capacity to perform, any such function. Davidson's argument here seems a conclusive refutation of his own thesis.

Metaphor in my view involves withdrawing a term or rather a schema of terms from an initial literal application and applying it in a new way to effect a new sorting either of the same or of a different realm. Davidson's denial that the metaphorical and literal applications of a term can be distinct and that a statement false when taken literally may be true when taken metaphorically seems to me to constitute a fundamental confusion about metaphor.

3.—As Ted Cohen has often stressed,[4] and as I illustrated in *Languages of Art*[5] by the case of a picture that is both metaphorically and literally blue, a metaphorical truth is not always a literal falsehood. Wherein then, Cohen asks in effect, lies the metaphorical character of the literally true "No man is an island"? Quite clearly, the metaphorical reading is different from the literal one: in the metaphorical reading, a schema of terms that taken literally sort geographical units is applied to sorting organisms, with the result that no men fall under "island". "No man is an island" is metaphorical insofar as it implicitly continues "; rather, every man is part of a mainland". Likewise "No lake is a ruby" is as metaphorical as "That lake is a sapphire"; for in both cases a schema of terms for sorting jewels is being applied to bodies of water.

Furthermore, as shown by our doubly blue picture, a literal extension of a term and a correlative metaphorical extension need not be altogether separate; they may, though different, have items in common. Although "blue" applies both literally and metaphorically to the picture in question, many other things that are either literally or metaphorically blue in this way are not both.

But what if all and only things literally blue were also metaphorically blue? Still the distinction between literal and metaphorical use, in the face of extensional equivalence, will not require resort to nonextensional "meanings" or "senses". Difference in meaning between two extensionally equivalent terms amounts to difference between their secondary extensions—that is, the extensions of parallel compounds of those terms.

4. E.g., "Notes on Metaphor", *Journal of Aesthetics and Art Criticism* 34 (1976): 358–59.

5. *Languages of Art,* 2d ed. (Indianapolis, 1976), p. 83. However, in some other passages in that book, I have not taken this sufficiently into account. For further interesting discussion of this and related matters, see Israel Scheffler's forthcoming *Beyond the Letter* (London, 1979).

For example, although all and only unicorns are centaurs, not all and only (or indeed many) unicorn pictures are centaur pictures; and although all and only featherless bipeds are laughing animals, not all and only featherless-biped descriptions are laughing-animal descriptions. Likewise, when a literal and a correlative metaphorical use coincide extensionally, the significant difference is between secondary extensions: the literally-blue descriptions (descriptions as literally blue) are not all and only the metaphorically-blue descriptions (descriptions as metaphorically blue).[6]

Ordinarily, I have said, a term effects a literal sorting that upon metaphorical transfer is reflected in a new sorting. But where a term with a null literal extension—a term such as "unicorn" that does not apply literally to anything—is applied metaphorically, the new sorting cannot of course thus reflect any literal sorting by that term. Here again, secondary extensions are involved. The metaphorical sorting reflects, rather, the literal sorting of descriptions that is effected by such a compound of the term as "literally-unicorn description (or picture)".

A different and curious case was inadvertently introduced in the course of a recent paper of mine on another topic.[7] I suggested that Sir Agilulf, the hero of Italo Calvino's novel *The Nonexistent Knight,* is, among other things, a metaphor for "the real world": as the mythical knight existed only in and as some sort of armor, the chimerical one-real-world exists only in various versions. But how can a literally null term have a different, metaphorical application that is also null, since there is at most one null extension? The answer is that there are many null labels—that is labels with null extension—and that the compound term "Sir Agilulf description", taken literally, sorts out certain from other null labels. This sorting is reflected in the sorting of one-real-world descriptions from other null labels when we take "Sir Agilulf" to be a metaphor for the nonexistent one-real-world.

4.—Such special cases, though, must not leave the impression that metaphor is a mere literary luxury, a rare or esoteric or purely decorative device. By so putting old words to new work, we save enormously on vocabulary and take advantage of established habits in the process of transcending them. Metaphor permeates nearly all discourse; thoroughly literal paragraphs without fresh or frozen metaphors are

6. On the notion of secondary extensions and parallel compounds, see my "On Likeness of Meaning" and "Some Differences about Meaning" in *Problems and Projects* (Indianapolis, 1976), pp. 221–38; see also pp. 204–6. As Israel Scheffler has pointed out to me, I assume here that the modifiers "literally" and "metaphorically" are incorporated in the original terms; otherwise, an intermediate step is needed. Incidentally, were "literally blue" and "metaphorically blue" coextensive, there might also be this further difference: that the sorting of pictures by feeling under color terms might still differ from the literal sorting under these terms in what falls under some term other than "blue".

7. See n. 3 above.

hard to find in even the least literary texts. In terms of multiple application of words—and other symbols—and of schemata consisting of them, we can understand how various figures of speech are related to each other and to literal discourse, and also how metaphor constitutes so economical, practical, and creative a way of using symbols.[8]

In metaphor, symbols moonlight.

8. On the ways, metaphorical and otherwise, of making worlds, see my *Ways of Worldmaking* (Indianapolis, 1978).

Afterthoughts on Metaphor

VI

How Metaphors Work: A Reply to Donald Davidson

Max Black

1.—Perplexities about metaphors.[1] To be able to produce and understand metaphorical statements is nothing much to boast about: these familiar skills, which children seem to acquire as they learn to talk, are perhaps no more remarkable than our ability to tell and to understand jokes. How odd then that it remains difficult to explain what we do (and should do) in grasping metaphorical statements. In a provocative paper, "What Metaphors Mean,"[2] Donald Davidson has recently charged many students of metaphor, ancient and modern, with having committed a "central mistake." According to him, there is "error and confusion" in claiming "that a metaphor has, in addition to its literal sense or meaning, another sense or meaning." The guilty include "literary critics like Richards, Empson, and Winters; philosophers from Aristotle to Max Black; psychologists from Freud and earlier to Skinner and later; and linguists from Plato to Uriel Weinreich and George Lakoff." Good company, if somewhat mixed. The error to be extirpated is the "idea that a metaphor has a special meaning" (p. 30).

If Davidson is right, much that has been written about metaphor might well be consigned to the flames. Even if he proves to be wrong, his animadversions should provoke further consideration of the still problematic modus operandi of metaphor.

2.—The commonsense of metaphors. Before addressing Davidson's main

---

1. I shall use "metaphor" throughout this paper as a concise way of referring to metaphorical *statements.*
2. Donald Davidson, "What Metaphors Mean," pp. 29–45 in this volume. All further references in text.

contentions, I shall list some assertions, all of which I believe to be true, about a paradigmatic instance of metaphorical statement. It will be convenient to use the remark (R) with which Davidson opens his paper: "Metaphor is the dreamwork of language."[3]

I believe that all of the following assertions are true of R and that corresponding assertions would apply to many other metaphorical statements.

1   The *thought* that metaphor is the dreamwork of language (that R, for short) might have occurred to Davidson, and probably did, before he committed it to paper.[4]

1.1   If this happened, Davidson *affirmed* that R and he did not merely entertain the thought or use R as an example of metaphor.[5]

1.2   Thereby he expressed a distinctive *view* of metaphor, his topic.[6]

1.21   Davidson had won some new *insight* into what metaphor is.

2   When he wrote out R at the start of his paper, he was *making* that remark—and not quoting the sentence or, as some logicians say, "mentioning" it.[7]

---

3. The full sentence is: "Metaphor is the dreamwork of language and, like all dreamwork, its interpretation reflects as much on the interpreter as on the originator" (p. 29). I shall use "R" sometimes to refer to Davidson's *remark*, sometimes to refer to the *sentence* he used.

4. This rather obvious point deserves emphasis, since most students of metaphor overemphasize the quasi-performative aspects of metaphorical utterance. The uses of metaphorical statements are not confined to the role they play in communication with others. R, unlike such a clear performative as "I promise . . . ," makes sense in private thought. It would seem to me farfetched to regard such private utterance as a degenerate case of communication, like a chessplayer "playing with himself."

5. Alternatively, one might say that he *committed* himself to R. I use "affirmed" here in a sense sufficiently broad to permit a command or a question to be affirmed, in order not to beg the question whether somebody affirming a metaphor can be making truth-claims.

6. Probably most of those who agree would find it hard to spell out what having a view amounts to.

7. We lack a convenient label for such straightforward, primary uses of language.

Max Black is Susan Linn Sage professor of philosophy and humane letters emeritus at Cornell University and senior member of the Cornell program on science, technology, and society. His many influential works include *Models and Metaphors, A Companion to Wittgenstein's Tractatus,* and, most recently, *Caveats and Critiques.*

2.1   In so doing, he was writing *in earnest,* not joking or pretending or playacting.

2.11   He *meant* what he wrote.[8]

2.2   In making the remark he was *saying* something, not merely doing something else such as nudging his reader to find similarities between metaphors and dreamwork.[9]

2.3   A reader could understand or misunderstand Davidson's remark.[10]

3   In Davidson's use of *R,* the word "dreamwork" was being used metaphorically, and the remaining words literally.[11]

3.1   Davidson was not using *R* as he would have done had he intended *R* to be taken literally.[12]

4   In making the remark, *R,* Davidson chose words precisely appropriate to his intention.[13]

4.1   He said and intended to say that metaphor *is* the dreamwork of language.

4.11   Davidson would not have been satisfied to say instead that metaphor is *like* linguistic dreamwork; or that the one can be *compared* to the other; or that in metaphorizing[14] we are regarding one thing *as if* it were another.

    8. Or: *intended* that he should be taken as speaking in *propria persona,* straightforwardly (4.1) and seriously.

    9. I intend "saying" here to mean much the same as J. L. Austin's "constating," i.e., the presenting of claims that might be disputed (see 6 and 6.1). We shall see that Davidson emphatically disagrees with 2.2.

    10. Of course, a promise or a bet can be misunderstood, so accepting 2.3 need not commit one to accepting 2.2.

    11. I call these the *focus* and the *frame* of the sentence respectively. See "Metaphor," chap. 3 of my *Models and Metaphors* (Ithaca, N.Y., 1962), p. 28. See also my "More about Metaphor," *Dialectica* 31 (1977): 431–57.

    12. If only because *R,* taken literally, is plainly false, as Davidson points out in similar cases.

    13. I am assuming that Davidson, like other careful writers, would not say "Metaphor *is* dreamwork" unless he intended to say just that and not something else. In the propositions 4 and 4.11, I am urging that the categorical use of the copula in a metaphor of the form "A *is* B" serves a distinctive purpose (though, to be sure, a somewhat obscure one). Thus I regard 4.11 as an important weapon against theorists who wish to reduce metaphor to simile or comparison.

    14. I shall use this word to refer both to the production of metaphorical statement (whether in thought, speech, or writing) and also to the comprehension of another person's metaphor.

5   In affirming *R*, Davidson was implying and intimating various un-
     stated remarks.[15]

5.1 He was implying, but not explicitly saying, that metaphor and
     dreamwork have some similar or analogous properties.[16]

5.2 He was using "dreamwork" to *allude* to certain Freudian doc-
     trines.[17]

5.3 Davidson was *suggesting* various unstated contentions, left to the
     reader to develop at discretion, for example, that a metaphor has a
     latent as well as a manifest content.

5.4 He might reasonably be taken to be suggesting also various *evalua-
     tions* of metaphor consonant with the parallel Freudian doctrines
     about dreams.

6   A reader could *disagree* with Davidson's remark (e.g., by objecting
     that the underlying analogy was "too thin"—or by saying
     "Metaphor is sometimes *waking* work").[18]

6.1 Reasons could be offered for and against *R*.[19]

7   *R,* or any other metaphorical remark, might be criticized as inept,
     misleading, obscure, unilluminating, and so forth.[20]

7.1 A metaphorical statement, such as *R*, can fail or succeed.[21]

     Summary: A metaphorical statement, such as *R*, can be affirmed (1.1)
in private thought (1) and hence need not be addressed to another
person. In either case the statement expresses a view of its topic (1.2) and
some putative insight (1.21). When a statement is seriously communi-

     15. It would be arbitrary to restrict a metaphor's content to what is *explicitly* expressed
by it. I take the metaphor's author to be committed (4.11) to its implications.
     16. It is tempting to say that *R* implies that metaphor is *like* dreamwork. But the latter
assertion implies that metaphor is *not* dreamwork! Only different things can be sensibly
compared.
     17. Here and in 5.3 I am trying to acknowledge, however inadequately, the aspects of
a metaphor's working that cannot plausibly be subsumed under implicit "*saying.*"
     18. Thus using one metaphor to oppose another, as can sometimes happen.
     19. The truth of this and the preceding assertion, 6, supports my own view that
metaphors can imply truth-claims (see 2.2).
     20. I shall not discuss here the vexed question whether metaphors can be true or false.
     21. Anybody inclined to agree with Davidson that "there are no unsuccessful
metaphors" (p. 29) might be asked to consider Hegel's metaphor of the solar system as a
syllogism whose three terms are the sun, the planets, and the comets (from Julien Benda,
Du style d'idées [Paris, 1948], p. 143).

cated (2, 2.1), its user, if expressing himself precisely, means just what he says or writes (2.11). The author of a metaphor *says* something (2.2), although he will also typically be alluding to (5.1), suggesting (5.3), and evaluating (5.4) other things. When a statement is metaphorical, the sentence used, part only of which consists of a word or words used metaphorically (3), is not intended to be taken literally (3.1). In appropriate and precise formulation, a metaphorical statement cannot be replaced by literal statements of resemblance or comparison, or by allied *as-if* statements (4.11, 2.2), but will usually imply these and other unstated implications (5, 5.1). Metaphors can be understood or misunderstood (2.3) and can be rejected or endorsed (6.1). Metaphorizing may fail or succeed (7.1).

In thus setting out the commonsense of the production and understanding of metaphorical remarks, I have abstained from using the verb "to mean" except in one instance (2.11) where it can be replaced. Yet, it would be natural to add further comments about what Davidson *meant* by his metaphorical remark and what he would properly be taken by a competent reader as intending to mean. At a pretheoretical commonsensical level, one would suppose that Davidson could hardly have thought R (1) without meaning something by the words that occurred to him, and it is hard to understand how he could have affirmed R (1.1) unless he meant something by that remark (2.11). Nor could he have acquired insight into the nature of metaphor (1.2 and 1.21) otherwise. I have also claimed that he was *saying* various things, many of them implicitly (2.2, 4.1, 5, and 5.1).

The propositions I have formulated concerning a reader's ability to disagree with R (6) and to offer reasons for such disagreement (6.1) further strengthen the case for thinking that the producer of a metaphor such as R is usually making some *assertions*. Davidson denies this. But it is time to see precisely what he is claiming.

3.—Davidson's contentions. A careful reading of Davidson's essay will show that he is concerned to argue three main propositions, the first two of which reject a crucial part of what I have called the "commonsense" of metaphor, while the third states his own position.

(*A*) The producer of a metaphorical statement says nothing more than what is meant when the sentence he uses is taken literally.

(*B*) The sentence used in making a metaphorical statement has in context nothing more than its literal meaning.[22]

22. I have expressed these propositions in my own words. Davidson's most explicit statement of his own view is: "a metaphor doesn't say anything beyond its literal meaning (nor does its maker say anything, in using the metaphor, beyond the literal)" (p. 30). Also: "Metaphor runs on the same familiar linguistic tracks that the plainest sentences do" (p. 41).

(C) A metaphor producer is drawing attention to a resemblance between two or more things.[23]

4.—Some comments on these contentions. On (A): Davidson uses "says" throughout in a more restricted way than would fit my own usage of "affirmed" (for which see n. 6). He would of course not deny that a metaphor producer "says," or perhaps even "affirms," something in the weak sense of uttering the words in question seriously. What he does emphatically wish to deny is that in such utterances any *truth-claims* are made. Sometimes he makes this point by denying that a metaphorical statement has "a specific cognitive content," one that "its author wishes to convey and that the interpreter must grasp if he is to get the message" (p. 44). Anyone who "attempts to state the message, is then fundamentally confused . . . because no such message exists" (p. 45). If such a message were "said" or asserted by the author, his words would have to be taken as "standing for, or expressing, [some alleged] fact" (p. 44). If we are led by a metaphor to appreciate some fact, as may happen, that is because the metaphor works like "a picture or a bump on the head." In Davidson's usage, then, to "say" something metaphorically would be to express some supposed *fact* or facts; the theory that a metaphor ever does so is just "false" (p. 44).

One might suppose that since Davidson regards the sentence used in a metaphorical statement as preserving its ordinary literal meaning, he might take its user to be asserting at least one supposed fact—in our prime example, the alleged fact that metaphor is literally dreamwork. But of course there is no such fact, as Davidson himself emphasizes, "For a metaphor *says* only what shows on its face—usually a patent falsehood or an absurd truth . . . given in the literal meaning of the words" (p. 41): what metaphorical statements, taken literally, assert is nearly always plainly false and absurd. Thus, (A) should be understood to mean that a metaphor producer is "saying" *nothing at all*. What, then, is a metaphor producer doing? We shall see when we come to examine (C).

On (B): Davidson devotes much of his paper to attacking the view,

23. "A metaphor makes us attend to some likeness, often a novel or surprising likeness, between two or more things" (p. 31). Davidson also says, more picturesquely, that a metaphor "nudges us into noting" a likeness which it "intimates" (p. 36); it "invites" us to make comparisons (p. 38); a metaphor "inspires or prompts [an] insight" (p. 45). I suppose it is the metaphor maker who literally invites, prompts, provokes, or nudges the receiver. "A simile tells us, in part, what a metaphor merely nudges us into noting" (p. 36). As for what a simile tells us, "In the case of simile, we note what it literally says, that two things resemble one another; we then regard the objects and consider what similarity would, in the context, be to the point" (p. 38). Davidson here, and throughout, apparently overlooks the fact that a simile can be *figurative*. Thinking of a similarity as a literal statement of mutual resemblance between two things will fail to explain why many similes are not immediately reversible. In ordinary usage, "An atom is like a solar system" does not always imply that "A solar system is like an atom."

supposedly held by contemporary theorists, that some of the words used in a metaphorical remark change their senses when so used. He says that the "central mistake" is "the idea that a metaphor has, in addition to its literal sense or meaning, another sense or meaning" (p. 30). He denies vigorously that in the metaphor "the Spirit of God moved upon the face of the waters" it is proper to "regard the word 'face' as having *an extended meaning*" (p. 32, my italics). He thinks that "according to [the current and erroneous] theory a word has a *new meaning* in a metaphorical context" (p. 35, my italics) and adds, provokingly, "the occasion of the metaphor would, therefore, be the occasion for learning the new meaning." In comparing and contrasting metaphors and lies, he claims that "the difference . . . is not a difference in the words used or what they mean (*in any strict sense of meaning*) but in how the words are used" (p. 41, my italics).[24]

Much of this vigorous polemic is beside the point. I know of no theorist who claims that the words used in metaphorical remarks thereby acquire some new meaning in what Davidson calls, as we have seen, the "only strict sense of meaning."[25] I would guess that the strict sense he has in mind is the "Literal meaning . . . [that] can be assigned to words and sentences apart from particular contexts of use" (p. 31). Well, certainly, when Wallace Stevens called a poem a pheasant, he was not permanently changing the standard dictionary sense of "pheasant," a feat almost never accomplished by a single use of a familiar word. One may indeed agree with Davidson that awareness of the "ordinary [literal] meaning"[26] is necessary if the metaphor is to be recognized and understood.

The question to be considered, then, is not the idle one of whether the words used in a metaphorical remark astonishingly acquire some permanently new sense but rather the question whether the metaphor maker is *attaching* an altered sense to the words he is using in context.

24. Davidson does, however, agree with Paul Henle, Nelson Goodman, "and the rest in their accounts of what metaphor accomplishes, except that I think it accomplishes more and that what is additional is different in kind [from meaning anything or saying anything]" (p. 31). I shall examine what Davidson thinks a metaphor "accomplishes" in my comments on proposition (*C*) below. He is, by the way, mistaken in saddling the writers under attack with thinking of "metaphor as primarily a vehicle for conveying ideas, even if unusual ones" (p. 30). Aristotle et al. can answer for themselves; but no moderately attentive reader of my own writings on metaphor could suppose that I ever maintained that metaphorical statements are *primarily* used "for conveying ideas." I have argued merely that such statements can and usually do have a "cognitive content," or do "carry a message," by virtue of implying assertions with truth-value. Like all of Davidson's opponents, I have stressed that much more than the expression of propositional truth is at work in metaphorical discourse.

25. Webster gives four main senses of "mean"; I wonder how many of these Davidson would regard as "strict"? Alas for Ogden and Richards' efforts to display the endemic ambiguities of the word.

26. "The ordinary meaning [of a metaphor] in the context of use is odd enough to prompt us to disregard the question of literal truth" (p. 40).

Did Stevens mean by "pheasant" something having a tail and able to fly, thereby committing himself to the absurd idea that a poem literally *is* a bird? Or was he rather using his remark to *say* something about poetry (the question addressed in proposition (*B*) above)?

The use of a sentence having a familiar standard sense or meaning in order to say something unusual is too familiar to arouse perplexity. When a chess master says, while watching a match, "No pie from that flour"—or rather makes the corresponding Russian remark[27]—what he means could be of no interest to a baker. So, *pace* Davidson, I see no reason on general grounds to be suspicious of the claim that metaphor makers are indeed saying various things, without thereby inducing any permanent change in the standard meaning of the words used metaphorically.

On (*C*): A sympathetic interpretation of Davidson's positive conception of how metaphors work would be to regard him as supporting the view, advanced by some other writers,[28] that anybody making a metaphorical remark is performing a distinctive speech-act, whose force could be more perspicuously expressed by some such formula as "I (hereby) draw your attention to a likeness between (say) metaphor and dreamwork." I think he might accept this, or something like this, given his reiterated emphasis on how a metaphor producer is *using* words to "nudge," "intimate," "provoke," and so on rather than to say anything. To be sure, Davidson's many remarks about the *effects* of a metaphor (acting like "a bump on the head") might suggest that he is more interested in what Austin would have called the perlocutionary effects of metaphorical discourse than in any postulated illocutionary force of metaphorical utterance. Either way, there are serious objections.

1. On the speech-act approach, it is hard to make sense of what happens when somebody expresses a thought *to himself* (see proposition 1 in my list of commonsensical truths about metaphor, above). Any clear cases of speech-acts that come readily to mind involve communication with an audience: it makes little sense to think of promising *oneself* something, or warning, advising, pronouncing judgment, and so on, to oneself. What then, on Davidson's view is a soliloquizing thinker, using metaphorical language, supposed to be doing? Nudging and provoking himself to pay attention to some covert likeness? But surely he has already done so? What then is the point of saying to himself that metaphor *is* dreamwork? Is he perhaps pretending to talk to himself, as if he had

27. "No pie from that flour!" (nothing will come of it) was Tal's comment after the fourth game of the Karpov-Korchnoi match in Baguio apropos of Karpov's use of a dubious opening variation (*Chess Life and Review*, January 1979, p. 44).

28. See, for instance, Dorothy Mack, "Metaphoring as Speech Act," *Poetics* 4 (1975): 211–56; and Ina Loewenberg, "Identifying Metaphors," *Foundations of Language* 12 (1975): 315–38. Ted Cohen's "Metaphor and the Cultivation of Intimacy," pp. 1–10 in this volume, might also be read as sympathetic to this approach.

not already been seized by an unobvious resemblance between the two things in question?

2. There seems, in Davidson's view, just as little point also in drawing *another* person's attention to a likeness between two things, since, according to him, "all similes are true . . . because everything is like everything" (p. 39). If the hearer agrees with Davidson that "all similes are trivially true" (p. 40), how is he supposed to be prodded by Davidson's dreamwork remark? Is he to attend to the "trivial" similarity between the two things mentioned?

3. If Davidson's view were correct, there would be a readily available and more perspicuous way of expressing a metaphorical thought, whether to oneself or to another person, which would bypass the difficulties listed above that attend any commitment to metaphorizing as speech-act. Why not simply say "Metaphor *is like* dreamwork"? Given that the two things mentioned do not, at first blush, look very much alike, such a remark should do all the nudging, provoking, and intimating that Davidson attributes to the usual metaphorical form. If so, we shall have to explain why all of us have an inveterate and, as I think, justified impulse to say in such cases that A *is* B and not merely that A *is like* B (see propositions 4.1 and 4.11 above). The only plausible reply that occurs to me would be to assimilate metaphor to hyperbole (as in "There are hundreds of cats in the garden")—as an exaggerated and somewhat hysterical style of talk to be eschewed by careful thinkers.

4. I believe, therefore, that Davidson's position reduces to a reformulation of the ancient and, as one might have hoped, discredited theory that I have in the past called a "comparison view."[29] I still think that my earlier conclusion that "a comparison view . . . suffers from a vagueness that borders on vacuity"[30] holds against any such view and specifically against Davidson's latest, though unacknowledged, espousal of it.[31]

5. The gravest objection to Davidson's vigorously argued standpoint then is that, while rejecting current views, it supplies no insight into how metaphors work and fails to explain why the use of metaphors seems to so many students of metaphor an indispensable resource.

---

29. See my "Metaphor," *Models and Metaphors*, pp. 35–37, where citations from earlier defenders of such a view are supplied.

30. Ibid., p. 37.

31. Davidson echoes my older criticisms of the view that "equates the figurative meaning of the metaphor with the literal meaning of a simile" when he says that the literal meaning is "usually a painfully trivial simile. . . . trivial because everything is like everything, and in endless ways" (p. 37). He doesn't seem to notice that the objection applies equally to his own position, even if one continues to insist that a metaphor does not *say* anything but rather provokes and intimates, etc., something like the perception of symmetrical similarities.

5.—The case against assigning meaning to metaphors. I have been arguing in the last section that Davidson's view of how metaphors work is not
as he seems to think a new and illuminating view of the topic but is
rather, if I am not mistaken, one that treats metaphors as perversely
cryptic substitutes for literal similes. I have claimed that this way of
looking at metaphors does not explain how strong metaphors work to
express and promote insight. Now somebody who is more sympathetic to
Davidson's position than I am might retort that the alternative current
views are in no better shape. It seems advisable, therefore, to complete
this examination of Davidson's paper by evaluating his specific objections
to what might be called, for short, any *semantic* interpretation of
metaphor (of which my "interaction view" would be a special case).

So far as I can see, Davidson presents five objections, reproduced
below with a brief reply appended to each.

First objection: "There are no instructions for devising metaphors; there is
no manual for determining what a metaphor 'means' or 'says';
there is no test for metaphor that does not call for taste" (p. 29).

First reply: That the meaning of a live or active metaphor cannot count as
part of its standard meaning, and is therefore to be found neither
in dictionaries or encyclopedias, is a point that has often been made
by students of metaphor. Thus I have said in the past that the
producer of such a metaphor "is employing conventional means to
produce a nonstandard effect, while using only the standard syn-
tactic and semantic resources of his speech community. Yet the
meaning of an interesting metaphor is typically new or 'creative',
not inferrible from the standard lexicon."[32] This point leaves untouched
the contention at issue, that a metaphor *producer* means something,
possibly novel, by his metaphorical statement.

Second objection: "It is no help in explaining how words work in metaphor
to posit metaphorical or figurative meanings" (p. 31). Davidson
contends that "simply to lodge [the] meaning in the metaphor is
like explaining why a pill puts you to sleep by saying it has a dormi-
tive power" (p. 31). He contrasts such pseudoexplanation with the
"genuine explanatory power" of an appeal to "Literal meaning and
literal truth conditions [that] can be assigned to words and sentences apart from particular contexts of use" (p. 31).

Second reply: One must agree that it would be pointless and obfuscating to
invoke some ad hoc "figurative" sense, not otherwise specified, to
explain "how metaphor works its wonders" (p. 31). Nevertheless, it
would help us to understand how a particular metaphorical utterance works in its context if we could satisfy ourselves that the
speaker is then attaching a special extended sense to the metaphorical "focus" (selecting, as I have explained elsewhere, some of the

---

32. "More about Metaphor," p. 436, italics added.

commonplaces normally associated with his secondary subject, in order to express insight into his primary subject). This view is not open to the charge of invoking fictitious entities.

We may compare explanations of ironic talk: it really does help us to understand what somebody means by saying of a colleague's contribution to a college meeting, "X is so *amusing!*" to realize, as we immediately do, that "amusing" here has a sense contrary to its standard sense. Throughout his essay Davidson seems fixated on the explanatory power of standard sense; but when such an explanation is plainly defective, there can be no objection in principle to invoking what the speaker means when speaking metaphorically.

Third objection: The view "that in metaphor certain words take on new, or what are often called 'extended,' meanings [as when somebody calls Tolstoy an infant] . . . cannot, at any rate, be complete," for if in such a context the word "infant" applies correctly to the adult Tolstoy, then "Tolstoy literally was an infant, and all sense of metaphor evaporates" (p. 32).

Third reply: Recognition of an "extended" nonce meaning is not intended to be a "complete" explanation of how metaphor works. There is no implied claim, either, that in such use a word "applies correctly." If Davidson's objection were sound, then to perceive that an ironical speaker meant by "amusing" something like "unfunny" would be to make all sense of irony "evaporate." Irony remains irony, even when understood; and so does metaphor.

Fourth objection: "If a metaphor has a special cognitive content, why should it be so difficult or impossible to set it out?" (p. 42). Davidson challenges my old contention that a literal paraphrase "inevitably says too much—and with the wrong emphasis."[33] "Why," he asks, "inevitably? Can't we, if we are clever enough, come as close as we please?" (p. 42).

Fourth reply: Why not, if we are clear about coming "close" and do not mistake an explication for a translation? I supplied a partial answer to Davidson in the passage preceding the one that he reproduces: "the set of literal statements so obtained will not have the same power to inform and enlighten as the original. For one thing, the implications previously left to a suitable reader to educe for himself, with a nice feeling for their relative priorities and degrees of importance, are now presented explicitly as having equal weight."[34] I went on to say that explication or elaboration of a metaphor's grounds (such as I later supplied in "More about Metaphor," pp. 443–45, using the example of "Marriage is a zero-sum game") can be extremely valuable "if not regarded as an adequate cognitive substitute for the original."

33. "Metaphor," *Models and Metaphors,* p. 46.
34. Ibid.

The point is of general application. Toynbee's remark, in connection with American nuclear policy: "No annihilation without representation," could no doubt be spelled out to render his allusion to the familiar slogan boringly explicit. I suppose any sensitive reader would feel that something of the force and point of the original remark would then have been lost. As in aposiopesis, a metaphor leaves a good deal to be supplied at the reader's discretion. To say something with suggestive indefiniteness is not to say *nothing*.

Fifth objection: "Much of what we are caused to notice [by a metaphor] is not propositional in character" (p. 44).

Fifth reply: Agreed. But it is going too far to claim that in understanding a metaphor "What we notice or see is not, *in general,* propositional in character" (p. 45, my italics). A metaphor may indeed convey a "vision" or a "view," as Davidson says, but this is compatible with its also *saying* things that are correct or incorrect, illuminating or misleading, and so on.

6.—Verdict. If a "semantic" conception of metaphor is open to no more serious objections than those advanced by Davidson (lack of recipes for producing metaphors, absence of explanatory power in the theory, incompleteness of the semantic view, difficulty of paraphrasing a metaphor's cognitive content, presence of nonpropositional insight in metaphorical thought), its advocates have no cause for alarm and may rest unabashed in their imputed "error and confusion." The verdict must be "nonproven."

In my opinion, the chief weakness of the "interaction" theory, which I still regard as better than its alternatives, is lack of clarification of what it means to say that in a metaphor one thing is thought of (or viewed) *as* another thing. Here, if I am not mistaken, is to be found a prime reason why unregenerate users of appropriate metaphors may properly reject any view that seeks to reduce metaphors to literal statements of the comparisons or the structural analogies which *ground* the metaphorical insight. To think of God *as* love and to take the further step of identifying the two is emphatically to do something more than to *compare* them as merely being alike in certain respects. But what that "something more" is remains tantalizingly elusive: we lack an adequate account of metaphorical thought.[35]

35. I have made some preliminary suggestions in sect. 8, "Thinking in Metaphors," of "More about Metaphor," pp. 446–48.

Index

Abrams, M. H., 66, 66 n
Absence, idea of, in metaphor, 82–84
Abstractions, and language in Condillac, 20–23; and symbols in Kant, 24–25
Advertising, 67
Aestheticism, 26; and ontology, 86–88; as escape from reality, 79–86. *See also* Autotelism
Alan of Lille, 169
Allen, Woody, 40
Allusion, and meaning, 163; as property of context, 164
Ambiguity, 32–33, 36, 77, 176, 177; and reference in poetry, 151–52
Analogy, 24, 49, 52, 146, 157, 160
Aristotle, 5, 30, 43, 52, 62, 68, 71, 74, 142, 143, 144, 145, 146, 155–56
Autotelism, of poetry, 71–76; Baumgarten on, 73–74. *See also* Aestheticism

Bachelard, Gaston, 147, 149
Barfield, Owen, 42, 44
Barthes, Roland, 151
Baudelaire, Charles, 117
Baumgarten, Alexander Gottlieb, *Reflections on Poetry*, 73–74, 83, 84
Being, 22–23. *See also* Ontology
Berggren, Douglas, 152
Black, Max, 30, 31, 37, 43, 44, 129, 145, 147, 149; interaction theory of, 42, 97, 143, 190, 192; "Metaphor" (article), 3, 29 n; system of associated commonplaces of, 145 n; on translation and meaning, 165–66
Bloom, Harold, 80–81
Booth, Wayne C., 5, 163
Brain, injury and the breakdown of metaphoric competence, 134–39
Breton, André, 114
Burke, Edmund, 60, 61, 63

Campion, Thomas, "There is a Garden in her face," 77–78, 168, 172

Catachresis, 19, 85
Cavell, Stanley, 44 n
Character, as revealed through metaphor, 55–56, 59–61, 63, 176
Cognitive content, 3–6, 30, 42–45, 150, 170, 186, 187 n, 191. *See also* Ideas; Meaning
Cohen, Jean, 143
Cohen, Jonathan, 122
Cohen, Ted, 40, 52, 178
Community, creation of, through metaphor, 6–10
Condillac, Etienne Bonnot de, *Essai sur l'origine des connaissances humaines*, 20–23. *See also* Language; Metaphor; Ontology
Context, and metaphoric comprehension, 129; relation to meaning, 34–35, 39–42, 51, 57–58, 119, 173, 185, 187; and truth-value, 176
Criteria for evaluating metaphors: accommodation to audience, 55; activeness, 54; adequacy, 91; appropriateness, 55, 91; coherence, 54; concision, 55; effectiveness, 53–56; novelty, 36, 54, 108, 190; sincerity, 111–12; taste, 29; in theology, 91
Critic, role of, in interpreting metaphor, 45
Criticism, and ethical responsibility, 69; relation to culture, 61–70, 176
Culler, Jonathan, 73

Davidson, Donald, 4, 50, 162, 163, 166, 168–70, 176–92 *passim*
de Man, Paul, 2, 5, 49, 167
Demetrius, 53 n, 54
Derrida, Jacques, 83–84, 167
Descartes, René, 22, 80–86
Doctorow, E. L., 62 n
Donne, John, 35

Effectiveness. *See* Criteria for evaluating metaphors

193